Contents

Strange acknowledgements of several kinds

We have numerous people to thank, not least of all each other, for persevering during the (sometimes painful) process of translating our passions into a book. Those people include Pamela Bruder-Freeman, Dumitru Chitoran, Gavin Fairbairn, Nicola Groves, Sneja Gunew, Jalna Hanmer, Amanda Hawley, Ian Hunter-Smart, Patricia Johanson, Simon Lee and his ethical and 'running stream' visions, Myra Macdonald, Cam McDonald, Michael Posluns, Sheila Scraton, Arle Sklar-Weinstein (whose insights and explorations inspired the material on art and craft in Chapter 6), Willie Thompson, Paul Tyrer (without whom the manuscript might still be in our computer), Dave Webb, Angus Wells, Bud Whiteye – and everyone whose e-mails we failed to respond to on account of being too busy with writing. The editorial staff at Edinburgh University Press are – to a man and woman – kind, attentive, efficient and insightful; we thank Sarah Edwards, James Dale, Eddie Clark, and Nicola Wood, whose sharp eye and quick wit made the copy-editing process almost enjoyable.

There are those to whom we wish to pay special tribute. On Valerie's part, they include the one with boundless energy and a gift for turning fury into prose, lover of olives and humans (probably in reverse order); Pete, centre of the universe and not at all (as an impertinent writer once suggested) a 'myth'; the magnificent MMZ and her parents, Peggy Jane and David and uncle Daniel; Rachel, Bill and Susan – ethical judge and champion punster; the rest of the family (you know who you are; we know where you live); the life-saving support of Dr Shahid Junejo; the early inspiration of Jenny Wells Vincent and the incomparable Paul Robeson; the music and spirit of Evelyn Pittman in the early Oklahoma days.

On Simone's part, they are D, for ensuring that my passions came before mundane necessities and for allowing me to hog the limelight; the night owl, for being the sort of mentor who sends e-mails at three in the morning; Rebecca Sutcliffe – student extraordinaire, who deserves much of the credit for the material on asylum seekers in Chapter 1; Pete, for the olives and a space to think out loud – in that order!; Ngahuia

Media and Ethnic Minorities

Media Topics
Series editor: Valerie Alia

Titles in the series include:

Media Ethics and Social Change
by Valerie Alia
0 7486 1773 6 (hardback)
0 7486 1771 X (paperback)

Media Policy and Globalisation
by Paula Chakravartty and Katharine Sarikakis
0 7486 1848 1 (hardback)
0 7486 1849 X (paperback)

Media Rights and Intellectual Property
by Richard Haynes
0 7486 2062 1 (hardback)
0 7486 1880 5 (paperback)

Alternative and Activist Media
by Mitzi Waltz
0 7486 1957 7 (hardback)
0 7486 1958 5 (paperback)

Women, Feminism and Media
by Sue Thornham
0 7486 2070 2 (hardback)
0 7486 2071 0 (paperback)

Sexuality and Media
by Tony Purvis
0 7486 2265 9 (hardback)
0 7486 2266 7 (paperback)

Media Discourse
by Mary Talbot
0 7486 2347 7 (hardback)
0 7486 2348 5 (paperback)

Media and Ethnic Minorities

Valerie Alia and Simone Bull

Edinburgh University Press

Edinburgh University Press Ltd
22 George Square, Edinburgh

Typeset in Janson and Neue Helvetica
by TechBooks, India and
printed and bound in Great Britain by
MPG Books Ltd, Bodmin

A CIP record for this book is available from the British Library

ISBN 0 7486 2068 0 (hardback)
ISBN 0 7486 2069 9 (paperback)

Te Awekotuku and Allison Morris for inadvertently inspiring a young Maori woman coming into a political consciousness; Biko Agozino for uplifting use of awesome intellect; and, last but not least, Maia Orana whose infrequent eruptions in the middle of the night called to mind an Ethiopian proverb about resilience in the face of adversity: 'When the great lord passes, the wise peasant bows deeply and farts silently.' If ever a slogan were needed to inspire ethnic minorities to forge new images using their own media, this would be our pick.

Preface

Consistent with the colonial roots of much contemporary scholarship, publications concerning media representation of ethnic minority peoples have tended to be limited in scope and written from 'outsiders' perspectives. To provide a range of counter-colonial perspectives, this text presents a mix of voices – of 'insiders' and 'outsiders', scholars and media practitioners. One of our main objectives is to deconstruct the myth of passive minority consumption and (non-)participation in the processes of production, considering media from the 'mainstream' and an array of alternative and ethnic minority locations and sources.

While we seek to understand the relationships between media and ethnic minorities in a broad international and intercultural context, this volume features the authors' comparative research on experiences of Inuit and First Nations in Canada and of Maori in Aotearoa (New Zealand). These are cultural communities with whom the authors have worked closely and/or personally identify, but their experiences reflect those of a wide range of minority communities around the globe. The analysis is broadened by consideration of Native Americans and African Americans in the United States; Sámi in northern Europe; Aboriginal peoples in Australia; and Roma communities of Europe, the Republic of Ireland, and the United Kingdom.

We concede at the outset that media are not necessarily the 'controlling will' in the nations and communities they service. The act of offering a portrayal does not guarantee that an audience will wholeheartedly accept it, much less react in some predictable fashion or take from it what the producers intended (Spoonley 1993). Consumers are actively involved in investing media representation with meaning, and tend to access information from a variety of sources. Nonetheless the media serve not only the public but various political agendas and play an important, though not exclusive role in shaping public opinion. Mass media present particular dangers to the well-being of ethnic minorities, but also, opportunities for empowerment. It is our intention to examine both these aspects of the media–consumer relationship, focusing on the media participation, representation and consumption of ethnic minorities. We hope that we can contribute in some small way to a better understanding of the evolution, contemporary realities, and future possibilities of multifaceted media-minority relationships – locally, nationally, regionally and internationally.

Persistent blind spots

In September 2004 Valerie Alia wrote a letter to *The Independent on Sunday* which the editors declined to publish, finding it 'interesting' but not sufficiently important for their readers. It is reprinted here to emphasise a point we wish to make about the persistence of blind spots in media representations of ethnic minorities.

Sir:

Jenny Gilbert's otherwise commendable portrait of the distinguished dancer, Arthur Mitchell (2004: 14–15) contains a serious error. It is not true that the New York City Ballet was 'wholly Caucasian' when its founder, George Balanchine, hired Mitchell in 1955. By that time, Maria Tallchief had been the company's leading ballerina for eight years. For several of those years, she was not only Balanchine's muse and interpreter but his wife. Born in Oklahoma, Tallchief was the first great American ballerina. A Native American of Osage and Scots-Irish-Dutch parentage, she carries the honour name of Wa-Xthe-Thomba ('woman of two worlds').

It is telling that the editors considered their error too insignificant to correct. To achieve this error, they had to reconstruct Maria Tallchief as 'Caucasian'. A similar blind spot is evident in the extensive media coverage of the September 2004 launch of the Museum of the American Indian in Washington, DC. In a manner unheard of in coverage of major architectural openings, most of the media reports omitted the name of the internationally distinguished architect who designed the museum everyone called exceptional. The reports were frustratingly semi-accurate, misleading, incomplete and confusing. The architect, Douglas Cardinal, is Canadian Métis of Blackfoot, Ojibway and European descent. Métis is a term used in Canada and parts of the US to refer to people of mixed First Nations and European-North American descent (though it originally was applied only to people of First Nations-French origin). Although most Canadian media have long called Douglas Cardinal Métis he is misidentified in most of the US media as simply 'Blackfoot'. He designed Canada's magnificent national Museum of Civilisation. To add further insult to the widespread omission of his name and biographical details, Cardinal himself was absent from the 2004 celebrations that accompanied the museum launch. This commemorated an earlier insult: following a dispute between the architect and a contractor, in 1998 the Smithsonian Institution (the organisation that runs the complex of museums of which the new museum is a part) fired Cardinal. Although it remains his design – his building – he has been virtually wiped from the record. Disputes are rampant in the world of building design, budget and construction. Seldom is the name of the designer obliterated from the project or the record. The questions we must ask are, 'Why were the media complicit in this case?' and 'Was the architect's ethnicity a relevant factor in the decisions made by the media and the museums?'

Notes on terminology

'Indian' is a term used to sell things – souvenirs, cigars, cigarettes, gasoline, cars, recreational vehicles, golf courses, movies, and books. 'Indian' is a figment of the white man's imagination. (Keeshig-Tobias 1990: 67)

In this book we use names such as Inuit, First Nations, Maori, Native Americans, African Americans, Sámi, Aboriginal, Roma and Celtic to identify and distinguish the ethnic minority groups under discussion. Although there are numerous 'official' generic definitions, our preference is to accept culturally specific, autonomous naming (for instance, 'Lakota' rather than 'Native American'). Following people's own preferences sometimes results in references that look contradictory. For example, in Alaska the term 'Inuit' is used as a political generic, in the context of the circumpolar, pan-Inuit movement, and within the Inuit Circumpolar Conference (ICC). In daily usage at home, people prefer either 'Eskimo' as a generic, or the specific cultural name (Yup'ik or Iñupiat); therefore, except in international references, we have followed that usage. To the best of our knowledge the above names and spellings (for example, of Aboriginal with a capital 'A') are those most widely used by the peoples themselves. However, even the most conscientiously chosen names can reduce diverse clusters of people to homogeneous groupings, and are incapable of reflecting unique identities. Many – perhaps most – people are of mixed ethnicities. Transcultural boundary-crossing, 'hybridisation', marriage and other alliances complicate the matter of how to categorise people (see, for example, Gunew 2004; Appadurai 1996). Whenever possible, we refer to smaller, discrete units within the broader groups, using their ways of naming themselves, and have adopted terminology derived from the languages spoken by those whose voices we are borrowing (for example, Pakeha rather than non-Maori; Qallunaat rather than non-Inuit). Except in the case of proper nouns, where meanings are not defined within the text, the notes clarify and help to decode key words and concepts for those unfamiliar with the languages concerned.

Introduction: 'race', ethnicity and representation

In his classic 1963 text, *Invitation to Sociology*, Peter Berger argued that sociologists should have 'difficulties with any set of categories that supply appellations to people – "Negroes," "whites," "Caucasians",... "Jews," "Gentiles," "Americans," "Westerners"...all such appellations become exercises in "bad faith" as soon as they are charged with ontological implications' (American Sociological Association (ASA) News online 2002). 'Why should we continue to measure race?' asks sociologist Troy Duster.

> If biological research now questions the utility of the concept for scientific work in this field, how, then, can racial categories be the subject of valid scientific investigation...our social and economic lives are integrally organized around race as a social construct....Sociologists are interested in explaining how and why social definitions of race persist and change [and] the nature of power relationships between and among racial groups...['Race' comprises] a fluid and contingent set of classifications that vary across regions and nations, and over time and space even within in the same society. (ASA News online 2002)

Social scientists 'are not able to rid themselves of a clearly absurd tradition of grouping persons according to certain anatomical attributes' (Yehudi Webster quoted in *Anthropology Newsletter* 1998: 3). Yehudi Webster points to a split in the social science community. He contends that sociologists remain committed to the continuing study of 'race relations' and is concerned that 'their collaboration with political representatives in the dissemination of "race" is beginning to reach new heights'. By contrast, anthropologists have sought to distance themselves from the study of 'race' and from collaborating with government programmes to do so. Webster cites a statement by the American Anthropological Association calling on the US Census Bureau to 'phase out classification by race' (*Anthropology Newsletter* 1998: 3).

1

Disciplinary boundaries and definitions

We do not consider 'ethnicity' to be synonymous with race. Nor do we adhere to pseudo-racial definitions wherein physical characteristics and 'blood quantum' dictate identity and, too often, become an alibi for oppression. In the US the General Allotment (or Dawes) Act of 1887 used a blood quantum test to confiscate more than 100 million acres of land from 'mixed blood' Native Americans. Nor is it satisfactory to rely on census figures. Census data present a snapshot, frozen in space and time, while identity is never static. Few of the world's people can be said to be monocultural, and the number of people claiming a particular ethnic identity fluctuates according to politics, fashion, personal preferences and other factors. Language is also insufficient to determine identity, especially in the wake of efforts to strip minority peoples of their original languages (for example, the punishing of indigenous children for speaking their own languages in missionary schools). Although language proficiency does not guarantee the knowledge and skills requisite for effective communication, the inability fluently to speak one's ancestral language is sometimes used to discredit both insiders and outsiders. Some ethnic minority groups have rules of descent; others use a combination of membership criteria. The United Nations (UN) offers a useful working definition of 'an ethnic minority' as:

> a group of citizens of a State, constituting a numerical minority and in a non-dominant position in that State, endowed with ethnic, religious or linguistic characteristics which differ from those of the majority of the population, having a sense of solidarity with one another, motivated, if only implicitly, by a collective will to survive and whose aim it is to achieve equality with the majority in fact and in law. (Deschênes 1985: 31)

This definition is not universally applicable. It presupposes a group's residence within a State – an assumption that is irrelevant for Kurds and Roma (Gypsy) Travellers (among countless others) whose ethnic identities cross many State boundaries.

Anthony Giddens defines an ethnic group as 'one whose members share a distinct awareness of a common cultural identity, separating them from other groups around them'. He observes that in 'virtually all societies ethnic differences are associated with variations in power and material wealth' and that where ethnic differences are also racially defined, 'such divisions are sometimes especially pronounced' (Giddens 1997: 582). For van den Berghe race, class and ethnicity are stratified in similar ways and are imbedded in our genes and psyches (van den Berghe 1978: 22).

Nobility, savagery and history: outsider representations

There are two contradictory themes running through 'outsider' representations of indigenous and other minority peoples. On one hand, they are romanticised and portrayed as quaint, '...bare-chested warriors in flax skirts' (Marks 2004). On the other hand, they are demonised as urban criminals; hence the hackneyed line: 'Police said there had been no law and order problems' (BBC 2004a), as if any 'minority' gathering would automatically degenerate into a riot. Such portrayals stem from centuries of oppression, misrepresentation, misunderstanding and philosophical debate. Descriptions of Sámi living 'in wonderful savageness' can be traced as far back as the Roman author Cornelius Tacitus, whose tract, *Germania*, dates to AD 98 (Lehtola 2002: 22). The seventeenth-century English theorist Thomas Hobbes saw the 'uncivilised' minorities as mere savages (Oakeshott 1962). In 1751 Benjamin Franklin referred to the Iroquois Confederacy or League as 'Six Nations of ignorant savages' (Wearne 1996: 38). In the nineteenth century Kipling referred to the recently colonised people of the Philippine Islands as '...half devil and half child' (Kipling 1940: 321). Over the years, indigenous peoples of the Antipodes have been depicted as savage vagrants who unproductively occupy potentially productive land (Evans, Grimshaw, Philips and Swain 2003). That attitude is seen in many parts of the world, especially where outsiders wish to appropriate lands and waters for their own occupancy and profit. Nineteenth-century anthropology, firmly rooted in theology, is replete with savage imagery:

> John Wesley, teaching that mankind in its natural state was fundamentally bad, drew lively pictures of savage customs to illustrate the degeneracy of those who were not saved: 'The natural religion of the Creeks, Cherokees, Chickasaws and all other Indians, is to torture all their prisoners from morning to night, till at length they roast them to death... Yea, it is a common thing among them for the son, if he thinks his father lives too long, to knock out his brains.' (Douglas 1999: 12)

By contrast, eighteenth-century Swiss theorist Jean Jacques Rousseau equated civilisation with the degeneration of humankind. He saw human beings as 'primitive' but possessed of a natural disposition to compassion or pity. Hence his belief that the 'uncivilised' were 'noble savages'. Both views – of 'savage' and 'noble savage' – are grounded in an ideology that supports the inferiority of ethnic minority peoples and has served to justify policies and practices of assimilation, ethnocide and genocide (Ross 1998).

In recent years, the rules have changed concerning who can represent whom, and in what ways. A number of academic associations have adopted codes for the proper conduct of research, and drafted statements setting out the principles they intend to follow. The American Anthropological Association, for example, has said that anthropological researchers 'have primary ethical obligations' to the people 'they study' and with whom they work. They should consult actively 'with the affected individuals or group(s) [to establish] a working relationship that can be beneficial to all parties involved . . .' (American Anthropological Association 1997: 3). The only problem with this statement is that it implies that no researchers are themselves members of the communities under study.

This volume examines such themes and modes of representation in the context of a growing worldwide movement of minority peoples to present their own images and voices in 'mainstream' media and at the same time, to create and control their own media. We outline some of the issues that face minority communities around the globe, using case studies of indigenous media and their links to socio-political movements, non-governmental organisations (NGOs) and other international and transcultural organisations and institutions. It is our intention to raise awareness of emerging worldwide media and socio-cultural movements and progressive policies, as well as the persistent racist policies that are not relics of the past but, all too often, features of modern governance. We consider these policies in the light of the experiences of Roma/Gypsy Travellers in Ireland, Scotland, England, Europe and elsewhere; and of pan-indigenous movements and organisations such as the Inuit Circumpolar Conference. Tracking some of the current work on Diaspora and homeland, we explore the place of language, culture, identity and media in liberation struggles and new political entities; and of cultural maintenance, regeneration and renewal among Inuit in Canada and Maori in Aotearoa. We examine representations of minorities by dominant society outsiders as well as indigenous self-representation through media creation and production in film, television, radio, print, and new media. Our analysis is situated in the context of the international, multicultural movement we have called the 'New Media Nation' (Alia 2004).

The politics of ethnicity: a question of boundaries

Like identity, cultures evolve and adapt to meet new circumstances. The presence of well-developed media does not signify a culture destroyed or assimilated, but a culture defending itself, campaigning to be heard (Wearne 1996). In his novel, *Emergency*, Richard Rive uses music to capture the complexities of a multifaceted, culturally complex experience of crossing ethnic and geographical boundaries. In a beautifully orchestrated passage, he interweaves Western classical music with South African traditional song, depicting a *new* culture, less singular or 'pure', but just as real as the old:

> Moldau from Ma Vlast. My country. Patriotic music, the stirring of national consciousness... what we need in this country is the development of all indigenous cultures for the furtherance of a truly South African art form. Solo flutes described the River Moldau... he knew every part of it, recognized every instrument, every note. Hell, waiting for the strings to take up the motif in the middle of pass-burnings and rioting, while on the run from the Special Branch. Fiddling while Rome burnt. The swelling of the mood indicating rustic revelry... The green banks of the Moldau strewn with the dead of Sharpeville and Langa. (Rive 1970: 35)

Rive's work is full of irony, bitterness and hope. The River Moldau of Czech composer Bedrich Smetana's homeland is at once outrageously out of place in South Africa's Sharpeville and entirely appropriate to the Sharpeville context. Reaching across cultures, Rive connects this universal song of Diaspora to his own song, using the intersection between cultures to portray the cultural and political isolation of a Western-educated, Africa-identified man of 'mixed race' origins, living as a dissident in apartheid-era South Africa.

Such cultural mixtures do not always come guilt-free. Jadine, an African-American character in Toni Morrison's ironically titled novel, *Tar Baby*, feels guilty 'for liking Ave Maria better than gospel music and Picasso better than an African mask'. ' "Sometimes [I long] to get out of my skin and be only the person inside – not American, not black – just me" ' (Alibhai-Brown 2004: 8). In her equally ironically titled book, *Some of my Best Friends are...*, Yasmin Alibhai-Brown writes: 'I know exactly how [Jadine] feels. It is not that we wish we were white. Just that we cannot just be cows in a branded herd throughout our all too brief lives' (Alibhai-Brown 2004: 8).

Amin Maalouf expresses a more fully integrated and unembattled identity. Having spent half his life in Lebanon and half in France, he has tired of being asked whether he feels 'more French' or 'more Lebanese'.

> So am I half French and half Lebanese? Of course not. Identity can't be compartmentalised. You can't divide it up into halves or thirds or any other separate segments. I haven't got several identities: I've got just one, made up of many components combined together in a mixture that is unique to every individual. (Maalouf 2000: 3)

Maalouf's little gem of a book, *On Identity*, is a call to end holy wars and ethnic cleansing, and the earlier stages of ethnic tugs-of-war that pressure people into confusing cultural preferences and practices with political allegiances. It is no easy task to define the underlying categories and concepts that express such complex realities. The following journal entry, from a trip across Canada by rail, demonstrates the difficulty of expressing 'ethnicity' and setting definitions:

> I was immersed in writing. A railway employee passing by glanced at a word on the page in front of me and asked, 'What's ethnicity?' My reply got stuck in mid-sentence. 'It's ... it means ... how you see yourself,' I said. That didn't work: blank look. I tried again. 'Uh ... your background, roots, feelings ... How you think about connections ...' Embarrassed, I stopped again. *She* was losing patience, and *I*, confidence. She looked again at the strange word on the paper. Suddenly her face lit up and she said, 'Ethnic. Is it like "ethnic"? Like in the newspapers when they write about "ethnic"?' 'Sort of,' I replied, eager to end the awkward dialogue and get back to work. It was an inadequate response. I did not want to launch into a discussion of how mass media perpetuate incorrect usage of the word 'ethnic' to imply minority status. I did not say ... that social scientists, journalists and public officials all have different ways of using 'ethnic' to separate or unify the people they depict or control. I did not [say] that people in the dominant sub-culture (Anglo- or Franco-Canadians in Canada, Anglo-Americans in the United States, people of Anglo-Celtic origin in Britain) are not called 'ethnic' while those in minority sub-cultures are. I was neither fair nor honest in replying to the woman on the train. I just wanted to get back to my writing. I left her out of the dialogue that properly involves us all. It was also an admission of inadequacy. After years of study and thought, I still am unable to say in a simple sentence what ethnicity means. (Alia 2004)

The concept of 'Other' permeates portrayals of ethnicity and divisions marked by ethnic (or pseudo-ethnic) boundaries. We read about 'ethnic' political districts, 'ethnic' communities, music and food. In the popular media, in government documents, even in communications from social agencies, we almost never read about Anglo-Saxon 'ethnic' groups. Apart from the social scientists who address ethnicity specifically, much of the scholarly literature suffers from the same ethnocentric bias. 'We' are the 'real' culture. 'They' are 'ethnic'. It is so imbedded in our daily talk and construction of society that even people who know better refer to 'ethnic radio' and 'ethnic policy'.

There are many ways to view ethnicity. For Young (1999: 90) it is only one of several structural axes (which also include age, class and gender) from which people 'evolve their own subculture' in order to develop solutions to the problems their structural positions engender. Further, '... the structural predicaments which give rise to problems for different groups are varied and stratified throughout society. Subcultures overlap ... People in the same structural position can also evolve different subcultures and these will change over time' (Young 1999: 90). The problem with this approach is that if you keep subdividing society into more and more finely differentiated subcultures you end up at a point where you are a culture unto yourself. According to Barth, we should study the constitution of ethnic groups and the nature of the boundaries between them (Barth 1969: 9). In this view, an ethnic group: (1) is biologically self-perpetuating; (2) has members who 'share fundamental cultural values'; (3) constitutes 'a field of communication and interaction'; and (4) has a membership 'which identifies itself and is identified by others as constituting a category'. For Barth, self-identification determines group ethnicity and is preferable to identity imposed from outside. Barth does not sufficiently account for the subtler effects of colonial domination in determining group identities and relationships.

By claiming that every ethnic group experiences a continuous process of dissolution and change, Banton (1983) also overlooks the effects of colonisation. In Aotearoa, for example, Maori society underwent a period of exceedingly rapid and fundamental change on contact with Pakeha. Land Court evidence suggests most descent groups were hybrid prior to colonisation (Ballara 1991). Thereafter, the Pakeha image of Maori society (and of a 'Maori race') took hold. It depicted pyramidally structured 'tribes' or *iwi*, made up of 'sub-tribes' or *hapu*, further subdivided into 'extended families' or *whanau* (Ballara 1991), an image that has come to be ingrained in Maori themselves. Further, Banton thinks group continuity is learned. Even though they have more in common with French or German students, English schoolboys are taught to identify with the Englishmen featured in history textbooks (Banton 1983: 101). Banton's thesis fails to account for the persistence of externally coerced identity and change such as those experienced by Inuit, discussed below.

Ethnic solidarity occurs whenever a group defines its boundaries in cultural terms. In examining the transition from 'tribal' to 'complex' societies, a process in which culturally divergent groups form a newly identified city or state, Michael Hechter (1975) suggests a continuum of integration. He studies the Anglo-Celtic experience as an instance of internal colonialism. While the ruling class abandoned Celtic culture to

Anglicise, the lower classes did not, and Celtic culture became a weapon used to mobilise against the English. Where such a cultural division of labour appears, political demands are often formulated in terms of ethnicity rather than social class (Hechter 1975: 345).

In ancient Greece, the word *ethnikos* meant 'heathen' or 'pagan'. It evolved into the Greek *ethnos* and in the mid-nineteenth century began to take on the meaning of physically observable 'racial' characteristics. In the US at the time of the Second World War, the term 'ethnics' became 'a polite term referring to Jews, Italians, Irish and other people considered inferior to the dominant group of largely British descent' (Eriksen 2002). The *Oxford English Dictionary* published the earliest English language dictionary definition of ethnicity in 1972, but the US sociologist, David Riesman, had used the term at least two decades earlier (Glazer and Moynihan 1975: 1). According to Eriksen, early twentieth-century social theorists erroneously assumed:

> that ethnicity and nationalism would decrease in importance and eventually vanish as a result of modernisation, industrialisation and individualism. This never came about. On the contrary, ethnicity and nationalism have grown in political importance in the world, particularly since the Second World War . . . In many parts of the world . . . nation-building – the creation of political cohesion and national identity in former colonies – is high on the political agenda. Ethnic and national identities also become strongly pertinent following the continuous influx of labour migrants and refugees to Europe and North America, which has led to the establishment of new . . . ethnic minorities in these areas. (ASA News online 2002)

We wish to emphasise the political and power discrepancies that characterise minority–majority relations. Minority status is more than simply a numerical or a cultural issue. Perhaps the key phrase in the UN definition on page 2 is 'non-dominant'. In the mainstream media, 'minority' and 'ethnic' are often used interchangeably, while power discrepancies are ignored and all minority groups are assumed to be disadvantaged or marginalised. This must be examined in relation to apartheid societies, in which the minority holds the greatest political power – a reality that clarifies the fact that oppression and domination are not determined by population size.

Notes on 'visible' and 'invisible' minorities

There is an unspoken hierarchy of minorities, often linked to the length of time in which an ethnic community has inhabited the host country:

In less than half a biblical lifetime, Toronto's Italian community has all but completed the transition from 'ethnic group' to mainstream. And what is most fascinating about the transition is that it came about not in a flurry of assimilation, but through a total redefinition of 'mainstream,' a reworking of the criteria that go into making a Torontonian. (Gault 1984)

When Italian Torontonians became Torontonians of Italian descent they achieved a new kind of political and social status. These days the media often carry reports claiming that Jews living in the US are not only 'normal' citizens but 'privileged' in US society, given special treatment by the Christian right that dominates the presidency of George W. Bush. It is a judgement strikingly out of kilter with the experiences of most Jewish immigrants to North America, including the personal experience of one of the authors. Her family arrived in the US at a time when Jews and other minorities were excluded from playing tennis at Forest Hill, the US equivalent of Wimbledon, as well as from the prestigious 'Ivy League' colleges and other institutions of career-building and higher learning. The 'preferential' treatment her family experienced in the first half of the twentieth century included not only such exclusion from universities, colleges, social and recreational organisations, clubs and professions, but verbal and physical abuse, sometimes at the hands of adherents to the very faith that dominates the Bush White House. The journalists need to contextualise their observations. There are political reasons for current relations between governments (not 'American Christians' and 'American' or 'Israeli Jews' but two governments with Christian and Jewish politicians in them). In oversimplifying the categories, the media not only distort the news but contribute to conflicts between people and among nations. Discrimination based on religious, cultural and other identifying categories remains a part of daily life, passed on from one group to another, with the least powerful often those most recently arrived.

Society loses by fostering such exclusion-by-category. The protests against 'affirmative action' and other enforced change ignore the reality that improving media portrayals may require a generation or two of inclusion-by-category. Amin Maalouf calls 'identity' a 'false friend', encouraging divisive allegiances that foster crimes 'in the name of religious, ethnic, national or some other kind of identity' (Maalouf 2000: 9). Similarly, Harold Isaacs asks:

How can we live with our differences without . . . being driven by them to tear each other limb from limb? This is at bottom a question of power, of the relative power or powerlessness of groups in relation to one another. If there is any substance to the now-universal demand of all groups for some more decent equality of status in all societies, how might this demand be met? What new politics might meet these needs, what new institutions? What new pluralisms? (Isaacs 1989: 218)

Educating media, informing the public

Isaacs' questions are indeed the questions of our time. Identity politics have led to rigidifying boundaries. An alternative is to encourage a 'soft' or permeable boundary system of intersecting identities and affiliations. In practice, this might look something like Stuart's proposal for journalism education in Aotearoa, which would produce:

> truly bicultural journalists, both Maori and Pakeha, who can report comfortably from both cultures. This means making Pakeha reporters aware of Maori processes and perspectives, of teaching them about Maori culture, while teaching Maori reporters able to use western communications processes and teaching them Pakeha culture. Each approach must happen in a way which allows the students to maintain their own identity. And both involve different approaches to teaching. (Stuart 2002: 56)

Those approaches are not only needed in Aotearoa. British journalists are desperately in need of sensitivity and diversity training, and journalism of better hiring practices. 'Why are Britain's newsrooms still so "hideously white"?' asks a headline in *The Independent on Sunday* (Cole 2004: 18). In 2000 a group of senior broadcasters and other media executives and practitioners founded the Cultural Diversity Network, dedicated literally to changing the face(s) of British media. The *Independent* mapped the staffing changes of 'quality' and tabloid newspapers:

> The bald facts to emerge were these: on the *Birmingham Evening Mail* seven out of 93 editorial staff are from minority ethnic backgrounds; on the *Bradford Telegraph & Argus*, two out of 65; *Leicester Mercury*, four out of 120; *Manchester Evening News*, six out of 112; *Oldham Chronicle*, one out of 34; *Yorkshire Evening Post*, none out of 68. (Cole 2004: 18)

These numbers do not reflect the proportion of ethnic minorities in the population of media consumers. Some newspapers serve communities with ethnic minority populations of 10 to 40 per cent. Yet these areas are covered by mainly white reporters 'with little understanding of the cultures and religions of the communities they were reporting...' (Cole 2004: 18). Roger Borrell, editor of the *Birmingham Evening Mail*, recalls arriving there to take up his post [in 2001]:

It was like walking into the *Johannesburg Star* circa 1952 . . . There were plenty of black people around, but they were cleaning the toilets. It seemed appalling to me, having just walked through the streets and seen the mix there. You can't reflect the community unless you reflect its mix. (Cole 2004: 18)

Editors say they receive too few applications from members of ethnic minorities and attribute this in part to the scarcity of minority ethnic students on journalism courses. These are shocking figures in a time of increasing celebration of ethnic diversity and concern about interethnic tensions. We lose, by continuing to foster exclusion-by-category. Protests against 'affirmative action' and other enforced change notwithstanding, we are convinced that if changing requires a generation or two of *inclusion* by category, so be it. That is how women got the vote, and African Americans in the US, and indigenous people in Canada. It is how Jewish people and women got into medical school. It is how African American people in Valerie Alia's hometown of Oklahoma City got to use the same drinking fountains, restaurants, washrooms and schools as Caucasian people – and that did not happen until the end of the 1950s. 'Two-thirds of whites say they are biased against minorities', reads an *Independent* headline from late 2004. The accompanying article describes a 'damning report' identifying several types of bigotry, ranging from what Johan Galtung would call 'structural violence' to outright physical violence (Cole 2004; Goodchild 2004; Galtung and Ikeda 1995). The media can help to defuse, or escalate physical and structural violence. Examples of structural violence are found, not only across the whole of society, but in media newsrooms.

Overview of the coming chapters

The issues examined in this book are by no means 'conventional'; some would get little more than passing mention in a standard media studies text. The material here reflects a commitment to what Linda Tuhiwai Smith calls 'decolonising' our methodologies. She cautions against continuing the kinds of research that have made 'research . . . one of the dirtiest words in the indigenous world's vocabulary' because of 'the ways in which scientific research is implicated in the worst excesses of colonialism' (Smith 1999: 1).

Chapter 1 reflects on the institutionalised racism found in media representations of ethnic minorities. Drawing on the work of anthropologist Mary Douglas, we argue that filth is disproportionately imputed to ethnic minorities courtesy of media myths of criminality. In Chapter 2 we consider how dominant cultures cope with the threat of danger discussed in Chapter 1, by reducing ethnic minorities to a romanticised ideal. Chapter 3 focuses on the long-term effects of media-sponsored colonial racism, as manifested in competing insider accounts of violence among ethnic minorities. In Chapter 4 we examine the complexities of outsider representation, taking as a case in point the culture of silence that has grown up in mainstream media around accounts of compulsory schooling. In Chapter 5 we expand on the concept and history of the 'New Media Nation', a term indicating the scope and impact of the international movement of indigenous media. Chapter 6, which deals with cultural appropriation, includes some discussion of historical scientific appropriations and associated media complicity. In Chapter 7, we bring it all together and suggest some ways of moving forward. Our approach makes this in some ways an atypical textbook. We offer basic principles and survey key theories and perspectives. However, rather than simply surveying existing theory, our comparative research on Inuit in Canada and Maori in Aotearoa forms the foundation of the book. Using this research as a starting point, we explore the various ways in which ethnic minorities are represented, by 'insiders' and 'outsiders', in particular locations, cross-culturally and internationally. The reader is invited to reach past the conventional ways of memorising names and theories and to critically and creatively engage with the material.

Exercises

Colonising and decolonising identity

1. Listen to the track entitled 'E5-770 My Mother's Name' from Lucie Idlout's (2002) àlbum of the same name. If you do not have this CD, complete the exercise starting with part 2.
2. Go through your wallet and consider the plastic cards you find there. How do these cards determine or declare your identity? In smaller groups, talk about your names, namesakes and nicknames. Discuss how they reflect your identity – for yourself, within your family, community and society.

Further reading

Alibhai-Brown, Yasmin (2004) *Some of my Best Friends are ... Collected Writings 1989–2004*, London: Politico's.
Hall, Stuart (ed.) (1997) *Representation: Cultural Representations and Signifying Practices*, London: Sage/Open University.

Hechter, Michael (1975) *Internal Colonialism: The Celtic Fringe in British National Development, 1536–1966*, Berkeley, CA: University of California Press.

Maalouf, Amin (2000) *On Identity*, London: The Harvill Press.

Said, Edward (1986) 'An Ideology of Difference', in Gates, L. H., Jr (ed.), *"Race," Writing, and Difference*, Chicago, IL: University of Chicago Press, 38–58.

1 The rise and rise of imputed filth

We rely heavily on the media to inform us about the world at large. At best, they offer integrity, illumination, reflection and information. At worst, they are weak reeds that succumb to distortion, sensationalism and misrepresentation. Too often, they manufacture minority criminal stereotypes. In this chapter, we describe and analyse such media representations, drawing on anthropologist Mary Douglas' theory of the 'rise and fall of imputed filth' (Douglas 1992: 86). In her work on comparative religion, Douglas (1999) posits that dirt is essentially disorder, and the elimination of dirt represents a positive effort to organise the environment. Because of its potential to disrupt order, dirt/disorder 'symbolises both danger and power' (Douglas 1999: 95). In the broader social context, disorder and danger are attributes that tend to be assigned to those on the fringes of the dominant social system. Since 'fear of danger tends to strengthen the lines of division in a community' the supposed dangerousness of marginalised people often serves as a pretext for further marginalisation (Douglas 1992: 34). For example, 'belief in [the] sinister but indefinable advantages [of Jews] in commerce justifies discrimination against them – whereas their real offence is always to have been outside the formal structures of Christendom' (Douglas 1999: 105).

Douglas' original phrase, adapted for the title of this chapter, implies that those deemed filthy do not comprise a fixed category, and the accusation of filth shifts from one target to the next. It includes 'betraying leaders' (Douglas 1992: 86), 'the disenfranchised majority', and 'outsiders' (Douglas 1992: 98). While we accept that accusations of filth are bound to shift, we observe that the accusations are visited disproportionately on ethnic minority peoples, supported by the legacy of racial hierarchies. Such hierarchies equate majority culture ancestry with 'civilisation' and 'rationality', while those of 'other' racial and cultural origins are regarded as inferior. In 1876, Cesare Lombroso claimed that ethnic minorities possessed the same characteristics as 'habitual delinquents'. Thus, by the late nineteenth century, the link between 'filth' and ethnic minorities was already well established. Over time various ethnic groups have been portrayed as filthy via the label of deviance. In the UK, this has frequently included African-Caribbean and Asian groups. It has also included ethnic and religious groups commonly (though not always accurately) thought of as 'white', such as Irish, Maltese, Russians, Jews [sic] (Pearson 1983). Note that 'Jews' constitute the only religious group in that list, which otherwise focuses on national origins.

Sometimes the 'experts' perpetuate the problems. Over the centuries Jews have often been refugees and seekers of asylum; but 'Jewish' refers to a religion (Judaism) and Jews of many ethnicities and nations (divided into two main categories of *Sephardic* – Middle Eastern, Spanish, Portuguese; and *Ashkenazic* – European origins) practise their faith in many different ways. To understand our point, consider whether Pearson would be likely to list 'Irish, Maltese, Russians' and *Christians*. Across geography and time, refugees and asylum seekers of various cultural origins are constructed as folk devils. The frequently-heard epithets of 'dirty Jew/Gypsy/Indian', or any other stigmatised group, and terms such as 'the great unwashed' make Douglas' point all too literal. Once accusations of filth are levelled they are extremely difficult to shake off. The media are not just innocent bystanders or neutral observers; they are culpable. It is useful to reflect on the rise and rise of imputed filth in media representations of ethnic minority peoples.

Filth is not stratified solely along racial lines. Douglas (1992: 95) notes that, 'after 1170 vagabonds, beggars, and heretics were the category charged with leprosy [a disease that amounts to a proxy for filth], while the rich and powerful suddenly seem to have become practically immune.' While there may well be an element of 'class' stratification at work, socio-economic status often serves as a proxy for ethnicity. While the target of the accusation may vary, the purpose is generally the same – to bring the filthy under restraint. Following Douglas, let us consider how symbolic criminalisation has constructed ethnic minorities as filthy, and therefore dangerous, with the help of the media. Stereotypes of Australian Aborigines and First Nation peoples are compared with those of Maori. The stereotypes tend to fluctuate between the extremes of Noble Savage and good-for-nothing petty criminal. Further examples of minority criminalisation include the moral panic over African-Caribbean criminality in the UK that has continued since the 1950s and contemporary demonisation of asylum seekers and Roma/Gypsy/Travellers. This is linked to ongoing immigration debates, and in particular, the new criminalisation that is emerging from Islamophobic anti-terrorism propaganda.

The filthy few

In the US, the stereotype of the drunken, suicidal, lazy, primitive and criminal 'Indian' is as popular today as it was in the nineteenth century, when Native Americans were perceived as irresponsible, childlike, 'drunken Injuns'. Newspapers of the time tended to celebrate, in racist parlance, the apprehension of Native American 'offenders' (Ross 1998). The same phenomenon persists in modern newspaper treatments of Native Americans who are criminalised for upholding their traditional fishing rights. When Native Americans fish 'illegally' in order to maintain traditional rights enshrined by treaty, newspapers invariably focus on their 'criminal' culpability and irresponsible behaviour. 'Natives' are characterised as over-fishing and creating a black market, compared to governments and companies, portrayed as managing fisheries carefully (cf. Ross 1998). During the pioneering days of film making, African Americans and Native Americans 'were vilified or portrayed as being racially inferior by American film makers' in practically the whole genre of Hollywood 'Westerns' (Mita 1996: 42). In Australia, media representations of issues and events pertaining to Aboriginal peoples have increased considerably since the 1960s. These representations have been predominantly negative, over-emphasising drunkenness and crime and offering biased and inflammatory views. In the aftermath of the infamous headline, 'Aboriginal gangs terrorise suburbs' (*West Australian* 1990), portrayals of Aboriginal peoples as threats to law and order were linked to battles over land rights (Sercombe 1995).

In their seminal text, *Policing the Crisis* (1978), Hall et al. analyse the 1972–3 moral panic around muggings in the UK, linking it with a crisis in the capitalist economy that gave rise to increasingly hostile confrontations between police and ethnic minorities. The panic was sparked when an elderly white man was stabbed to death in the course of a robbery by three young people – one African-Caribbean, one Maltese, and one of 'mixed' origins. Newspapers were quick to portray mugging as a quintessentially 'black' crime. High-ranking police officers and politicians such as Enoch Powell lent their weight to this view. Indeed, long before the panic erupted the police had linked mugging predominantly to African-Caribbean youth and had mobilised resources to combat it (Agozino 2003). The official consensus, which held that settler communities offended at lower rates than the majority population, changed dramatically in the mid-1970s, with the accumulation of unofficial police statistics documenting higher arrest rates for African-Caribbean youth in London.

Following close on the heels of this development, Margaret Thatcher was elected in 1979 to her first term as Conservative Prime Minister. She expressed public sympathy with the whites who feared being 'swamped by alien culture' and promised to bring in more law and order. One of the effects of Thatcher's policies was that over-policing of ethnic minorities provoked riots among black and minority ethnic communities in several British towns and cities in the 1980s. The riots were extensively and often irresponsibly reported, helping to cement beliefs about 'black criminality' in the public imagination.

In nineteenth-century Aotearoa, threats to the ideal of the crime-free society did not come from Maori. At that time, Maori were regarded as Noble Savages and any threat they may have posed was mitigated by the widespread belief that they were a dying race. The threat was from 'undesirable immigrants', 'strangers' and 'outsiders', who in those days were largely Pakeha (Pratt 1992). Urbanisation of most of the Maori population after the Second World War brought Maori and Pakeha into widespread contact for the first time since the mid-nineteenth century (King 1997), and negative representations of Maori intensified correspondingly. In addition to their labour, Maori (and Pacific Island peoples) brought their cultures with them to the cities – mostly into areas of urban decline (Spoonley 1993; Awatere 1996). In the North Island cities, Auckland and Wellington, such areas became identified as 'problem' places. With the economic downturn of the early 1970s adding major unemployment into the mix, Maori and Pacific Island peoples came to be perceived as threats to law and order (Spoonley 1994). The media had found a scapegoat, providing a satisfactory outlet for majority readers' frustrations, in the face of a weakening economy and rising unemployment.

In all of these examples, the minority group challenges its assigned marginal status by claiming a right or possession that is currently denied. As we demonstrate below, the media response to such challenges is often to impute filth, and thus make the case for continued discrimination against the minority group, based on its perceived disorderliness or dangerousness, rather than on the facts.

It is interesting to note that a very few ethnic minorities have escaped media imputations of filth. For Chinese minorities in many 'Western' nations, criminal stereotyping has followed almost the reverse trend, from nineteenth-century 'yellow-fever' racism to 'model' minority status. 'Yellow-fever' measures are evident in efforts to prevent Chinese from emigrating to Western countries and, after their arrival, assignment of a range of deviant labels. Chinese were depicted as incorrigible gamblers and opium addicts. Their hard work in gold mining, railway building and other industries was dismissed as a second-class and sometimes dishonest occupation. Frequently, racist legislation denied them fundamental rights. For example, Chinese Americans were prevented from testifying in court cases involving whites, as were African Americans and Native Americans (Ross 1998). Yet nowadays, Chinese are widely regarded as a model minority through stereotyping that renders them diligent, inward looking, tightly knit and self-regulating. Other minorities, such as South Asians in the UK, have also managed to acquire these traits, which (before 9/11, at least) help to shield them from criminal justice surveillance. We postulate that the minority groups which tend to be assigned characteristics considered desirable are those which, within recent memory, have not publicly claimed any 'rights'.

Media negativity

Maori representation by Pakeha image-makers has been influenced by dominant discourses which have constructed limited notions of who we are, derived from colonial representations of Maori. These discourses of Maori can be expressed in three paradigms: the native/inferior Other, the deficient/depraved/negative Other, and the activist/radical/excessive Other . . . (Pihama 1996: 191)

For many people, the news media are the principal source of information about 'law-and-order' issues (McGregor 1993). The nature of the editing process, cuts to budgets, staff and space and other factors, means that newspapers, radio and television outlets (and to a lesser degree, online news services) seldom provide comprehensive service. In addition, they are driven by their particular editorial policies and perspectives. Instead of offering a representative sample of all available news items, media coverage of news, including crime news, has built-in biases. The shorthand style of media reporting, with its emphasis on sound bites, summaries and headlines, is a fundamental problem (Spoonley 1990; Thompson 1953, 1954, 1955; Alia 2004). Newspapers have separate staff for producing headlines and cutlines (captions accompanying photographs) and separate photographers as well. A headline is seldom written by the reporter who researches and writes the story. Even where accuracy is desired, headlines do not always reflect the stories they introduce. In the worst cases of tabloid journalism, they provide a 'sales pitch', a chance to sensationalise and sometimes, to distort (Alia 2004). Many newspaper readers do not read beyond the headlines, and those who do may already be primed to a certain attitude (Thompson 1953, 1954, 1955). Where coverage of minorities is concerned, this can cause more than the usual problems.

Newspaper headlines have tended to reinforce the racial aspect of offending in Aotearoa (Thompson 1953, 1954, 1955; Duncan 1972; Jones

1998). For example: 'Probation for Maori' (*New Zealand Herald* 1935); 'Maori's attack on white girl' (*Truth* 1947); 'Maori guilty of murder' (*New Zealand Herald* 1950). Further, the appearance of factuality makes news ideologically powerful (Spoonley 1993). If the media get things wrong, they create an impression that is very difficult to counter (Spoonley 1990). This is particularly problematic in small countries like Aotearoa where crime from any one part of the country receives a lot of coverage throughout the rest of the country (Robinson 1984; Allison 1989). Yet, if public surveys are to be believed, the media are not highly regarded, suggesting that the relationship between news reporting and public opinion is not necessarily that of a biased press shaping unresisting wills (Williams and Dickinson 1993; Ditton and Duffy 1983). The consumer is also actively involved in investing news with meaning (Spoonley 1993).

An overview and discussion of the broader picture is found in Chapter 4 of *Media Ethics and Social Change* (Alia 2004c: 52–67). The book also addresses questions of crime coverage, for example, in the excerpt and discussion of US 'muckraker' Lincoln Steffens' satirical piece, 'I make a crime wave' (Alia 2004c: 165–8). Several scholars have looked at crime news involving Maori (see Thompson 1953, 1954, 1955; Kernot's survey of newspaper reports 1990; Spoonley 1993; Jones 1998). Thompson is the most authoritative. From the beginning of October 1949 to the end of September 1950, every news item directly involving Maori or Maori affairs was recorded and scrutinised. Thompson measured the material using five factors which are useful for examining coverage of minorities in general as well as more specific coverage of Maori. These are: (1) the quantity of information devoted to various aspects of Maori news; (2) the story's potential impact on readers' attitudes towards Maori; (3) devices of reporting and sub-editing that might introduce distortion into the account; (4) the relationship between editorial opinion and manner of presentation of the item; (5) the central idea presented and developed in each news item.

More than 10,000 news items were studied (Thompson 1953: 372, 1954, 1955). In the papers of Auckland, Wellington, Christchurch and Dunedin, almost 50 per cent of the attention value for the year (1949–50) was concerned with crime, sport and accidents (Thompson 1953: 372, 1954, 1955). In all of the other daily papers sampled, the average attention value given to these three items was 60 per cent of the year's total; the proportion found in individual papers ranged from 52 to 70 per cent (Thompson 1953, 1954, 1955). The news reported within these categories was more remarkable for its unusual rather than its representative character (Thompson 1953: 373, 1954, 1955). By and large, the weekly newspapers presented a picture of Maori affairs that confirmed some of the main impressions given by the dailies (Thompson 1953: 375, 1954, 1955). 'The *NZ Truth* typically devoted almost three-quarters of its Maori news to crime, and a large proportion of the remaining items reported various incidents... [that] were discreditable to Maori' (Thompson 1953: 375, 1954, 1955).

The dominant characteristics implied in media coverage reported in the thematic and favourability analyses included portrayals of Maori as: generous and hospitable, good rugby players, artistic, musical, good craftsmen and good soldiers (Thompson 1954: 1–2, 1955). Unfavourable themes were more common, implying that Maori: are lazy and irresponsible, abuse Social Welfare benefits, are content to live in dirty and overcrowded conditions, are morally and socially irresponsible, are ignorant and superstitious, are political opportunists, hold large areas of land irresponsibly (Thompson 1954: 3–5, 1955). Stress on the Maori character of those involved in crime was a feature of all but one daily newspaper in Thompson's sample; *The Press*, of Christchurch (Thomson 1954: 216). Even in that case, Thompson (1954: 217–18, 1955) observed widespread use of the terms 'half-caste' and 'quarter-caste', and these terms were reserved almost exclusively for crime reports. However, newspapers did not tend to give greater space or attention to 'race-labelled' crime news and, 'when crime news was reported in its most sensational [forms], the sensational quality of the reporting appeared to take its cue from the nature of the event rather than from the racial background of the participants' (Thompson 1954: 218, 1955). Nonetheless, Thompson (1955: 33–4) concluded that 'the practice of race-labelling Maori crime news was widespread, unjustified and, inasmuch as it was virtually limited to Maori, discriminatory'. Thompson believed that the bias was still operating in 1969 (Duncan 1972). Jones' (1998) less extensive survey of labelling in newspaper reports seems to confirm this. While metropolitan dailies such as the *Herald* and *Auckland Star* were largely avoiding labelling Maori in crime and accident reports by 1955, the national weekly *Truth* continued to favour this practice (Jones 1998). In March 1955, out of fourteen crime reports involving identifiable Maori, eight were labelled as such, whereas only one out of six reports involving identifiable Maori in the *Herald* included any labelling (Jones 1998).

Towards the end of the 1960s, Maori academics and social commentators argued that the overwhelmingly negative media portrayals of Maori were symptomatic of institutionalised racism (Carmichael and Hamilton 1967). 'Maori became more vocal in their demands, and broadcasting was on the priority target list. By now the problem was to decide which was better, being invisible, or accepting the negative images of TV and the newspapers' (Mita 1996: 45–6). Institutionalised racism reflects the idea that racism 'permeates society on both the individual and institutional level, covertly and overtly' (Carmichael and Hamilton 1967: 21–7). Unlike 'institutional racism', to which Macpherson referred in his report on police misconduct surrounding the racist murder of black teenager Stephen Lawrence in London in 1993, institutionalised racism questions the assumption that people are unaware (or 'unwitting' as Macpherson put it) of the inherent racism of institutionalised practices.

The longevity of negative portrayals of Maori speaks volumes about the extent of institutionalised racism in the mass media. The subsequent newspaper surveys of Spoonley (1993) and Kernot (1990) provide further evidence of race labelling, though their work is less authoritative than that of either Thompson or Jones. In a month-long survey of crime reports appearing in the *Dominion* and *Evening Post*, Kernot noted that it was only non-Pakeha who were racially identified, and minority group labels were often used in the reporting of criminal cases (Kernot 1990; Spoonley 1993). Spoonley (1993) surveyed news reports (excluding overseas and sporting news) 'in four papers over a six-week period in April and May 1986. Two city newspapers were selected along with a provincial newspaper and a Sunday paper' (Spoonley 1993). This modest survey revealed that labels such as Maori, Pacific Islander, or Polynesian were used three to four times more than labels such as Pakeha (Spoonley 1993). This was particularly true of violent and sexual offending, reinforcing the belief that Maori and Pacific Island peoples were responsible for such crimes, and therefore a 'breakdown of law and order' (Spoonley 1993).

Labelling of crime news is not confined to newspaper reporting. McGregor and Comrie (1995) studied crime news, news about or concerning Maori, political news and health news on television. If a story about a Maori issue overlapped with one of the other categories it was coded as Maori news. Weekday news was chosen over weekend news bulletins, where staffing and resource allocation are reduced, and to avoid days on which programmes included in the study were not broadcast. A total of 915 stories was coded: 389 between *TV One News*, *Top Half* and *Holmes*; 164 between *TV3 News* and *TV3 Features*; 236 between *Morning Report News* and *Features*; and 126 from *Mana News*. Of the total sample, 26 per cent of stories related to crime and 19 per cent related to Maori issues. Maori stories were examined to see what type of news was covered. Treaty issues comprised 19 per cent of the stories broadcast, while 'policy' and 'culture' each comprised 11 per cent. Stories featuring employment, health, education, welfare issues and housing amounted to 18 per cent. Unfortunately, the authors do not state what percentage of the Maori news stories was devoted to crime. However, coders were asked to indicate whether news stories about Maori issues were predominantly good news, bad news or neutral. Unsurprisingly, over half the stories were coded as predominantly bad news (for Maori and about Maori).

In their research on the reporting of Maori news published in 1991, using questionnaires followed by personal interviews with a sub-sample, Massey University and the Race Relations Office surveyed almost 200 news executives working in the 'mainstream' media in Aotearoa. The results showed that news executives generally had little social contact with Maori and thus were less likely to think of news opportunities involving Maori people or to have sufficient breadth of social experience properly to select and present stories about Maori people and issues (McGregor 1991). This, and the fact that journalists and media executives are themselves unlikely to be Maori, may help to explain why Maori news is rarely reported from a Maori perspective.

In the Aotearoa study, no news executives were fluent speakers of Maori and none could conduct an interview in Maori, though most understood a few terms in common usage. Most rated their understanding of Maori culture as 'some' or 'moderate', with a small number rating themselves as 'good' or 'thorough' (McGregor 1991).

> Because of the monocultural domination of the media and related industries there has been an absence of Maori media professionals and those who have come through have had to teach themselves to a large extent... the situation has not stopped us from telling our stories. (Mita 1996: 49)

This calls to mind the experiences of Enos (Bud) White Eye, a journalist from the Delaware First Nation in Canada who has broadcast for CBC and written for several newspapers:

> In breaking 'hard news' stories involving Native people, the first one to get interviewed is the white guy and he gets about ten paragraphs. The reporter drags the chief in at the bottom, in a one-paragraph interview, or the story has no First Nations interviews at all. (Alia et al. 1996: 96)

In Abel's (1997) study of television news coverage of Waitangi Day commemorations in 1990, 1994 and 1995, Maori were most likely to appear in stories on crime or 'deviance' or as part of an official welcome to an overseas dignitary (Abel 1997). Moreover, a predetermined news frame portrayed protesters as a potential threat to law and order and to the State, regardless of the facts, in an attempt to construct a strong, dramatic story (and perhaps, to foreground a political agenda):

From the start, dominant (Pakeha) culture has represented the Maori as they, outsiders to the New Zealand norm, objects of ethnographical (and more recently sociological) research or tourists' curiosity-seeking. In film such representations have sometimes been respectful, sometimes demeaning... but have always carried a Pakeha perspective, owing principally to the exclusion of Maori from positions of influence within the film and television industries... (Campbell 1996: 106)

It is interesting that Maori women, who constitute the vanguard of the renaissance movement in Aotearoa (Greenland 1984), are typically absent from such representations. The invisibility of Maori women in media representations of Maori was particularly pronounced during the occupation of Pakaitore Marae (Moutoa Gardens) in Wanganui in the early 1990s. Maori women who were part of a core group of about 150 from a local *iwi* (tribe) spurred protest. Some of those women were elderly and at least one was a middle-aged Catholic nun. Because the women maintained low profiles, however, the media tended to assume that the activists were all 20- to 30-year-old men, and published photographs out of context which effectively reduced the audience's understanding of the men's activism to senseless delinquency. Letters to the editor certainly constructed the activists as 'hoons', 'criminals' and 'welfare dependents' (Wall 1997). Not only was the purpose of the occupation displaced, the stereotype of the [male] Maori criminal was reinforced and the role of Maori women in the protest was minimised, if not overlooked altogether. The possibility that it is easier to posit Maori men (rather than Maori women) as dangerously violent, and their delinquency as disorder, calls to mind Stuart Hall's articulation theory; in particular, the idea that race, class and gender are joined in such a way that each cannot be understood in isolation from the others.

Whatever the explanation, sexism is deeply imbedded in representations of ethnic minority people. The First Nations Canadian novelist, poet and academic, Lee Maracle, asks:

How often do we read in the newspaper about the death or murder of a Native man, and in the same paper about the victimisation of a female Native, as though we were a species of sub-human animal life? A female horse, a female Native, but everyone else gets to be called a man or a woman. Across the Pacific, Maori women writers Patricia Johnston and Leonie Pihama make reference to Joseph Banks's description of young Maori women who were as 'skittish as unbroke fillies'. (Smith 1999: 9)

Having discussed the process of media misrepresentation through selection of predominantly negative subject manner, next we examine explicit demonisation of minorities, taking Roma and asylum seekers as cases in point.

The demonisation process

Readers of *The Mail on Sunday* were invited to 'indulge' their 'inner gypsy' and Anglo-Saxon children were invited to play in a 'genuine gypsy caravan'. It is telling that in these countries where playing at being 'gypsies' is considered an exciting prospect for outsiders and their children, actual Roma are widely ostracised. A boy reported that people 'pick on us because of where we come from' and businesses refuse to serve them (Gillan 2003: 9). As a child in the south-western US state of Oklahoma, Valerie Alia heard the same language and witnessed similar treatment of African Americans, who were forced to use separate drinking fountains, toilets, and other facilities, were refused service at 'Whites only' restaurants and, when they needed public transport, were confronted with large signs telling them to 'step to the back of the bus'.

In the north-east of England where one of the authors lives, a heavy obstruction placed to prevent vehicle access onto a piece of land is known colloquially as a 'Gypsy bund' – a barrier to stop a veritable flood of undesirables. The tabloid newspapers prominently mention arrests of Gypsies, attribute crimes to Gypsies, and monitor their whereabouts with dark hints of an imminent crime wave in the affected localities. There is a definite split between the romanticised 'Gypsy' who (in person or in absentia) performs for tourists, and the 'real' Roma depicted in the news media. It is as if the same readers, listeners and watchers are not expected to access both the news media and the media designed for promoting tourism and toys. The news consumer is hard pressed to find Roma represented as anything other than criminals, vagrant menace, or exotic exhibitionist Others. News media seldom mention the systematic efforts to marginalise, move and decimate Roma populations in Western and Eastern Europe, Ireland and Britain.

The divided treatment of Roma as demonised 'filth' and romanticised 'exotic' is reminiscent of the 'genuine Indian (or First Nations, or Native American) experiences' on offer in the US, Canada and other locations. In both cases, people who are widely derided and considered second-class citizens – or non-citizens – are turned into exotic objects and performers for the tourist trade. A good deal of fear and loathing surrounds the depiction and treatment of Travellers in Ireland. In 2003, we were told that Irish people who were otherwise welcoming and tolerant warned a visiting Canadian to be vigilant and keep away from 'Travellers'.

Similarly, visitors to 'Indian country' are warned to keep their distance from Native American people, but invited to partake of 'genuine spiritual experiences' in sweat lodges and shamanic rituals. The 'Indian' and 'Gypsy' wannabes join touristic costume parties and sometimes even visit indigenous communities. They seldom engage with members of the cultural communities they visit.

It is obvious that Roma are not the only people to be demonised at the hands of the British press. In the UK, the well-being of refugees and asylum seekers continues to be undermined by racism. The same is undoubtedly true around the globe, particularly in the wake of 9/11 and Iraq. Such racism takes place on the streets, in schools and in workplaces. It is difficult not to notice the swastika graffiti on Jewish businesses and mosques and National Front (NF) recruitment stickers on every other power pole. Fascist organisations, government ministers and the media share responsibility for exploiting and redirecting the disillusionment caused by unemployment and poverty towards asylum seekers and refugees. 'Immigrants are one of the easily available scapegoats for the recurring economic and social ills of a system in crisis' (Hall et al. 1978: 50). Coverage of ethnic minority issues in the British media has generally been of two distinct but complementary kinds. First, immigration issues are formulated as a 'problem'. Second, minority people born in Britain are also perceived as 'problems'. In both cases, deviance underscores the 'problem' (Bowling and Phillips 2002; Pickering 2002).

If people can be labelled 'deviant' when they have not broken any rule (Becker 1963: 9, 17), and discourses emerge from relations of power (Foucault 1980: 114), then politicians and media practitioners are ideally positioned to demonise (Young 1999) asylum seekers and refugees as 'bogus', 'economic migrants', 'terrorists', and to instigate a moral panic (cf. Cohen 1972). Demonisation is important as it allows the problems of society to be blamed upon fictional Others who are already on the periphery of society (Young 1999: 110; Trowler 1991: 65). Asylum seekers have become the new 'folk devils', the subjects of verbal and physical abuse fired by resentment and unreasoned hatred.

Where a moral panic is followed by social and legislative action, the public is reassured that there is strong leadership from the government (McRobbie and Thornton 1995: 562). The government's predilection for implementing repressive legislation against asylum seekers and refugees, as in the Nationality, Immigration and Asylum Act (2002) – the fourth major piece of asylum legislation in a decade – can be seen as an attempt to win support. However, 'folk devils can and do fight back' (McRobbie and Thornton 1995: 559) and seize opportunities to capture media (and therefore, public) attention and foreground their own agendas, perspectives and voices. Other voices contribute to the moral panic-driven debate, representing interest groups, pressure groups, lobbies and campaigning expertise. 'Folk devils' are sometimes supported in the very mass media that castigate them. National headlines such as 'Asylum: the real cost' (Shipman 2002) imply that asylum seekers and refugees are taking resources from 'native Britons'. Those headlines are counteracted by others, such as: 'Resist the attacks on asylum seekers' (*Socialist Worker* 2003). Even so, a survey of stereotypes and prejudices in Britain showed that xenophobic opinions and sentiments are widespread. Twenty-five per cent of respondents agree that immigrants increase crime rates; 48 per cent believe that immigrants take jobs away from those born in Britain, and 64 per cent want the number of immigrants to the UK reduced (Dowds and Young 1996).

Whether it be Iraqis in the United Kingdom, Indonesian 'boat people' in Australia, or Mexican border jumpers in the US (McMaster 2001), racial hostility 'is once again at the centre of politics in Britain and indeed across the globe' (Mahamdallie 2001: 3), assuming new forms and new antagonisms in a range of situations (Gilroy 1987). In recent years, representations of asylum seekers have merged with criminal imagery. In this scenario, refugees are portrayed as 'bogus' and destined to 'milk' the state of resources, or as dangerous and motivated by criminal intent (Weber 2002). Thanks to media misrepresentations, the distinctions between refugees, legal immigrants, illegal immigrants, terrorists and Muslims have become blurred (Weber 2002; Pickering 2002). This has led to criminalisation at three mutually reinforcing levels: the *symbolic level* – asylum seekers are considered 'dangerous' and the media are prone to distort and sensationalise their supposed deviance; the *literal level* – asylum seekers are charged with criminal offences for 'crimes of survival' (such as theft and prostitution) and 'crimes of arrival' (people effectively forced into illegality when they are denied legal means of entry); and the *procedural level* – asylum seekers are treated as if they were criminals (for example, the fingerprinting of all asylum applicants over the age of 14 years at point of entry) (Weber 2002; Weber and Gelsthorpe 2000).

A number of key myths can be distilled from media representations of asylum seekers and refugees. In her analysis of Scottish newspapers, Mollard (2001: 9–13) identifies the *numbers myth*, the *ineligibility myth*, the *cost myth* and the *social cost myth*. Baird (2002: 12) has proferred a fifth, the *criminality myth*. The *numbers myth* exaggerates the number of asylum seekers and refugees entering Britain. The idea that there are too many refugees trying to come into 'our' country (Baird 2002: 9) is evident in National Front discourse of asylum seekers 'swamping Britain', even though asylum seekers account for a minuscule proportion of the population (Statistics Department 2001). The Committee to Defend Asylum Seekers (2002; Nasim 2002: 18) reports that most asylum seekers end up in third world countries, with only a tiny minority in 'developed' countries. Thus, the 'frenzied political debate' over a supposed 'flood' of asylum seekers is not justified by the figures, which show that in the last decade, applications for asylum have fallen by almost half across Europe. Indeed, figures for asylum claims do not go up and up as the right wing claim; they go up and down from month to month (Mahamdallie 2001: 9). For example, during the first quarter of 2002, 2,480 Iraqi nationals applied for asylum in the UK. The number rose to 4,300 in the third quarter of 2002, but by the first quarter of 2003, the number was back to 2,135 (Home Office 2003). Despite such facts, the general public receives an inaccurate view of the number of asylum seekers taken in by Britain. A 2005 survey found that the average person thinks asylum seekers and refugees make up about 23 per cent of the UK population, yet research shows the actual figure is 1.98 per cent – less than two per cent (*The Independent* 2005: 36).

The *ineligibility myth* questions the 'genuineness' of asylum seekers and refugees, asserting instead that they are 'economic migrants'. The reality is that most asylum seekers are not motivated to come to Britain by *pull* factors such as economic benefits, but by *push* factors such as 'fleeing persecution, violence or threats of violence' (Home Office 2002). Even if the majority of asylum seekers were economic migrants (which they are not), it is the developed world (of which Britain is a part) that creates the need for economic migration. Weber and Bowling (2002: 123) link hostility towards asylum seekers with global capitalism, arguing that the 'developed world' sees migration from the 'less developed world' as a threat to their way of life, yet has produced the need for 'economic migration' by exploiting the 'less developed' world.

The *cost myth* inaccurately inflates the amount of financial assistance given to asylum seekers and refugees by the State, and portrays asylum seekers and refugees as receiving better services than local residents. Immigrants are portrayed as parasites who have come to Britain to fill 'our' hospitals and classrooms, take 'our' jobs, and use 'our' social welfare systems (Baird 2002: 9). In truth, Britain's hospitals could scarcely run without the immigrants who staff them at every level – from consultants and doctors to cleaning staff. The *cost* mythologisers fail to mention the several billion pounds' worth of net contribution immigrants make to public finances each year (Hayter 2002), or the fact that immigration can increase employment opportunities by bringing new skills that help to develop new sectors. The media often portray asylum seekers and refugees as jumping housing queues; in truth, many are forced to live in woefully substandard accommodation (Committee to Defend Asylum Seekers 2002).

After a number of myths had appeared on its letters page, the *Sunderland Echo* published a two-page myth-busting article. It quoted a spokesman for Sunderland Council who said that, contrary to the myth-makers, 'no council tax money is spent on providing accommodation or special services for asylum seekers' (*Sunderland Echo* 2003). According to a report by Oxfam and the Refugee Council, 85 per cent of organisations working directly with asylum seekers said their clients go hungry, while 95 per cent said their clients could not afford to buy shoes or clothes (Penrose 2002: 4). The *cost myth* diverts attention from the benefits of immigration, the real causes of social problems – such as unemployment and substandard housing – and the very real poverty faced by refugees and asylum seekers themselves.

The *social cost myth* portrays asylum seekers and refugees as a threat to 'the British way of life'. Baird (2002: 9) argues that asylum seekers and refugees are portrayed as 'different from us', as not sharing 'our' values, customs, languages or religion and as swamping 'our' culture. This view was promulgated by former British Prime Minister Margaret Thatcher in her infamous 1978 speech claiming that 'people are really afraid that this country might be rather swamped by people with a different culture' (Callinicos 1992: 16). Subsequent politicians have echoed Thatcher's views. They deny that they are being racist or xenophobic when they do so (Brown 2002), while promoting racism in a new guise. Racism today has fluidity; its immediate focus can shift quickly and is not necessarily defined by colour (Mahamdallie 2002: 27). Racist treatment of asylum seekers is as likely to be aimed at Eastern Europeans (Brown 2002) as people of colour; its main objective is still to create mechanisms of inclusion and exclusion (Gilroy 1987: 41). The 'new racism' specifies who may legitimately belong to the national community. Since asylum seekers and refugees are portrayed as a threat to national identity, clearly they are not a welcome addition.

Baird's (2002: 12) *criminality myth* reflects the tendency of media representation to criminalise asylum seekers and refugees and treat them as 'terror suspects'. Some newspapers consciously use crime reporting to promote opposition to immigration (Hayter 2001), and thus contribute to the stereotyping of ethnic minorities (Trowler 1991). The suggestion is that 'we' do not know who these people are, that they often enter the country illegally and are therefore criminals or possibly even terrorists (Baird 2002). The media seized upon this view after the events of 9/11. While the national media consistently link asylum seekers with crime, Karpf (2002) notes that the media failed to inform the public that, during a three-year period in Kent, reported crime fell at the same time that the population of asylum seekers rose. It is not just the media that criminalise refugees and asylum seekers. It is also the case that asylum seekers can and do fight back. Imprisoned refugees at the Woomera detention centre in Western Australia dug their own graves and sewed their lips together in order to draw media and public attention to the prison-like conditions they were forced to endure (Barkham 2002: 17).

Islamophobia

The 'new racism' directed at refugees and asylum seekers stems, in part, from a broader moral panic over immigration and terrorism. That panic was sparked by the terrorist attacks of 11 September 2001, when operatives from the Muslim terrorist organisation Al-Qaeda hijacked planes in the US and flew them into the World Trade Center and Pentagon complexes, killing several thousand people. The resulting fear of Muslims (people who adhere to the Islamic faith), or Islamophobia as it is commonly known, has thrust religion to the forefront of debates on ethnicity. In the 1994 National Survey of Ethnic Minorities in the UK, respondents were asked to indicate which two of twelve elements of self-description were most important to them. The majority of South Asians picked religion and nationality, in that order. There are more than 1 million Muslims living in Britain; many consider Islam to be a central part of their lives. However, individuals classified as Muslim in the UK are not a homogeneous group. Their countries of origin differ; they speak different languages and follow different schools of Islamic thought. There are two main strands to Islam, Shi'a and Sunni, which subdivide further; 90 per cent of Muslims worldwide are Sunni.

Islamophobia is not a new phenomenon so much as a transformation of old phobias about African-Caribbean and other ethnic minority communities – an example of how the target of filth accusations shifts while remaining firmly imbedded among ethnic minorities. Islam has been associated with extreme political and personal violence in the past. In recent years public fears about Muslims seem to have intensified in response to several high profile incidents. The first of these is the so-called Rushdie Affair of 1989. Salman Rushdie was born in India to a Muslim family. At the age of 14 he was sent to school in England. When his parents left India for Pakistan, Rushdie stayed in England to continue his studies at King's College, Cambridge. After graduating in 1968 he moved fluidly between Pakistan and Britain, working in television, theatre and advertising before settling on a writing career. In the late 1980s, he published a novel called *The Satanic Verses*. There was nothing particularly demonic about it. However, one of the characters in the novel speculates that a passage in the Qu'ran may not be the word of God. Since the Islamic faith is deeply committed to the view that the Qu'ran is in fact the word of God, it is considered unacceptable to question this. In 1989, the pre-eminent Iranian Muslim leader, the Ayatollah Khomeini, issued a *fatwa* – a death warrant – against Salman Rushdie. Rushdie went into hiding. Muslims all over the world expressed support for the *fatwa* by staging public burnings of the book. No doubt many more began a quest to find and kill Rushdie.

In 1994, another novelist, the Egyptian Nobel prize-winner, Naguib Mahfouz, was assaulted for similar reasons. Events such as these, and the 1991 Gulf War, brought Muslims into the media spotlight and adversely affected their treatment in the UK. This then affected other ethnic minorities. Racist slurs were used to bait and ridicule. Ahmed (1993) argues that media representations of Muslims reflected a choice of language that implied that Muslims inhabit a 'criminal culture'. Across the globe, latent stereotypes of Islam and the Orient were reinvigorated so that Muslim communities came to represent a threatening enemy within (Saeed 2002; Saeed, Blain and Forbes 1999).

The Bradford disturbances of June 1995, and April and July 2001, involving (among others) Muslim Pakistani youths, again placed British Muslims in the public eye. Then came 11 September 2001 and the Bali bombings. Those and related events undoubtedly exacerbated racism, victimisation and criminalisation of Muslims of South Asian and 'Middle Eastern' appearance (Pickering 2002). Women who wear the *hijab* (veil) do so to deflect the male sexual gaze; as such, it is both a sign of respect and a form of protection. At the same time, the *hijab* can arouse aggression, harassment and hostility from those in the non-Muslim community. Particularly since 9/11, Muslim women wearing the veil have been targets of hate crime. Poynting (2002) provides evidence linking Australian media discourse vilifying ethnic minorities, particularly those of 'Middle Eastern appearance', to an upsurge in racist hate crimes. Of particular concern is the way in which categories such as 'Muslim' and other 'non-Christian' religions have merged with 'Arab' and 'terrorist' in public discourse. According to Poynting, around the time of the Gulf War, most racist attacks in Australia were directed at Muslim women and girls wearing *hijab*. Sikh men wearing turbans and other non-Muslims of 'Middle Eastern' appearance were also targeted.

There is no reason to believe that Australia is unique in this respect. It appears that distinctions between refugees, legal immigrants, illegal immigrants, terrorists and Muslims have become so blurred that the non-Muslim public views all such 'outsiders' as 'dangerous' (Weber 2002).

Conclusion

'Unlike any location in metropolitan Europe, colonial locations were regarded collectively by Orientalist scholarship (Said 1979) as places characterised by lawlessness and chaos' (Agozino 2003: 3). Newspapers capitalise on this. The mass media are filled with disproportionate references to the supposed deviance of the 'new' colonial subjects – ethnic minorities. This suggests that accusations of filth do not shift arbitrarily, but fall disproportionately on ethnic minority peoples, and provides indelible evidence of institutionalised racism. Rather than helping to overcome unfounded fears, those who control the tools of communication encourage audiences to dread the Other, thus contributing to the general climate of 'dangerisation' in which the world is viewed through 'categories of menace' (Lianos and Douglas 2000: 267). It is obviously simplistic to analyse media representation of ethnic minorities solely as a process of imputing filth, and the coming chapters provide a range of analytical tools and frameworks. Along with the motivation for imputing filth comes the accompanying threat of danger. How is the threat posed by the filthy to be assuaged? By reducing ethnic minorities to a romanticised ideal – a point to which we will turn in the next chapter. When the objects of romanticism fail to live up to the ideal, as they inevitably will, the majority have further justification for imputing filth.

Exercises

1.1 'Filth' and 'Grime'

1. Find a volunteer to read out to the class the satirical extract below:

GRIME MAGAZINE

Sunday, 1 April 1984

Blacks commit more crime than whites. It's natural because of biology. Dark skinned persons have evolved to blend into the landscape better, especially at night; therefore they have a greater ability to commit secretive and heinous acts. (*Queen's English Dictionary*). Naturally they have all the appropriate behaviour patterns necessary for their evolutionary niche. Jumping, for example, assists in accessing their crime areas, as well as making a quick getaway if a pig or other predator turns up. Yet obviously jumping has other uses, as in basketball and other such sociocultural artefacts. Similarly, the evolved criminogenic

---

abilities can find other applications at times and places other than those for which they were originally developed. The jumping prowess of black men is also an evolutionary device designed to make them more attractive to potential mates. Pigs too have evolved to meet the demands of the ecosystem, I would assert. They can fly, albeit in a rather clumsy manner, and I imagine this makes them fearsome predators. Notice that they too tend to wear dark clothing presumably in order to frequent similar surroundings. This may be one reason why they make frequent captures. Frequent captures imply a high breeding rate among the criminogenic group, and here too jumping may be important, particularly for the male. For women, pregnancy is probably a hindrance to jumping. If they cannot jump far enough, they would not be expected to take as much part in criminal activity, or they would get caught more.

2. Now, watch the Australian Aboriginal satire, *Babakiueria*. Divide into groups. Each group will produce a mock news broadcast focusing on media stereotypes of ethnic minorities.
3. Taken together, the 'new racism' and moral panics over immigration make the treatment of refugees and asylum seekers a controversial and highly emotional topic. In these circumstances it is hard for students to take a balanced critical approach. Indeed, the latest asylum opinion poll conducted by the MORI Social Research Institute (2003) reveals that many young people in Britain are ill-informed about the asylum process and harbour negative views of asylum seekers. Conduct an asylum myth-busting quiz. Write a list of questions, and display them on a whiteboard or overhead projector.

Sample questions
- In 2005, what percentage of the world's asylum seekers came to this country?
- Which country took in the most asylum seekers?
- Between 2005 and 2006, what were the top five countries of origin for asylum seekers in this country?
- Do asylum seekers receive more in economic benefits than citizens of this country?

Write down your answers, then swap answer sheets with the person next to you. Read out each question and ask students to volunteer answers. Supply correct answers, accompanied by evidence.

4. Question for discussion

Presented in a format that encourages belief, and drawing on enough stereotypes to be plausible to some readers, the absurd *Grime Magazine* argument on 'Black criminality' above masquerades as a rational thesis. How much more powerful are the oft-repeated, unchallenged and contradictory themes that appear every day in the overwhelming majority of our mainstream media?

Further reading

Ames, M. M. (1992) *Cannibal Tours and Glass Boxes: The Anthropology of Museums*, Vancouver: UBC Press.

Cultural Survival Quarterly (periodical).

Douglas, M. (1999) *Purity and Danger: An Analysis of the Concepts of Pollution and Taboo*, 2nd edn, London: Viking.

Étienne, M. and Leacock, E. (eds) (1980) *Women and Colonization: Anthropological Perspectives*, New York: Praeger [out of print; subject to availability].

Hall, Stuart (ed.) (1997) *Representation: Cultural Representations and Signifying Practices*, London: Sage/Open University.

Pratt, Mary Louise (1992) *Imperial Eyes: Travel Writing and Transculturation*, London: Routledge.

Suggested viewing

Latcho Drom
Pow Wow Highway

2 Nanook, Nyla and their successors: representations from the outside

In this chapter we look at 'romantic' depictions of minority peoples in mass media, and the ways these trivialise, ignore, or contradict the people, places and events they purport to represent. To demonstrate the processes and products of representation, we provide case studies of Robert Flaherty's documentary, *Nanook of the North*; the Disney Studio's feature-length cartoon film, *Pocahontas*; a recent feature 'celebrating' 'Indian fashion' published in our local newspaper, the *Sunderland Echo*; belated global coverage of one of the most important general assemblies held by the Inuit Circumpolar Conference, in Greenland in 1989; and a Sunday magazine feature on the Canadian Inuit community of Holman Island in the Northwest Territories, published in 1991 in the British newspaper, the *Sunday Telegraph*. Some of these representations are well-intentioned; others show a blatant contempt for the facts. Such representations, seen in many media, locations and times, are characterised by rampant errors – mislabelling of places and people, misnaming of people (or omitting their names altogether), and getting even the simplest factual details wrong. In these instances, the basic fact-checking that is considered standard practice in most media organisations is entirely missing from the production process. Far from innocuous, such misrepresentations leave the public woefully misinformed.

Nanook of the North

Northern peoples, particularly Inuit, first came to the attention of Outsiders in 1922 with the release of Robert Flaherty's ground-breaking work, *Nanook of the North*. Although *Nanook* is widely considered to be the first 'documentary' film, the term was not used until several years later, in John Grierson's reference to Flaherty's 1926 film, *Moana* (Alia 1999: 17–18). Flaherty's self-declared intention was to show Inuit 'not

34

from the civilized [sic] point of view but as they saw themselves' (Griffith 1953: 36). Today, 'documentary' is supposed to be factually based. But the father of documentary, Flaherty, staged scenes and constructed sets from the start, and set the tone for future work in which people, land and events are at least made to *appear* to be real. His method drew from early ethnography – a field involving description of cultures – which has undergone radical transformation and examination over the years (e.g., Malinowski 1922; Dietz, Prus and Shaffir 1994).

The production of ethnographic text is now widely considered to be subjective and narrative. Subjectivity is less accepted in the world of 'documentary' television and film, which is generally linked to journalism. One major difference between Flaherty's film and the documentaries of today is that his fictionalisation is made more transparent for the viewer. Current ways of production and commentary pretend distance, objectivity and factuality. Yet all documentaries present subjective realities from their makers' points of view. Sherrill Grace (1996) thinks Flaherty's documentaries have more in common with fictional romance than anthropological documentation – a position that requires further thinking, since we could also argue that anthropological documentation is itself a form of fictional romance.

Flaherty was a complex man of his times, an innovative experimenter in a relatively new medium and an interested, admiring, sometimes patronising observer of Inuit life. He went on from *Nanook* to other locations and people, leaving the Inuit to live out their (mostly brief) lives and also to care for his descendants. Flaherty's appreciation of Inuit and their accomplishments is tempered by paternalistic and racist assumptions about their 'primitiveness' (Flaherty 1924). He expressed appreciation and admiration for his Inuit companions and assistants. He apparently regarded his Inuk partner Alice Nuvalinga (the actress who portrayed 'Nyla' in *Nanook*) with genuine – and limited – affection, and as no threat to his 'real' wife. Some twenty years later, Robert Peary – far less benevolent in tone or intention – portrayed his own Inuit assistants and companions as mere childlike servants (Alia 1987: 64). Flaherty's detractors have focused on the film's failure to reproduce life literally, but its ability to convey the spirit and culture of Inuit must also be acknowledged.

Nanook played a crucial role in representing Inuit to those Outside (the term northerners in Canada and Alaska use to refer to those living outside the Arctic and sub-Arctic regions). As Sherrill Grace puts it, Robert Flaherty is a sign in the 'semiotics of north' (Grace 1996: 3). Spin-offs from his film included 'Eskimo Pie' ice cream bars – available for decades in every town and city in the US, and still available in Aotearoa – popular songs and a multitude of books. Flaherty's own 'real life' was reinvented to the extent that, according to Grace, none of his biographies mentions his Inuit family. That is striking, because his descendants remain prominent and present in today's Arctic. The Canadian political and social leader, Martha Flaherty, is his granddaughter. Just before the final credits, the 1994 film about Flaherty, *Kabloonak*, makes passing reference to her forebears – in the past tense – in printed text that informs viewers that 'Nyla's' (Alice Nuvalinga's) son is no longer alive, but entirely neglects his living relatives. Flaherty declared:

> I am not going to make films about what the white man has made of primitive peoples ... What I want to show is the former majesty and character of these people, while it is still possible – before the white man has destroyed not only their character, but the people as well. (Barnouw 1974: 45)

The sort of false impressions that Flaherty's *Nanook of the North* constructed are an example of what Blythe (1994: 22) calls the 'Myth of Authenticity' – 'a myth in which erotic/exotic worlds can be constructed as authentically different from European or American cultures by piling up various racial and cultural differences'. Charles Goldie's paintings of Maori (suitably captioned 'The Passing of the Maori', 'The Last of Her Tribe' and so on) are similarly emblematic of Pakeha trying to recover what they could of a so-called 'dying race'.

Native American 'Princesses'

The representation of Martha Flaherty's grandmother is reminiscent of the 'Indian princesses' documented by Gail Guthrie Valaskakis in her exhibition and book (co-authored with Marilyn Burgess), *Indian Princesses and Cowgirls: Stereotypes from the Frontier* (1995). 'Near Sitting Bull's grave, there is a bullet-ridden obelisk raised in memory of the Indian woman who accompanied Lewis and Clark on their expedition across the West ... Sacajawea ...' (Valaskakis 1995: 11). Sacajawea, also called 'Sakakawea', an Hidatsa word meaning 'bird woman', was transformed in popular imagery (for example, a 1920s advertisement for Oriental Dyeing and Cleaning Works) into an 'ageless' 'shapely Indian princess with perfect caucasian features, dressed in a tight-fitting red tunic, spearing fish with a bow and arrow from a birchbark canoe suspended on a mountain-rimmed, moonlit lake' (Valaskakis 1995: 11).

Such images and attitudes continue to influence depictions of First Peoples. In the 1996 movie, in North America titled *Smilla's Sense of Snow* and in Scandinavia, Aotearoa, and elsewhere following the original title of Peter Hoeg's novel, *Miss Smilla's Feeling for Snow*, the British actor,

Julia Ormond, portrays the Greenlandic lead. A Native American Barbie doll-styled cartoon image of Pocahontas features in the eponymous 1995 children's film produced by Disney studios. She looks strikingly like the Sacajawea of the 1920s, although her slightly less Caucasian face features Oriental-looking eyes. The lyrics to one of the main songs, 'Savages', are supposed to provide parallel stereotypes – whites looking at Native Americans and vice versa. The realities of colonial history and the continuing inequalities of power and misrepresentation suggest the 'Indian' stereotypes are the ones that will most affect the movie's audience:

> What can you expect from filthy little heathens?
> Their whole disgusting race is like a curse.
> Their skin's a hellish red.
> They're only good when they are dead!
> Savages, Savages . . . (*Pocahontas* 1995)

The US film industry awarded the musical score an Oscar with nary a thought for its disconcerting lyrics. Viewers in the UK had to contend with additional confusion. Despite the years of seeing Hollywood Westerns with their cowboys-and-Indians themes, 'Indian' is generally understood to refer to people from India rather than to descendants of the people Christopher Columbus misidentified on landing. In the US there are still sports teams (and peanuts!) called 'Redskins' and 'Indians'. Brand names such as 'Redman' fruit appear in flaming red logos on fruit boxes in American supermarkets. 'First Nations people do not typically feel flattered by Disney's *Pocahontas* or mascots like the Washington Redskins', said singer-songwriter, Buffy Sainte-Marie (1998).

Alex Karoniaktatie Jacobs calls the appropriation and (mis)representation of First Nations identity and culture the 'politics of primitivism' (Jacobs 1986). In *Freeze Frame*, her study of the depiction of Alaska Eskimos in the movies, Ann Fienup-Riordan dissects this 'politics of primitivism', considering the 'disjunction between how life is lived in Alaska and how it is represented in film' (Fienup-Riordan 1995: xx). In the movies, Eskimos are usually 'primitives', 'noble survivors in a hostile land' (Fienup-Riordan 1996: 4). In 1932, *Igloo* was supposed to be about Canadian Inuit; it featured (western Alaskan) Ray Mala and an all-Iñupiat cast (Fienup-Riordan 1996: 4). Other films feature such 'Inuit' as Anthony Quinn, Yoko Tani, Gloria Saunders, Lotus Long, Carol Thurston, Joan Chen, Meg Tilly and Lou Diamond Phillips.

In 1969 the National Film Board of Canada first produced a work created primarily by indigenous people, *These Are My People*, directed by Michael Mitchell, a Mohawk. That same year, the Anik satellite system was launched, paving the way for the first indigenous television network,

Television Northern Canada (TVNC). Today, there is a strong body of films and an international network, the First Nations Film and Video World Alliance, with members in Canada, Vanuatu, Mexico, the United States, Greenland, Australia, Aotearoa, and the Solomon Islands.

The persistence of the exotic

The exoticising of land and people persists in many of the publications produced for consumers and travellers, which depict the homelands of many peoples, not as places of residence, but as places of exploration, tourism and trade. It is also true that many people wish to increase tourism and trade and become partners in exploration, and there is a growing tendency in print and broadcast media at least superficially to consider social, political and environmental concerns (for example, *Lonely Planet* and *Rough Guide* publications and television programmes). However, even today's environmentalists often focus more on land, flora and fauna than on the effects of environmental problems on people. *The Beaver* remains the voice of Canada's Hudson's Bay Company (founded mainly by Scottish immigrants to the Canadian North) and the portrayer of its history, although it has often published work by indigenous writers (for example, Peter Ernerk's article, 'The Inuit as Hunters and Managers', in *The Beaver* 67(1) Feb/March 1987: 62) (Petrone 1988: 283).

Much as women in male-dominated societies are put on pedestals, indigenous people are portrayed as 'noble savages', admired for their intriguing costumes, appearances and skills, but dismissed as having lesser intellect and fewer accoutrements of 'civilisation'.

Homes and playthings: a comparative excursion into nomadic lives

In the Introduction, we noted the marketing of Roma cultural products to British non-Roma, particularly the 'Hand made gypsy caravans for [children's] play' (Lavenders Blue Ltd 2004). Encountering this advertisement, we were struck by parallels from Valerie Alia's Oklahoma childhood, when elaborate child-sized 'Indian' *teepees* (tents used by some Native American tribes), brightly coloured turkey-feather headdresses and other accoutrements of fictional Native America appeared in countless backyards and streets across the US. Today, they are found in both child- and adult-sized versions throughout Europe, Britain and Australasia. These exotic playthings have nothing to do with promoting intercultural communication and mutual understanding, and everything to do with a kind of essentialist theatre. In fact, they (often inadvertently) perpetrate and perpetuate misunderstanding, miscommunication, mis-representation and racism. Parents who think it charming for their chil-dren to play at 'Gypsies' or 'Indians' would be hard pressed to encourage them to befriend real Roma or Native American playmates. Indeed, the continuing stigmatisation of Roma and indigenous peoples creates a stun-ning dissonance.

The writers live in the north-east corner of England. An issue of the local newspaper, the *Sunderland Echo*, carried a splashy new 'lifestyle' supplement with a two-page, full colour, lavishly photographed feature headlined, 'Celebrating the difference'. With the city experiencing well-documented bouts of harassment, assault and generalised intolerance of cultural difference, we were thrilled to see the paper offering positive coverage of ethnic minorities (or so we thought). On closer inspection, we saw seven sweet-looking, pale-faced girls, all but one of them blonde. It is unlikely that the editor meant to make a 'racial' statement with the cutely punning captions ('Sari, sari night'; 'Bolly good show', and so on), but like her companions, the girl whose photograph is captioned 'ALL WHITE HERE' is indeed 'all white'. So where's the 'difference'? It's all in the sub-heading: 'Bollywood comes to South Hylton' (a neighbourhood in our city). 'Bollywood' refers to the Indian film industry (Hollywood East). The girls are not learning about the real-life Indian children whose clothes they are wearing. They are playing *dress-up*.

The story describes a program in which members of Indian and other cultural communities were invited to bring their music, food, clothes and art to a primary school. But where are those people's children? Not in the photographs or the clothes. The journalist called it 'a true taste of India' and gushed: 'The girls felt like little princesses as they dressed in silks...' (Colling 2003). It is true that some Indo-British women wear the traditional long, flowing sari, but most girls of student age wear the same kinds of clothes or uniforms as their Anglo-Celtic classmates. The depiction of exoticised 'Others' serves more to perpetuate cultural stereo-typing than to promote genuine understanding and is, we would argue, unethical. A near-parallel might be to picture South Asian schoolgirls wearing Scottish-style kilts without actually encountering any Scottish children. There were clearly well-meant thoughts behind the week-long celebration. But despite the good intentions, there is no hint of dialogue between students of different ethnic backgrounds. The 'all white here' girl and the editor apparently do not know that in India, white is generally a funereal colour, girls from Indo-British communities are not all sari-wearing 'little princesses', and our city is home to significant numbers of people with variously hued hair and skin. Here was a missed opportunity to promote intercultural tolerance and understanding.

Trivialising peoples and politics

In June 1997, the Inuit Circumpolar Conference (ICC) celebrated its 20th anniversary at Barrow, Alaska. In 1987, the ICC brought the Inuit Regional Conservation Strategy to the United Nations – the first time such a strategy was developed by an indigenous people anywhere in the world. In 1992 the *Globe and Mail*, which bills itself as 'Canada's National Newspaper', finally decided that the then 15-year-old ICC merited serious coverage (Cernetig 1992). Since its inception, the ICC has held a general assembly every three years; the world's media missed a major international story in failing to produce news reports of its 1989 assembly in Greenland.

In October 1992, the *Globe and Mail* ran a large front-page photograph with the caption: 'The lifting of the Iron Curtain is redefining the Arctic'. It is certainly true that the so-called 'lifting' of the so-called 'curtain' had enormous impact on the North. It is also true that these changes affected Inuit and the ICC. It is not true that Aboriginal Russians did not join the ICC until the Soviet Union ended. Although this was the first *official* Russian delegation, it was not the first *delegation*. The first delegation had arrived with much celebration, three years earlier, virtually ignored by the world press. In 1989:

> I joined townspeople and assembly organizers on the small ferry dock, to await the arrival of the boat with delegates from all the polar nations. The flags of Canada, Greenland, the US and the USSR waited with us... Since its founding in 1977, the ICC has declared itself 'under four flags'. Until now, Soviet participation was only symbolic – the Soviet flag and an empty chair were placed at the head of each assembly. The flags remained, but no chair was empty. The flags welcomed Inuit from Chukotka Autonomous Region in the USSR, from Alaska, Canada's Northwest Territories, Labrador, Northern Quebec and Greenland. ICC President Mary Simon called the Soviet presence 'a milestone in Inuit history'. 'Our family of Inuit is today complete,' said Greenland Premier Jonathan Motzfeldt. (Alia 1989)

The Arctic policy document reported as news in 1992 was available in draft form at the 1989 assembly; the media practitioners who attended paid it scant attention. This comprehensive policy addressed every aspect of northern life – environmental, social, cultural and political. Its *Draft Principles on Communications* outlined policy for broadcasting, telecommunications and print services, and made Inuktitut-language services and extensive northern coverage a priority. That same year, the Soviet foreign affairs department invited ICC to Moscow for environmental talks; a year later ICC President Mary Simon accepted an additional Soviet invitation to the founding conference of the Arctic Peoples of the Soviet Union.

She spoke at the opening session in Moscow, where Mikhail Gorbachev's presence underscored the support of his (soon to be ousted) government.

Later that year, the *Moscow News* began reporting problems faced by northern peoples, including a cancer rate two to three times the national average among indigenous people in Chukotka. ICC representatives met with Vladimir Sangi, a distinguished poet and President of the new organisation of Soviet indigenous Arctic peoples. In 1990 Sangi said his struggle for this organisation spanned three decades (Alia 1992). By failing to cover these events, the news media did not just miss an opportunity to report accurately on indigenous people; they missed important information about the impending demise of the Soviet Union. Sangi predicted that 'this movement of Arctic minorities' would 'stimulate the whole destruction [of] this ugly federation' and would help to 'create within the borders of Russia a state of equal peoples' (Alia 1995: 21).

The *Globe and Mail* article offered some interesting observations and valuable – though belated – information. It also patronised the very people it called politically astute:

> When the Russian Inuit arrived in Inuvik, they were a heart-rending sight, more like figures from grainy photographs in an archive than citizens of a former superpower. They walked the sidewalks of Inuvik, dressed in ill-fitting clothes... [and] carried bulky Soviet cameras... (Alia 1995: 21)

If anything is 'heart-rending', it is the environmental and social destruction that continues to kill Aboriginal people in the Russian North. The reporter uses fashion terminology to refer to the Russian participants' accoutrements of poverty and difference, calls North Americans 'fashionable' and Greenlanders 'sophisticates' – crediting their sophistication to 'ties to Denmark' and Europe, not their own fashion sense. Why fashion sense is relevant in the first place is another matter. News coverage of dominant-culture politics mentions fashion only when describing women. We could postulate a hierarchy of discriminatory coverage (dominant-culture females, subordinate-culture males and females). In the classroom, we suggest that students apply a 'test of parallels' to measure equality of coverage. Consider news stories that describe female politicians (their clothes, hairdos, deportment... and politics) and ask whether the reporter would provide a similar description of a male politician's shirt or hairdo.

Although there have been some improvements, it remains the case that, even where journalists try to do their homework, the so-called 'authoritative' sources do not always make their research easier. The highly respected *Oxford Dictionary for Writers and Editors* tells its readers that Inuit are 'Canadian Native American people' whose language is

'Iñupiaq'. It further states that 'Inuk' means a member of 'a Canadian or Greenland Native American people', while Iñupiat is said to be 'an Alaskan Native American people, or the language of this people' (Ritter 2000: 172; Alia 2004c: 56). Another authoritative source, the *Oxford English Reference Dictionary*, defines 'Inuit' (which is in fact a plural form) as 'an Iñupiaq-speaking Eskimo, esp. in Canada' (Pearsall and Trumble 1996: 739). The situation gets even more tangled if our conscientious journalist consults yet another source, the *Oxford Colour Spelling Dictionary*. Here, we are told that the plural of 'Inuit' (which is already a plural!) is 'Inuit *or* Inuits' and the plural of 'Inuk' (a singular form meaning one person) is 'Inuk *or* Inuks' (Waite 1996: 277; Alia 2004c: 56).

Trying to untangle the inaccuracies piled upon each other in this magnificent mess is a dizzying affair. First of all, most Iñupiaq-speakers live in Alaska and Siberia. The separation of 'Inuk' from 'Inuit' as if these were names of different cultural groups in different countries (Canada and Greenland) is not only inaccurate, it is absurd. The word 'Inuk' is simply the singular form of 'Inuit'. 'Inuit' is an exclusively plural form, which therefore cannot refer to 'an' anybody. In the Inuktitut language, one person (of either sex) is *Inuk*; two people are *Inuuk*; and three or more people are *Inuit*. There are clear parallels with English, in which we identify one *person*, a *couple* (two people) and three or more *people*. It's as simple as that. You have to wonder why the 'authorities' keep getting it so very wrong. Inuit live in northern Canada, Alaska in the northern US, Greenland and Siberia.

'Native American' has nothing to do with Inuit. It refers to indigenous peoples of the United States who sometimes are called 'Indians'. 'Native American' sometimes is used to refer to non-Inuit indigenous people in Alaska but never to Inuit, anywhere. Inuit sometimes jokingly call themselves 'Inuks' but we have never heard this anglicised pseudo-plural used in any serious fashion, and it is certainly not correct. There is no such plural in the Inuktitut language – which is the dominant language spoken by Inuit. Iñupiaq is spoken by the people of that name, who live in Alaska and Siberia. It is never used to refer to Inuit in Greenland or Canada. This kind of carelessness amounts to a form of racism. It passes the mistakes on, from generation to generation, by presenting fiction as fact, in reference works and in the mass media that misinform the public. Imagine someone publishing (in a sourcebook used by journalists and editors) similarly erroneous information about white, English-speaking British people. Imagine hearing these kinds of errors in reference to white European or British people, broadcast on national radio and television.

We abhor the widespread misuse, in mass media, popular and academic texts, of words from indigenous languages, for example indicating a plural by adding an 's' to the end of a proper noun. In many cases the 's' is gratuitous, culturally inappropriate and ungrammatical, as in the false pluralising of 'Maoris' where the formation, 'Maori', already is a plural.

The British Broadcasting Corporation (BBC) is famed for the correctness of its English and is seldom found to err in the use of dominant world languages. Yet its radio and television writers often fail properly to research equivalent usage where minority languages are concerned. This unequal approach results in statements such as, 'Half the station's programmes must be in Maori, which is now spoken by fewer than a tenth of Maoris [sic]' (BBC 2004). Consider further examples of similar errors: 'Lego game irks Maoris' (BBC 2001); 'Maoris [sic] win return of preserved heads hidden away in museum' (Kelbie 2004); 'Global warming forces Inuits [sic] to abandon swamped homes' (Verrengia 2002). Yet there are always some writers – both cultural insiders and outsiders – who do their homework and provide correct usage to the media public: 'Fighting back – the Inuit forced from their homes to protect the US' (Butler 2003); 'The Sami – sometimes called Lapps...' (Kirby 2000) (though it can be said that in both cases, 'The' is superfluous – 'Inuit' and 'Sámi' would suffice; Sámi are indigenous people who live in northern Norway, Finland, Sweden and Siberia).

Consider whether any respectable editor would print or broadcast a reference to 'the Frenches'. To the speaker of a minority language, the double standard reflects a deeply entrenched lack of respect, especially when it comes from a major institution that markets itself as multicultural. A glance at the BBC's Internet home page reveals that the nation's major broadcast outlet prominently offers 'news in 43 languages', a link to its 'Asian Network' channel, and national information for residents of 'Wales/Cymru' (BBC 2004b). In the exclusive society of late modernity, the cherished value of 'diversity' is all too often merely an essentialist tool for explaining and excluding 'Others' (Young 1999: 88).

Translation is equally problematic. Inconsistency reigns supreme, with a marked tendency towards the superficial. Consider this excerpt from a BBC broadcast:

> About 10,000 mainly Maori protesters have marched through the New Zealand capital against plans to nationalise the country's beaches and seabed... At Wednesday's march, fifty Maori warriors led by organiser and academic Pita Sharples performed a haka war dance... (BBC 2004a)

Pakeha audiences may well have thought they were learning both about Aotearoa news and Maori culture. The problem is that a *haka* is not a dance, and this particular *haka* was performed to express dissent, not to provoke war. We have also found examples of excellence in translation and representation. Writing for the British newspaper, *The Guardian*,

Richard Adams (2004) recently produced a fine piece headlined 'Beyond the foreshore'. Although Adams was writing from the opposite side of the globe, he avoided using falsely anglicised plurals and provided accurate translation of Maori words like 'Pakeha' – 'the Maori name for the white settlers which now stands for their New Zealand-born descendants'.

Media mis/representations and 'imputed filth'

The 11.15 p.m. ITV news broadcast in the UK on 4 October 2002 described the Queen's annual visit to Canada. The audience was shown pictures of what was identified as 'Baffin Island', where Her Majesty 'was greeted by some of the local *Inuit Indians* [our italics]'. Baffin Island is Canada's largest island, the size of many a small country. Imagine hearing a major television broadcaster announce that the Canadian Prime Minister landed on 'the British Island' and was greeted by many of the local 'Englishmen Frenchmen'. The main community on Baffin Island is Iqaluit, which – as it has the only real airport – is probably where the Queen landed. Since 1999, Iqaluit has been the capital of Nunavut – a Canadian territory similar to the provinces and larger than most British counties. Nunavut (which the report did not even mention) covers nearly 2 million square kilometres – about one-fifth of Canada.

Contrary to the invention that appeared in the ITV news cast, there are no such things as 'Inuit Indians'. Inuit are people whom outsiders used to call 'Eskimos'. In Canada and the US, some non-Inuit indigenous people are called 'Indians' – an error dating back to Columbus' arrival in 1492, when he thought he had found India. Those people – who are entirely unrelated to Inuit – are variously referred to as Native Americans, Native Canadians, indigenous or Aboriginal people, or by one of the hundreds of culturally specific names such as Anishnabe, Cree, Tlingit, Lakota, Cherokee. Except for an occasional immigrant to the region, none of these 'Indian' people live in Nunavut. 'Inuit Indians' is something the writer made up. A further example comes from a 2003 science article in which *The Independent* refers to 'Inuits' – the equivalent of referring to male residents of England as 'Englishmens' (Burne 2003). Any reader would consider 'Englishmens' absurd; any editor would correct the error. In the case of 'Inuits' the editors, like countless others, missed the error. There is a tendency to assume that all such errors appear in the tabloid press. Sometimes the 'quality papers' are even worse, because readers take their greater accuracy and integrity for granted.

Media representations of the Arctic and its peoples are filled with the language of conquest and colonisation. Explorers are depicted as quasi-military conquerors who launched 'assaults' on the Pole. Indigenous people are portrayed as guides, assistants, or picturesque accoutrements whose lives revolve around helping explorers 'conquer' whatever piece of land or water they desire, and who teach them how to protect themselves against the conditions of climate and terrain. They are ignored, or treated as exotic items for study or observation, in need of 'civilisation'. Even Jane Campion's highly praised film, *The Piano*, '...served to validate colonial notions of Maori as the inferior/native Other who provided a backdrop to the real stories – those of colonial settlers...' (Pihama 1996: 192).

> Granted, the Maori characters are given a few resistant moments. Their appropriation of European dress and their mockery of Stewart gently mimics the role of the coloniser, a method which Homi Bhabha suggests can work to undo the structures of colonialism. However, the active military struggles against colonial occupation that were waging throughout this period are altogether absent from the film, although admittedly the film is rather vague about its exact period. The general passivity of the Maori in the film however lends a timeless essence; suspended outside history, they play nature to the white characters' culture. This is an old tactic, an opposition that draws on discourses of primitivism which have historically constructed the colonial Other as noble savage. (Goldson 1996)

In 1991 the *Telegraph* sent a team of journalists on a brief visit to Holman Island and published a photo-essay in its magazine supplement that infuriated members of the Holman (Uluqsaqtuuq) community and many others. Headlined 'Dressed to kill: Hunting with the Eskimos of Holman Island', it is a perfect example of 'imputed filth'. In a letter to the editor, which the *Telegraph* declined to publish, Holman's Mayor, Gary Bristow; Community Corporation Chairman, Robert Kuptana; and the US anthropologist, Richard Condon, wrote: 'thousands of... readers have had their opinions and attitudes about the Canadian Arctic falsely influenced by individuals with no understanding of even the most basic aspects of Canadian Inuit culture...' (Condon 1992; Bristow, Condon and Kuptana 1992). Among the most 'grotesque' of the *Telegraph*'s errors:

> 'Among hunters there is no code of honour,' the article proclaims...apparently measuring Inuit hunting against aristocratic English fox hunts. 'The hunter...is merciless and self-interested, gathering food only for himself and his family'... The unsuccessful hunter and his family could go hungry only steps away from someone else's well-stocked tent. (Thompson 1992: A3)

Inuit have long had an extensive food-sharing system. The *Telegraph* jour-nalists did not take the trouble to research it, or even to ask community members to explain it. Apart from their blatant errors, the *Telegraph*'s writers evidently considered subsistence hunting more 'merciless and self-interested' than the elaborately ritualised entertainments of British fox-hunting, in which the fox is used for sport, providing food and cloth-ing for no-one. At a time when British fox-hunting is increasingly under fire, the newspaper's treatment of Inuit 'barbarism' is curious indeed. It takes us back to the 'we'-'they' scenario: 'we' are enlightened; 'they' are uncivilised.

The *Telegraph* writer described 'Eskimos' who eat 'boiled duck and grease soup flavoured with feathers'. It is true that people sometimes eat duck soup. It is not made from feathers, though it is always possible that one might accidentally fall into the soup! The remark about 'grease' is gratuitous. All meat soup contains fat, unless it is skimmed. That com-ment, used to 'impute filth', could as easily be said of Yorkshire pudding. The *Telegraph* writers presented a portrait of fictional, 'wild' indigenous people much like the 'wild Indians' portrayed in Hollywood movies, in the mass media and in children's games. Even the efforts to place Inuit in the current century were misleading. Readers were told that Inuit track caribou by satellite and that snowmobiles have replaced dogs as the pri-mary mode of transportation, except during the summer migration, when 'the dogs come into their own'. Again, the reporter's imagination ran away with him. In reality, dog teams are never used in summer but *are* used almost exclusively in winter, less for Inuit hunting than to accompany tourists who come to Holman to hunt polar bears for sport. 'Perhaps the author is of the opinion that each snowmobile includes a satellite dish and computer screen? ... wildlife biologists ... track the wanderings of caribou on Victoria Island, making use of satellite technology. This tech-nology is *not* used by Holman hunters ...' (Bristow, Kuptana and Condon 1992).

Perhaps the greatest insult is the publication of photographs of Holman community members, without giving their names. In doing this, the newspaper editors are following 'a long colonialist "tradition" of photographing nameless "primitives"', a practice especially insulting in the case of 'the photograph of two of Holman's most respected elders, Jimmy and Nora Memogama' (Bristow, Kuptana and Condon 1992). To add further insult, the newspaper informs readers that the (unnamed) Memogamas are standing in front of a government-subsidised house in Holman. In fact, they were photographed several miles from town, stand-ing in front of their own hunting cabin that Jimmy Memogama built. The claim about government subsidy gives readers the clear message that these are welfare recipients who (like other members of ethnic minorities) are a drain on society and cannot care for themselves. It is a particular form of 'imputed filth', in which adults are infantilised and recolonised.

Some of the newspaper's errors should have led to the sacking of the writer and the editor who sent the story to press. The funniest one is a tale of a 'young white man who stepped off a train to stretch his legs; his frozen body was discovered the following spring' (Thomson 1991). It is possible that someone had a joke at the journalist's expense. Maybe people were poking fun at the journalist's ignorance and gullibility. Or perhaps the journalist knew the truth and was having a laugh at the reader's expense. No-one has ever stepped off a train at Holman. The nearest railhead is more than 1, 000 miles away, near the border with the province of Alberta.

Another article, in the venerable and internationally respected *New York Times* and republished in many US and Canadian newspapers, described 'Siberia's mystery nomads ... reindeer herders who dress in skins, practice ritual sacrifice ... eat raw fish ... and live year-round in reindeer-skin teepees ...' (Alia 1995: 20, transcript). The journalist did not consider such practices in the light of Jewish laws for ritual slaughter, Catholic communion – in which people practise symbolic cannibalism, ritually 'eating' the body and blood of Christ – or the Japanese culinary art of sushi. He also neglected to mention that indigenous Siberians have highly developed cultures, suffer from unprecedented levels of pollution and poverty, and rarely live past 40 (Alia 1995).

The *Telegraph* photo-essay and the *New York Times* portrayal of Siberian people are not just amusing examples of media ignorance. 'Each year ... Holman is visited by journalists who desire to write or photograph the definitive article about an isolated Inuit community ... the community has no way to ... monitor or comment upon their finished works ...' The worst harm is not the offence to ethnic minorities, but the misrepresentations, distortion and outright fabrications, which communicate those versions of 'reality' to thousands of media consumers. 'In an age when Inuit culture is being attacked by numerous animal rights groups, articles like "Dressed to Kill" ... perpetuate prejudice' (Bristow, Kuptana and Condon 1992: unpaginated).

Approaching inclusivity

Hamid Mowlana reminds us that the principle of inclusivity is an essential requirement of ethical media practice, yet it seldom enters into ethics texts or courses, let alone is identified as a central consideration.

Daily journalistic practice and codes of ethics increasingly pay closer attention to fairness and accuracy in reporting minority issues and people. The Canadian Daily Newspaper Publishers Association is committed to providing for 'the expression in its columns of disparate and conflicting views. It should give expression to the interests of minorities as well as majorities, and of the less powerful elements in society' (Canadian Daily Newspaper Publishers Association 1977). The journalistic code of conduct for the Republic of Ireland stipulates that a journalist:

> ... shall only mention a person's age, race, colour, creed, illegitimacy, disability, marital status (or lack of it), gender or sexual orientation if this information is strictly relevant. A journalist shall neither originate nor process material which encourages discrimination, ridicule, prejudice or hatred ... (Alia 2004c: 205)

Codes do not, however, guarantee, good practice, or immediately change the mind-sets of journalists and editors. In Britain, North America, Europe, Australia, Aotearoa, journalists and their subjects remain overwhelmingly Caucasian, and members of minority communities who do make it into the media still are too often relegated to stereotypical 'soft' categories and spaces. In the US, where African Americans are represented in the media, they make the music and sports pages and broadcasts far more often than the news pages and newscasts. When they do make the news, it is likely to be related to crime, drugs and corruption. There is progress, but it is stunningly slow (Mowlana 1989). Alternatively, those who do break into 'hard' categories and spaces tend not to 'rock the boat'.

Lest we seem entirely negative, we will mention one very positive portrayal, of young African-Caribbean-British students. 'Boy wonders: the black pupils making history' is introduced by a full-page photograph on the cover of the *Independent*'s *Education and Careers* magazine. Equally attractive photographs appear on the two-page inside 'spread', which is headlined 'Black boys do better'. The text describes a school programme in Hackney that is getting results. A year after introduction of the new programme, 'schools in Hackney have more than tripled the GCSE results of black schoolboys as a result of a drive to tackle under-achievement ... Among the strategies used are regular progress checks and changes to curriculum' (Cassidy 2005). The article is notable for its content and the appropriateness and attractiveness of the photographs that accompany the story. The main photograph, spread across two pages, shows two attractive, thoughtful-looking boys who appear to be deeply absorbed in their schoolwork. There is a gentleness to the scene, an everyday-ness. This photograph should not be special. What makes it so is the scarcity of images of this kind in the public media. These are not costumed musicians, high-powered athletes, drug-using or weapon-wielding gang members, or inmates in prison uniforms (stereotypical images that dominate media coverage of African-Caribbean boys and men). They are notable only for their attractive ordinariness. True progress will mean that eventually, such images will blend into the ordinary news day and the headline will be less about 'boy wonders' and 'making history' than simply going to school. Farther down that road, there will be no need of such stories at all.

Conclusion

We have commented above on a selection of 'outsider' media representations of ethnic minority peoples, and have demonstrated in each case that the content owes much more to the authors' imaginations than to ethical reporting. The result generally acts to support preconceived 'romantic' and paternalistic notions of a 'primitive' or 'savage' people. Needless to say, this is invariably insulting and degrading to the minority concerned. In the next chapter, we show that 'insider' representations can be equally contentious, and just as subordinate to politicised agendas.

Exercises

2.1 Consider the 'test of parallels' described in this chapter. Bring newspaper and magazine stories to class, which contain descriptions of men and of women. Apply the 'test of parallels'. If the treatment of women and men is not equal, rewrite the stories to make it so.

2.2 Consider two imaginary images:
   Image one: An Inuk man in carefully constructed, protective winter clothing is guiding a sledge across Arctic ice, in search of a caribou or seal, and has his son along to help. If they are successful, they will carry the animal or (depending on sizes and conditions) the hide and butchered meat, several miles back to their camp or community. There, women will scrape and prepare the fur-protected hides and turn them into essential winter clothing. Anyone who has survived an Arctic winter knows that 'fake fur' cannot protect against the extreme wind and cold; in this region, wearing fur can be a matter of life or death. The animal's fat will be rendered and used for food and heating oil. The meat will be shared among family and community and eaten raw; if there is enough, some may be frozen or dried. In Arctic conditions, raw meat often provides the only source of vitamins normally found in vegetables (vitamins A, C and so on).

Even though most northern communities have regular flights and import fruits and vegetables from the south, these are luxury items. Where they are available, they often arrive wilted and depleted, not only unappetising but inadequate to meet people's nutritional needs. What Inuit call 'country foods' – the foods they gather, fish and hunt – remain essential components of most people's daily diet.

Image two: Fifty people wearing elegant, formal riding clothes, astride their equally elegant, beautifully groomed horses, are moving swiftly through the English countryside. They are accompanied or preceded by their canine co-hunters. Somewhere in the distance, a tiny fox runs for its life. There is much exuberance; the riders are playing a ritualised game. The outcome is known from the start: the odds are stacked and the fox has no chance. When the riders have finished their game, the dogs will be fed, patted and praised; the horses cooled down, groomed, watered and fed. The people, too, will be festively watered and fed, though the 'water' is more likely to be whisky or wine and the food will bear no relation to the hunt. They will not eat their kill; its pelt will be too small to shelter anyone from winter. Its meat is insufficient even for dogs. It is a trophy, a prize for riding well. There is no connection between this hunt and the clothing and feeding of family and community.

Of the two images, which is a portrait of 'civilisation' and which of 'barbarism'? Or is each of the images a mix? Where might privilege and 'class' come into the discussion?

Further reading

Alia, Valerie (1999) *Un/Covering the North, News, Media, and Aboriginal People*, Vancouver: University of British Columbia Press, Chapters 2–4 and 7. Appendices A and B.

Alia, Valerie (2000) 'The Boundaries of Liberty and Tolerance in the Canadian North: Media, Ethics, and the Emergence of the Inuit Homeland of Nunavut', in Cohen-Almagor, R. (ed.), *Challenges to Democracy: Essays in Honour and Memory of Isaiah Berlin*, Aldershot: Ashgate, 275–95.

Clifford, James (1997) *Routes: Travel and Translation in the Late Twentieth Century*, Cambridge/London: Harvard University Press.

Crowe, Keith (1991) *A History of the Original Peoples of Northern Canada*, revd edn, Montreal: McGill-Queen's University Press.

King, J. C. H. and Lidchi, H. (1998) *Imaging the Arctic*, Vancouver: UBC Press.

Pratt, Mary Louise (1992) *Imperial Eyes: Travel Writing and Transcultura-tion*, London: Routledge.

Roth, L. (1995) '(De)romancing the North', *Border/Lines* 36, 36–43.

Suggested viewing

Atanarjuat
Pow Wow Highway
The Piano
Smoke Signals

3 Internalising 'outsider' representations: the Once Were Warriors syndrome

This chapter offers an analysis of Alan Duff's (1990) controversial novel, *Once Were Warriors*, and Lee Tamahori's film version (1994) of the same name. Each version presents a shocking portrait of urban Maori family life in 1990s Aotearoa. Both resurrect the influential and pervasive stereotype that Maori crimes of violence have their roots in the warrior past. Duff's depictions do not stand up to comparison with Irihapeti Ramsden's alternative 'once were gardeners' (see discussion, below) or Keri Hulme's complex tale of the clash between Maori and Pakeha identities and values in *The Bone People* (1983). Nor do they stand up to comparison with the Maori myth and legend to which Duff alludes. Nonetheless, his outlook may have encouraged some Maori to commit crimes, believing they are following their heritage. We call this way of internalising an outsider (mis-) representation – in this case the idea that the warrior is the enduring image of Maori society – and applying it to oneself the *Once Were Warriors* syndrome. We see the syndrome as a by-product of the long-term effects of media-sponsored colonial racism as described in the preceding chapters.

We also discuss the Canadian television documentary, *The Story of Joe and Elise* (Kuchmij 1995), which examines conflict resolution through native justice programmes and provides an equally problematic means of addressing violence and its remedies. The film documents a case in which the courts drew on Inuit and European-derived Canadian justice systems to impose a community-based sentence. The award-winning Ukrainian-Canadian film maker, Halya Kuchmij, is known for her well crafted and socially concerned films, and her particular interest in empowering ethnic minority people. In this case, her zeal for promoting humane and alternative systems of justice misses some of her own points. The film focuses almost entirely on justice for Joe Attagutaluk, leaving the issue of justice for his murdered wife outside the loop. The film maker gives viewers a rose-tinted-glasses view of the outcome of the trial, while marginalising questions of violence, abuse and gender relations that cut across cultural lines. In her decision to focus on the rehabilitation of a man (Joe) who killed his wife (Elise) during an alcohol-induced episode, Kuchmij almost entirely ignores the wife and her distinguished career – thus, in a sense, killing her twice. A third 'death' is dealt her by the omission of her treasured Inuktitut name, Kunatuloitok. An important part of her career was dedicated to addressing these very questions – of name and identity, violence and gender in her home community of Igloolik and nationally, through Pauktuutit, the Inuit Women's Association. Kuchmij's choice of perspective results in an oversimplified and almost romanticised depiction of the application of ideas of 'traditional' justice. There is some irony in the fact that, like the subjects of her film, the film maker is herself a member of an ethnic minority.

The reason for focusing on *Once Were Warriors* is that no previous book written by a Maori has generated as much controversy. In some ways its appearance was a defining moment in the history of Aotearoa. The film version alone was watched by at least a third of New Zealanders (Television New Zealand 1999). At the box office, it exceeded the blockbuster threshold in the first six weeks, on its way to raking in NZ$6 million. In October 1994, it toppled *Jurassic Park* as the most successful film in the history of Aotearoa (Calder 1996). If people from outside Aotearoa have seen representations of Maori, it is most likely to be Tamahori's film. Although it won the Booker Prize and received national and international critical acclaim, Keri Hulme's novel, *The Bone People*, aroused much less controversy until after the release of *Once Were Warriors*, when it was seized upon as a contrary opinion. This oppositional representation of the two works was fed by bitter personal disagreements between the authors, over the merits of each other's writing styles and identity as Maori.

We chose *The Story of Joe and Elise* as a subject of analysis for several reasons. The television documentary is based on a high profile case involving prominent and respected individuals. Joe and Elise Attagutaluk were leaders in their home community of Igloolik, as well as nationally. Elise's role in setting up a women's shelter is an irony lost on the film maker, who fails to mention this, or connect it to Elise's own death by violence. There is a personal connection as well, as Valerie Alia and Elise (Kunatuloitok) were involved in work on Inuit names and the effects of a government renaming programme known as 'Project Surname'. They planned a names project in Igloolik, the year before Elise was killed. The book they were to co-author ended with her death; the one eventually written is dedicated to her life (Alia 1994).

'Insiders' at odds

Alan Duff's debut novel *Once Were Warriors* (1990) rocketed to the best-seller list and has been extremely influential. The story takes place in a poor urbanised area of South Auckland where Beth and Jake Heke live in a state-subsidised house with five of their six children. Jake 'The Muss' is a 'hard-drinking, wife-beating, irresponsible, unemployed father' (Duff 1993: 62) unable to control the violent propensities he inherited (both genetically and culturally) from his slave ancestors. Highborn Beth, on the other hand, is angry that Maori accept second-class citizenship as a given. For her this stems from a cultural void. Jake's fighting ability, the only thing he 'inherits' from his culture, is responsible for all his few achievements and doubly responsible for his decline. By contrast, Beth's heritage helps her find the strength to pick up the pieces of her family. Similarly, teenage son Mark (Boogie) finds redemption through warrior discipline.

The film and book have become so entwined in the public conscious-ness it is difficult to separate the two. However, in the film, directed by Lee Tamahori (his debut) and starring Temuera Morrison and Rena Owen in the leading roles, there are a number of crucial differences from the book. The film is narrated predominantly from Beth's perspective, a result of Riwia Brown's brief to write the screenplay in such a way that Maori women could identify with it, whereas the book switches narration between the different chapters. In the book, Grace believes her rapist is her father, whereas in the film it is a friend of the family who violates her. The entire rationale for Duff's sequel, *What Becomes of the Broken Hearted?* (1996), is that everybody thinks Jake is a child molester. Class conflict un-derpins the 'Maori problem' in Duff's writing (1990, 1993, 1999), though it is still focused more on Maori–Pakeha than on Maori–Maori relations. The rich white folks versus poor brown folks theme, central to *Once Were Warriors*, is largely absent from the film. In the book, Grace hangs herself on the property of wealthy white folks. In the film, her suicide takes place in the family's back yard, turning what was originally a statement about class privilege and deprivation into an act destructive of both Grace and her own community.

The film and the book on which it is based caused a furore in Aotearoa and at numerous film festivals around the world. Apart from the ob-viously potent scenes of domestic violence, there is a complex cultural background to consider. Maori responses to *Once Were Warriors* tended to fall into two broad categories: some saw it as perpetuating negative stereotypes; others saw it as gruesome but true. Both perspectives were hotly debated in the aftermath of the book (and later the film) release.

Neither version was well received by Maori academics and prominent social commentators.

Like many others, Irihapeti Ramsden objected to Duff's insistence that Maori were and are incessantly violent. She saw Duff's portrayal as a regurgitation of outsider representations that are damaging to Maori, and offered an alternative – 'once were gardeners, once were astronomers, once were philosophers, once were lovers' (Ellison-Loschmann 2004: not paginated). Ramsden's point was that martial pursuits were well down the list of priorities for Maori. Moreover, far from being eternally fixed in the past, cultural identities fluctuate in accordance with the exigencies of history, culture and power (Hall 1997a). In the era of 'smithing', which we discuss in detail in Chapter 6, much of Maori history was derived from those who had been educated at a time of intense tribal warfare. Conflicts that might actually have occurred sporadically over centuries were telescoped into cohesive wars. The peaceful times between disappeared, thus over-emphasising warfare. In fact, signs of actual combat and of weapons themselves are quite rare in the archaeological record (Belich 1996).

Ramsden's belief that Duff's portrayal is clichéd seemed vindicated when reports of actual violence in the mainstream media evoked images from the film. This was bound to happen when word got out that actor Rena Owen was convicted of assault after a fight in a pub, dubbed 'the pool cue' incident. Where there were none of the cast's peccadilloes to report, references to the film appeared (and continue to do so) in the most unlikely places. A headline in the Australian newspaper, *The Age*, reads: 'More than once were warriors out of their tiny minds' (Masterson 2003). The associated story was about US pilots mistakenly bombing Canadian soldiers while 'high' on amphetamines. Some feared that the Heke family would be perceived as typical of modern Maori (Pihama 1996). Interestingly, most of the concern seems to have revolved around how outsiders would react, and what negative effects this might have on the country's image. Arguably, it is the insiders who stood to lose the most from the warped perceptions of their identity.

Duff's plot has been generalised to other minority groups. This is a form of essentialism – the anachronistic tendency to homogenise the experiences, preferences and aspirations of people who share a particular ethnicity (Young 1999). Assuming that ethnic minorities are all the same tends to imply that *Once Were Warriors* could as easily have been written about Native Americans. Such an implication might conceivably be of some use if it led to action on issues of violence within Native American communities. But it is just as unfair to claim that family violence is natural to Native Americans – according to Ross 'in pre-contact Native societies this type of abuse within families was a rare occurrence' (Ross 1998: 134).

Over-generalising the connections also obscures social issues of importance to Native Americans, such as the system of 'reservations' (or in Canada, 'reserves'). We must acknowledge here that indigenous peoples have sometimes themselves promoted generalisation across the 'fourth world', one of the negative by-products of a more generally positive pan-indigenous socio-political movement. We need to distinguish between essentialising or stereotyping, and the constructive search for, and use of commonalities. Comparisons are also made between *Once Were Warriors* and African American experience, as documented in numerous novels and (auto-) biographies (see for example, the works of Alice Walker, Toni Morrison, Richard Wright and others). There are limits here as well.

It is important to note that, like other indigenous peoples today, Maori constitute diverse groups living in a broad range of cultural and social realities (Durie 1994; Chapple 2000). Further, according to Young:

> If we reject essentialism, it follows that we must discard the notion of multiculturalism which proposes a mosaic of fixed essences glued to their historical past . . . To do this is not to deny pluralism and diversity . . . Rather it is precisely such a medley of cultures that gives vitality to the late modern world . . . It is a world of crossover and hybridization, not of separatism and assimilation; one where cultures constantly transform, disappear, yet where difference constantly re-emerges in new and synergic ways. (Young 1999: 108)

Many Maori were dubious about Duff's political stance. Maori are over-represented in all sorts of 'social problems' statistics; they are prominent among the unemployed, the incarcerated, the unhealthy, the poorly educated. Duff objects to institutional intervention aimed at reversing such trends and insists on individual effort instead (Heim 1998), a message he conveys in the novel through the character of Beth: 'This self-help idea was so beautifully all-embracing it was a wonder they, the Maori people in general, hadn't cottoned onto it before' (Duff 1990: 160). He concedes that some social problems among Maori may have been caused, in part, by colonisation rendering the old warrior culture redundant. Mostly, he thinks the problems arise from a failure of Maori to adapt to the colonial situation, thus effectively blaming Maori for their own 'underachievement' (Wall 1997).

The Bone People revolves around the lives of Kerewin, Simon and Joe, three Maori living in a remote South Island beach setting. Kerewin is a despairing artist who has shut herself off from the world. Her solitary existence is torn asunder by the sudden arrival during a rainstorm of Simon, a mute 6-year-old whose past is plagued by the trauma of abuse. In his wake comes his foster-father Joe, a Maori factory worker with a nasty temper. Throughout, the book addresses the problems of juggling traditions in 1980s Aotearoa. Whereas Duff's characters stereotype an entire population, Hulme's characters are too weird and idiosyncratic to be considered typical. The character of Joe Gillayley, in particular, represents a complex case of cultural hybridity. The differences in approach to Maori identity are mirrored in the authors' vastly different writing styles. There are also autobiographical echoes in the approach and work of each. Hulme lived as a hermit on the West Coast and, in her writing, draws quite deliberately on her mixed Maori and Celtic heritage. Although equally of 'mixed' inheritance, Duff apparently considered his upbringing typically Maori, rather than typically Pakeha.

In *The Bone People*, Kerewin and Joe experience a cultural void brought about by colonisation. Self-help is not explicitly mentioned, though Joe does search for his roots during a trip into the wilderness where he meets a *kaumatua* (elder). In some respects these characters cannot help themselves. Kerewin's martial arts practices cause her extreme pain; Joe's attempts at fatherhood destroy his foster-son, Simon. But Kerewin can be touched by Simon, and Joe's pain can be released by his mystic guide. In both the book and film version of *Once Were Warriors* it is only through Beth's efforts at self-help that other characters are liberated. Joe and Kerewin are outsiders in Pakeha society, just as the Heke family are. At some point, all of the characters are also outsiders in Maori society. By virtue of the cultural void they all occupy at some point or other, they lack many of the skills associated with Maori ethnicity, such as speaking the language.

In the case of Hulme's characters this sense of being on the margins of both cultures is exacerbated by the location in which *The Bone People* is set. It is not uncommon to hear North Island Maori jokingly point out that South Island Maori are somehow less real. Beneath the humour is a nugget of seriousness. This North Island–South Island distinction resembles Stuart Hall's 'second kind of otherness'. Hall (1993) postulates that identity is 'framed' by two axes that operate simultaneously: the axis of similarity and continuity (grounded in the past), and the axis of difference and rupture (grounded in discontinuity). Despite close ancestral ties, at some point North Island Maori started seeing South Island Maori as different, affected (emphasised by dialect – Ngai Tahu became Kai Tahu, for example).

It is clear in both versions of *Once Were Warriors* that Jake and his son Nig are not given validation by either culture. That said, Nig is offered a sort of counterfeit Maori culture by the gang, which Tamahori depicts as borrowing heavily from Maori motif, with tattoos and warrior aspect. Tamahori's inclination towards exoticising is as lamentable as Duff's will to misrepresent; both are remnants of the colonial enterprise. Perhaps because Hulme's book has never been turned into a visual medium, it has avoided a pitfall common to visual portrayals of ethnic identity. The film version of *Once Were Warriors* cast actors with uniformly brown skin. Because of the extent of inter-marriage between Maori and Pakeha, many Maori today are visibly indistinguishable from Pakeha.

In his defence, Duff at least draws on his own childhood experiences, and a story of that nature is bound to polarise people. This polarisation has led some to question Duff's identity as an insider. It is perhaps more interesting to speculate about how much criticism Duff might have encountered had he been an outsider. Tamahori (2003) is of the opinion that no outsider could get away with the sort of account Duff wrote. Given that Duff's views support predominant popular stereotypes, objections from Maori may have been stronger but it seems unlikely that Pakeha would object as strongly. The flip side to the question of whether or not a non-Maori could write this book is, would the story be as compelling if it revolved around a non-Maori family? Certainly the cinematic version benefits from the beautiful singing and tattooing. Of course, Stuart Hall's articulation theory, and the work of Mary Louise Pratt and James Clifford on borders, 'routes', and travel, would tell us that the insider/outsider dichotomy is far too simplistic (Pratt 1992; Clifford 1997). 'This politics of articulation eschews all forms of fixity and essentialism' (Rutherford 1990: 19).

Once Were Warriors and *The Bone People* are classic examples of post-colonial texts; they reflect a conscious effort to address a variety of cultural and political concerns of life in a decolonised nation. They are grounded in the complex historical, cultural and political contexts of Aotearoa. Indeed, both could be considered counter-colonial by virtue of wanting to liberate Maori through a revival of Maori practices. Whereas for Hulme the revival is on autonomous terms, for Duff it is on assimilationist terms. For example, he sees no point in addressing the culture void through Te Kohanga Reo, pre-schools dedicated to total immersion in Maori language. And yet, one of the more prominent features of his novel is the inarticulateness of the characters, which helps to explain their tendency to express themselves through violence.

Similarly, he links the art of *ta moko* – designs cut into the skin of the face with chisels, not dissimilar to wood carving techniques – with membership of a gang. In doing so, he reinforces the Maori culture–crime connection and extends the colonial ideology that saw the performance and wearing of *moko* criminalised in the first instance, under the Tohunga Suppression Act 1907. *Moko* are also prominent in *The Piano*. Despite the period in which the movie is set, there is no hint of the controversy surrounding the lucrative European trade in *moko mokai* (tattooed heads). Popularisation makes unhelpful associations worse. African American former world heavyweight boxing champion Mike Tyson, notorious for his violence outside the ring as much as inside it, these days sports a *moko* on the left side of his face. The *moko* in *Once Were Warriors* were created entirely from the artist's imagination (Kassem 2003) in order to avoid the culture–crime nexus, though it is difficult to believe that many viewers would be knowledgeable or perceptive enough to pick up on this. Aside from reinforcing stereotypes, the use of Maori motif in *Once Were Warriors* has further commodified Maori culture – an issue we examine in greater depth in Chapter 6.

The best use that can be made of Maori culture, Duff implies, lies in directing aggressiveness into harmless and socially constructive paths (Heim 1998: 49). This recalls Laura Nader's research on harmony ideology and conflict resolution within indigenous communities, in which she connects the discourse of harmony to the spread of Christianity and colonial policies. Harmony can come in many forms but its basic components are universal: emphasis on conciliation, recognition that resolution of conflict is inherently good; harmonious behaviour is inherently 'civilised'; consensus has greater survival value than controversy (Nader 1990). In pre-colonial times, many of these indigenous communities do not appear to have made extensive use of harmony models for conflict resolution; it was not uncommon for retributive measures such as banishment or death to be employed. Nonetheless, Nader has demonstrated that harmony models have been imposed on indigenous communities, allegedly to accord with their historical practice but with the intent of suppressing peoples by socialising them to conform. Because a retributive mindset poses a threat to the colonial enterprise, the promotion of harmony ideology helped colonists to manage and control indigenous populations.

Conversely, indigenous peoples may also use harmony ideology to resist external control. Even if it is not the preferred method for settling conflict, if it ensures a certain degree of autonomy in managing conflict resolution and avoids heavy-handed state intervention, appearing to be conciliatory has its advantages (Nader 1990). However, considerable care must be exercised to separate those methods of conflict resolution that constitute self-determination from those that merely replicate colonial attempts at assimilation.

Ultimately, Duff sees assimilation to Pakeha society as the solution to Maori social problems (Heim 1998), rather than requiring Pakeha culture to accommodate Maori mores. This reeks of the contemporary myth of the 'Frozen Maori', the idea that Maori traditions cannot change and remain Maori (Belich 1997). The ongoing reconstruction of tradition is a facet of all social life. Maori of the 1760s, no less than contemporary Maori, were moved by their own agendas to appeal selectively and creatively to the tradition of their ancestors; the same can be said for those ancestors, and so on indefinitely (Hanson 1989).

Neither account is superficial enough to suppose that past Maori society was egalitarian. This complexity is drawn out by Duff in the battle between the valorisation of the warrior-spirit (as exemplified by highborn Beth's redemption) versus the corruption of the warrior spirit (exemplified in slave-descended Jake's violence). The crucial difference lies in Duff encouraging liberation through adaptation of racial stereotypes with heavy colonial connotations. Arguably the image of Maori as warriors – a masculinised stereotype – was a necessary ingredient in imputing filth (Douglas 1992), and therefore helped to justify colonial violence. The stereotype applied to women, and exemplified in Beth, is the colonial version of the virgin/whore paradox. Ross (1998) describes a recent manifestation in the US, which is echoed in both the film and book version of *Once Were Warriors*:

> Native women have been reduced to the depraved squaw or the Indian princess . . . The princess image was recently repopularized by Disney's release of *Pocahontas*, in which we see a very sexy, and very young Indian princess. The princess is noble, virginal; the squaw is savage, whorish. The princess, of course, is too noble to ravage – only squaws are raped. (Ross 1998: 168)

International reception of *Once Were Warriors* and *The Bone People* was quite different. Readers (and viewers) are struck by the visceral qualities of *Once Were Warriors*. Perhaps because Hulme's book was published earlier, after winning the Booker Prize in 1985, people talked about how the Empire was striking back – the sort of sentiment one associates with literature that is both postcolonial and decolonised. Duff's work, on the other hand, has the air of a Maori working exceedingly hard to become an especially good Pakeha, and in the process playing to racist attitudes.

(Mis)representation

For Duff, Maori are:

> . . . without the sets of values which the European[s] have acquired over the years from the different and various cultures, including their own cultural evolution. It is because Maori have no overwhelming disapproval of violence . . . Maori culturally condone certain acts of violence . . . (Duff 1993: 65–6)

Certain acts of violence are condoned by most cultures, not least the technologically advanced and economically successful. The history of Aotearoa itself is replete with evidence of Pakeha condoning senseless acts of violence against Maori (Bull 2004). That said, taking liberties in works of fiction is scarcely new. What is worrying is that Duff's ideas reached a receptive audience in Aotearoa where racisms fester behind a harmonious veneer.

Stereotypes in *Once Were Warriors* help to reinforce and naturalise racialised notions of crime (Wall 1997). The key means by which they do this is through reinvigorating the idea that 'traditional' Maori society was characterised by relentless violence. The logic goes something like this: only primitive technology prevented the annihilation of Maori as a race. Then colonisation rendered the old warrior culture redundant. When Maori failed to adapt, the genetic propensity for conflict fulfilled itself in intra-racial violence and crime (Heim 1998). Duff may not have been the first to proffer this influential stereotype (see Philipp 1946; Bungay and Edwards 1983: 129–30; Sheffield 1958: 38; O'Malley 1973), but in recreating it he has set a precedent for others to follow. 'That my people . . . resort to violence in everyday life is both a consequence of their recent warrior past and of the imposition of western culture and values on top of Maori cultural values' wrote Sharples (1993: 13; see also Bungay 1998: 28). Moreover, Duff may have actually encouraged the commission of crimes by Maori who believe it to be their true heritage, which in turn exacerbates 'the Maori problem' he is so eager to rant about.

By representing Maori as hell-bent on their own destruction, *Once Were Warriors* plays directly into the hands of the mass media that have already constructed minority peoples as criminals. For example, through various procedures ultimately designed to dispossess Native Americans of their sovereignty, state and federal governments defined them as deviant and criminal (Ross 1998). In Australia, the 'face of the criminal' has become that of the Aboriginal (Sercombe 1995). Sporadic protests in Australia – for example in the Sydney suburb of Redfern in February 2004 – remind us that the criminal label is not one that Aboriginal people are willing to sit back and accept, especially taking into account notorious police brutality. On an international scale, Roma are almost universally criminalised. In the most vicious of cycles, they are attacked by governments using formal legal systems and by individuals and communities. Often, they are driven out of countries and communities and forced to continue the very mode of living for which they were demonised and criminalised in the first place.

The ancestors depicted in Maori traditions were almost without exception held in high esteem. Thus the image of order they portrayed was assumed to be exemplary. In Maori tradition, 'all [past] events were believed to show in numerous ways how people could live successfully in this world. The first actions of the ancestors established patterns of behaviour which were followed by later generations...' (Reedy 1997: 16). But how do we know what was done by our ancestors?

Reconstructing the past

Reconstruction of Maori life prior to colonisation is largely dependent on *matauranga Maori*, Maori knowledge forms or system (Binney 1984, 1987; Salmond 1983; Ballara 1991). This knowledge would originally have been passed down by word of mouth from generation to generation (Salmond 1983; Thornton 1985). But Maori were soon recording information for themselves and for Pakeha in manuscript books, letters, notebooks, and the like (Ward 1980; Salmond 1983; Parsonson 1980). Consequently, standardised, revised material was committed to print (Jackson 1975). Despite the proliferation of written material, important parts of the Maori historical record remain inaccessible – first, by virtue of the esoteric language in which they are written (Salmond 1985; Reedy 1993) and second, because numerous Maori families have manuscripts in storage, afraid to open them because they are regarded as *tapu* (set apart, sacred, forbidden) (Jackson 1975) or make them available to those whose integrity cannot be guaranteed (Ballara 1993).

Reconstructing Maori history is problematic for several further reasons. Missionaries left daily accounts of the small communities in which they worked (Parsonson 1980). But most missionaries were unsympathetic towards 'tradition', and had little interest in what they considered at best 'puerile beliefs' and, at worst, 'works of the devil' (Biggs 1964). The same attitude has been invoked in many other similar contexts (cf. Lehtola 2002). Consciously or not, they were instrumental in the distortion of Maori knowledge. Land disputes, as retold before Land Courts and the Waitangi Tribunal, are a notable cause of the 'reworking' of Maori history (Ballara 1991; Parsonson 1980; Ward 1990; Sissons 1991). That reworking found its way into more accessible formats through Pakeha officials who presided over the hearings and (selectively) published the stories they collected (Hilliard 1997; Soutar 1994).

Finally, in any narrative form of recording and transmitting knowledge, the fictitious and the symbolic are blurred (Binney 1984). Certain Maori myths, such as the tale of the Ngati Porou ancestor Paikea, are superficially about mass murder, and could be cited as further evidence of Duff's thesis. Yet Witi Ihimaera's story (later Niki Caro's award-winning film) *Whale Rider* is based on the Paikea legend, and forms the perfect counterpoint to the violence and devastation of *Once Were Warriors*. Out of all the possible interpretations of Maori history available to Duff, it is interesting that the warrior image is the one that he has chosen to 'simulate'. According to Baudrillard, simulation is a process whereby representation becomes more important than reality. In *Simulacra and Simulation* (1981), Baudrillard outlines a hierarchy of simulation involving four 'orders'. Duff's *Once Were Warriors* illustrates second order simulation – that which misrepresents an original.

Internalised imagery

Although we cannot determine whether Maori followed settled patterns of behaviour in pre-colonial times, because our knowledge of the past is constantly undergoing reinterpretation, people trying to rediscover and/or maintain their identity often introduce (perceived) past cultural patterns into present settings (Gluckman 1964). In the wake of *Once Were Warriors*, this was manifested in several public incidents in which 'warriors', motivated by alleged breaches of protocol, inflicted violence on innocent bystanders. In 1997, an Australian onlooker watching a cultural exhibition at Auckland Museum was struck without warning by a blow to the head from a *taiaha* (a long weapon of hardwood) wielded by a male performer. Later that year in Wellington, a cameraman was struck twice with a *taiaha* as he filmed a ceremonial procession carrying an historic *waka taua* (canoe used in times of war). The cameraman, himself Maori, was authorised to film the procession, but apparently gave unintentional offence by getting too close to the *waka* (*Evening Post* 1997). Self-consciously political 'arrests' of Maori are not new (Bull 2004). They reappeared in numbers in the 1970s and are still happening today (Te Awekotuku 1998). However, to call these incidents self-consciously political seems overly generous. Instead, we propose that they are symptomatic of the *Once Were Warriors* syndrome and stem from the 'invention of tradition'.

We do not see the *Once Were Warriors* syndrome as an 'invention of tradition' in the sense of Hobsbawm and Ranger (1983). For them, genuine traditions are those that emerge spontaneously, are not tools of power, and have existed since time immemorial. They set this against a phenomenon of 'invented tradition' *used by the powerful* [our emphasis] to fix their regimes within ritual forms and justify them by reference to fictitious historic precedent. Instead we follow Giddens (1999), whose views on the fluidity of cultural forms are echoed in articulation theory. Giddens sees all traditions as inventions, whether or not they are deliberately constructed; as powerful; and capable of transformation without notice. Similarly, articulation theory assumes that cultural forms will change as the need arises for communities to reconfigure themselves on the basis of selectively remembered pasts (Clifford 2001).

For Giddens, the distinguishing characteristics of tradition include collective action, ritual and repetition, the ability to provide a framework for action that can go largely unquestioned, and guardians capable of interpreting the real meanings involved in the rituals. Because the incidents described above appear to lack a political agenda, are carried out on the spur of the moment, by individuals, and are not directed at political targets, the *Once Were Warriors* syndrome could be considered an end result of the 'invention of tradition' as conceived by Giddens.

While we are in agreement with Hobsbawm and Ranger, and Giddens, that power underlies tradition, we would not want to see power treated as a unitary thing. When the inventors are politically dominant, as has often been the case in Aotearoa, the invention of tradition is part of a cultural imperialism that tends to maintain the asymmetrical relationship of power in favour of the politically dominant. The invention of Maori culture in Aotearoa has taken at least two distinct forms. Around the turn of the twentieth century, the primary aim was to assimilate Maori; in the present day, Maori seek to maintain their cultural distinctiveness and to assume a more powerful position in society. The Maori tradition invented by Pakeha is motivated by an assimilationist agenda. The Maori tradition that Maori (represented by powerful insiders) invent is one that contrasts with Pakeha culture, and particularly with those elements of Pakeha culture that are deemed least attractive (Hanson 1989), such as individualism and materialism.

It is perhaps inevitable that any minority will deliberately differ from the majority when they strongly disagree with practices and beliefs, but will not press the point where it does not matter. Cultural differences affect the ways in which this is done. Inuit value non-confrontational behaviour and decision-making by consensus. It is common to appear complicit, while privately disagreeing and working quietly and behind the scenes to challenge or change Qallunaaq (outsider/non-Inuit) approaches, policies and decisions. Colonisers often misunderstood this behaviour as perpetually happy, childlike, or malleable, and were sometimes surprised to find themselves mocked or challenged in subtler ways. Since the formal recognition in Canada of Nunavut Territory, some policies and practices have been reversed. For example, people renamed under the government programme called 'Project Surname' are formalising or taking back their original Inuktitut (Inuit language) names (Alia 1994).

Because of his status as an insider, Duff is acting as a vector for the perpetuation of colonial ideology. Through him, outsider portrayals are rejuvenated to the point where many Maori endorse the image of Maori family life Duff portrays. Archer and Archer (1970) found that Maori shared the same racial stereotypes held by Pakeha, including those that were unflattering or hurtful to themselves. More recently, participants in Te Whaiti and Roguski's (1998) research talked about how Maori youth were vulnerable to internalising stereotyped criminalisations of Maori. This bears a striking resemblance to what the great African-American scholar W. E. B. Du Bois called the 'double self' of black existence. This is where the status of oppressed people is composed not only of how they see themselves, but also of how others see them:

> It is a peculiar sensation, this double-consciousness, this sense of always looking at one's self through the eyes of others, of measuring one's soul by the tape of a world that looks on in amused contempt and pity. One ever feels his two-ness – an American, a Negro; two souls, two thoughts, two unreconciled strivings; two warring ideals in one dark body, whose dogged strength alone keeps it from being torn asunder. (Du Bois 1987: 8–9)

The *Once Were Warriors* syndrome also mirrors Stuart Hall's 'self-othering', the first of his three kinds of otherness (Hall 1997a: 394–5). With self-othering we start with an external image, as in Edward Said's *Orientalism* (1979), where we are constructed as different and other by someone else. This external image is then internalised to become a self-image, which in turn drives an inner compulsion to conform to what was originally an external image. According to Hall (1993), if not resisted, such a process produces what Fanon referred to as 'individuals without an anchor, without horizon, colourless, stateless, rootless – a race of angels' (Fanon 1963: 176).

Fleras and Spoonley (1999) speculate that the internalisation of negative images has already helped form Maori identities through the persistence of stereotypes such as the 'black singlet' persona of 1980s Maori comic Billy T. James (Blythe 1994; Wall 1997). The notorious black singlet character was an impoverished, happy-go-lucky blagger, often telling tall stories, looking for a free ride and slightly on the wrong side of the law (Wall 1997). The characters portrayed by Billy T. were not always notorious and negative. Some were talented, articulate, and self-assured – much like the man himself (Wall 1997). Still, it seems reasonable to wonder how many viewers perceived the satire underlying his characterisations (and then consciously processed this information) and how many had their existing prejudices and stereotypes confirmed. In the normal course of events, it would not seem fair to hold one man responsible for other people's perceptions. There is something insidious about an 'insider' generating negative stereotypes that could inflict a degree of symbolic and psychological violence on Maori lives and life chances, such that their sense of self-worth diminishes (Fleras and Spoonley 1999). Such conditions reflect what Johan Galtung has called 'structural violence' – 'the violence of repression and exploitation' (Galtung and Ikeda 1995: x).

Even where minority people believe recast versions of their heritage, this may not be detrimental. Valaskakis writes of the creative uses of mixed-cultural inheritance and the intricate relationship between tradition and transformation, coloniser and colonised:

> In the writing of outsiders, native American traditional practice is often misunderstood as feathers and fantasy or, worse, as oppressive reification of the distant past. But Indian traditionalism is not these; nor is it lost in transformation or revived as a privileged expression of resistance. It is an instrumental code to action knitted into the fabric of everyday life ... (Valaskakis 1988: 268)

Past and present are inseparable. Valaskakis' description of her Lac du Flambeau Chippewa childhood echoes experiences of people from many locations and ethnicities:

> We were very young when we began to live the ambivalence of our reality. My marble-playing, bicycle-riding, king-of-the-royal-mountain days were etched with the presence of unexplained identity and power. I knew as I sat in the cramped desks of the Indian school that wigwams could shake with the rhythm of a Midewiwin ceremonial drum, fireballs could spring from the whispers of a windless night, and Bert Skye could (without warning) transform himself into a dog. I knew that my great-grandmother moved past the Catholic altar in her house with her hair dish in her hand to place greying combings of her hair in the first fire of the day, securing them from evil spirits ... we were equally and irrevocably harnessed to each other ... I was both an Indian and an outsider. (Valaskakis 1988: 268)

Maori may find 'invented' or reinterpreted traditions more appealing and more useful in terms of mobilising pan-tribal political support (Levine 1991). Indeed articulation theory holds out hope for the combination of 'internal' elements with 'external' forms in processes of selective, syncretic transformation (Clifford 2001). Conversely, modelling behaviour on examples that were used to pacify and colonise in the first place could be detrimental to the pursuit of *tino rangatiratanga* (sovereignty, self-determination).

At least the film, for all its faults, has been a vehicle for greater minority representation in cinema. Subsequent Hollywood films in which the *Once Were Warriors* cast have had significant roles include *The Matrix*

(Julian Arahanga) (1999), *Star Wars II* (Temuera Morrison and Rena Owen) (2002), *Collateral Damage* (Cliff Curtis) (2002), to name but a few. The more on-screen appearances these Maori actors make, the more diffuse becomes their association with *Once Were Warriors* and the more likely they are to function as positive role models for young Maori, who could use a few more. Lee Tamahori's skills as a director are also in demand (*Along Came a Spider* (2001), *Mulholland Falls* (1996), episodes in the second series of *The Sopranos*, *Die Another Day* (2002)). It must be said that Duff's successes have helped positively influence the lives of young Maori, notably through his Books in Homes charity. Additional positive spin-offs include Jim Moriarty's musical adaptation of *Once Were Warriors*, performed at various venues around Aotearoa from March 2004. It is another of Moriarty's acclaimed theatre therapy events, this time spreading the message that domestic violence is unacceptable and that the cycle can be broken.

Masculinities and colour-blind violence

No discussion of *Once Were Warriors* would be complete without some reflection on domestic violence. Particularly striking is the film's realism. In the immediate aftermath of screenings, it was widely claimed that women's refuges and anger management groups were inundated with calls from people saying they had a 'warriors problem'. There was even some speculation that the film was one of the catalysts for change that included the introduction of the ground-breaking Domestic Violence Act 1995 (see Mahoney 2003). Although this latter claim seems a little grandiose, there is no doubt that *Once Were Warriors* drew considerable attention to the issue of domestic violence. As well, First Nations people in Canada noted commonalities with Maori and said they were especially impressed by the realistic portrayals of domestic violence and conditions of Aboriginal people, and more generally, were deeply moved by the film (Alia 1994–6). *Once Were Warriors* was a useful starting-point for discussion and for some, a therapeutic experience (Alia 1994–6).

Once Were Warriors is not just any old movie about domestic violence. It brings a minority experience of domestic violence to the fore. Ordinarily, that would be commendable. Where interest in domestic violence exists, however, certain perspectives are privileged, others marginalised as in any field of academic enquiry. Black and minority ethnic perspectives definitely fall into the latter category. Further, the Chief Executive of the National Collective of Independent Women's Refuges in Aotearoa, Merepeka Raukawa-Tait, has been outspoken in insisting that Maori themselves stop 'pussyfooting' around the issue of domestic violence.

First Nations people and Inuit in Canada expressed similar views; Inuit and First Nations women's associations developed programmes to support people in abusive situations, and Native American women expressed anger and anguish at the realities of gender relations in their homes and communities (Alia 1994–6).

Maori culture looms so large in *Once Were Warriors* it obscures the fact that domestic violence cuts across boundaries of class, age and ethnicity. Just as the occurrence of dowry-related deaths among South Asian women living in the UK is often seen by outsiders as unique and separate from the intimate partner violence that happens elsewhere, the heavy cultural overtones in *Once Were Warriors* make it difficult for people to divorce the violence from the Maori cultural context. 'The images of abuse and violence in *Once Were Warriors* are not cultural, they are an outcome of a history of colonial oppression and denial' (Pihama 1996: 192), as encapsulated in Jackson's Power to Protect theory of domestic violence among Maori. This theory holds that the abuse of power and the use of violence inherent in the process of colonisation is a central precedent of the abuse of power and use of violence in Maori communities today (cited in Glover 1993).

Manifestations of violence may vary according to culture, but the underlying power dynamics are the same, as are the extremes of brutality involved. Hence the comparisons audiences have made between *Once Were Warriors* and Gary Oldman's directorial debut, *Nil By Mouth* (1997). Oldman's film portrays a working-class London family embroiled in a devastating cycle of drug abuse and violence. An equally harrowing film to watch, it did not scale the heights of *Time Magazine*'s annual top ten films of the world list, as Tamahori's precedent-setter did. Imagine for a moment that it had been about a Jamaican family, and the likelihood that it would have made just as controversial a success soars.

The construction of masculinity is closely tied to the portrayal of domestic violence in *Once Were Warriors*. The film version, as a visual medium, is more relevant here. In the process of casting the actors for the leading roles, Tamahori ended up reinforcing stereotypical notions of masculinity. The men are built like brick shithouses, capable of drinking anybody under the table and emotionally aloof (except when drunk). The exception is the slightly greasy 'Uncle Bully', who rapes Grace. Outsiders could be forgiven for coming away from the film thinking that all Maori men are big and brave, a variation on the quintessential stereotype that all Maori (like all 'Negroes' in the 1950s, and African Americans in current usage) are big, brave, and good at sport. The film presents a skewed portrait of men who are aggressive toward their partners – who are just as likely to seem like timid nerds as 'warriors', outside the domestic sphere.

Unlike the film, real life reveals that Maori men come in all shapes and sizes and express their masculinities in a variety of ways. As Messerschmidt puts it (1993: 27) '... within each particular society, masculinity is constructed differently by class, race, age, and in particular social situations, such as the school, peer group, family and workplace'. Despite variations in the construction of masculinity, because of the 'single structural fact [of] the global dominance of men over women' (Connell 1987: 83), hegemonic masculinity prevails. Put simply, hegemonic masculinity is the practically universal set of beliefs that align masculinity with dominance, status, and independence (Connell 1987).

Of all the models of masculinity available to young Maori men in *Once Were Warriors*, Jake 'the Muss' most closely fits the mould of hegemonic masculinity. The prominence of Jake's masculinity over other models can be explained by the fact that hegemonic masculinity is 'always constructed in relation to various subordinated masculinities as well as in relation to women' (Connell 1987: 183). In both book and film, Jake's masculinity obliterates the available alternatives. Duff's book (and the film that followed) gives young Maori men a message that they may admire Jake's machismo and want to emulate him, and having done so, discover a convenient justification for their violence. Thus, while Duff may have drawn attention to the relatively neglected issue of domestic violence among Maori, he is less likely to be helping to challenge than to exacerbate the problems. Hence our argument that the sort of misrepresentation typified by *Once Were Warriors* poses a much greater threat to insiders than to outsiders.

The Story of Joe and Elise

It is ironic that Duff's thesis linking violence with Maori culture emerged around the same time as the popularisation of the notion that 'Maori justice' was based on restorative principles. After all, restorative justice is quite a contrast to the retributive justice of *Once Were Warriors*. This apparent contradiction between retribution and restorative 'native' justice programmes is illustrated in *The Story of Joe and Elise* produced for the Canadian Broadcasting Corporation documentary series, *Man Alive*. The 'story' takes place in the predominantly Inuit community of Igloolik, in the Canadian high Arctic (now part of Nunavut Territory). Despite the egalitarian implications of its title, the documentary is really Joe's story, with only occasional glimpses of Elise.

In public (especially to non-Inuit 'outsiders') Joe and Elise Attagutaluk seemed a model couple. Well-educated and known for their local and national community service (including Joe's help in founding IBC, the Inuit

Broadcasting Corporation, and Elise's in Pauktuutit, the Inuit Women's Association) they were considered by 'outsiders' and 'insiders' alike to be highly successful and exemplary. Then one day they returned to the drinking they had vowed to abandon, and had a fight. Joe assaulted Elise so severely she died of a cerebral haemorrhage. The subject of the documentary is Joe's 'fall from grace' and eventual reintegration into the Igloolik community.

The 'story' is full of mixed messages. We are informed in a foreboding way that as a child, Joe was shipped off to residential school (as was Elise), and in adult life became a prominent professional and activist (as did Elise). Joe's experiences in school and church are not introduced to help justify or explain his violence. Instead this material is used to explain how the Catholic faith helped to sustain him during his trial and incarceration. This is an unexpected revelation, because in his new role as elected chairman of the regional board of education he emphasises the importance of giving children opportunities to learn Inuit language and culture – lost to them thanks to the efforts of proselytising missionaries. Still, Joe is not the first person for whom a faith that originated in coercion has become a source of strength. We are not told whether he encountered any of the violent conditions experienced by many who attended church-run residential schools.

Where the documentary does set out to understand or justify Joe's violence, it does so by referring to his drinking habits. Elise's alcoholism is also in the spotlight – as though this has some bearing on Joe's violence. Apparently, Joe and Elise planned to stop drinking after their last shipment of alcohol ran out. According to his account, Joe got so drunk on the last of their supply, he killed Elise and woke up in jail with no recollection of what he had done. Perhaps for the sake of their six children, the community successfully petitioned to have Joe stay in the region until his trial. Eventually he pleaded guilty to manslaughter and was sentenced to five years at Yellowknife (Northwest Territories) Correctional Centre. Upon his release twenty-two months later, Joe flew home to Igloolik fearing how the community would treat him. As it turned out, the terminal was full of well-wishers. At Elise's grandmother's house, he found more people waiting to welcome him home. The community refused to condemn or abandon him. Their decision to embrace and support him seems based on the fact that it was a first offence, and on his vow never to drink alcohol again. Towards the end of the 'story' we see Joe with his new girlfriend and baby daughter, enjoying domestic bliss.

When Elise's sister, Alexina Kublu, is interviewed, she tells us that (though she thinks she should) she cannot really forgive Joe for killing her much-loved sister. This is one of the few hints that all is not as it seems, and the facts may contradict the warm glow we are presumably expected to feel after learning about dispute resolution in this remote indigenous community. By contrast, the *New York Times* recently ran a piece headlined 'Plagued by drugs, some tribes revive the ancient penalty of banishment' in which it is quite clear that traditional dispute resolution does not necessarily prize conciliation (Kershaw and Davey 2004) – just as Nader's research would predict. Of course, any account that finds nothing but fault with tribal justice should be treated with just as much caution as an account that paints a rosy picture.

Conclusion

We have seen that merely identifying 'insider' or 'outsider' representations does not necessarily tell us what is accurate or effective. Indeed, these designations need rethinking in the light of observations such as those of Valaskakis and others (including the authors). Representation can be a double-edged sword. On the one hand, it has the power to raise awareness. On the other, if it is the only source of information and is misleading, the consequences can be far-reaching. Giving voice to silenced minorities sometimes has the effect of homogenising their experiences. For example, the situation described in *Once Were Warriors* might be arbitrarily associated with other minorities. In depicting a particular minority, care must be taken to ensure the imagery is wise and constructive, because of the impact that an overwhelmingly negative characterisation can have. The validity and form of any image is dependent not only on who transmits it but also on who receives it (Soutar 1994; Te Awekotuku 1999). The receiver does not have to be an outsider in order for concerns about reliability and validity to emerge. That said, the concerns are likely to be much more significant where outsiders are involved. In the next chapter we consider the complexities of outsider representations of minority peoples and their ability to undermine or complement minority efforts at self-representation.

Exercises

3.1 Prior to class, select a relatively short extract from Nader (1990) for all students to read. In addition, half of the students should read Alan Duff's (1990) *Once Were Warriors*, and half should watch Lee Tamahori's film version of the same name. There should be some forewarning of the disturbing violence in both, and a list of contact organisations made available in case there are some students for whom either account touches a particularly raw nerve.

3.2 In class, divide into two groups, each composed of a mix of those who have seen the film, and those who have read the book. One group should be assigned to formulate amongst themselves arguments supporting the view that *Once Were Warriors* stereotypes Maori. The other group should formulate amongst themselves arguments supporting the idea that *Once Were Warriors* is gruesome but true. Each group should be allocated twenty minutes for this purpose. Then, not counting repetitive arguments, the groups should take turns at articulating an argument until one or other group runs out of ideas.

3.3 As a class, discuss how the portrayal of Maori in both the film and the book could be seen as an example of Stuart Hall's notion of 'self-othering'.

Further reading

Clifford, James (1997) *Routes: Travel and Translation in the Late Twentieth Century*, Cambridge and London: Harvard University Press.

Duff, A. (1990) *Once Were Warriors*, Auckland: Tandem Press.

Hulme, K. (1983) *The Bone People*, New York: Penguin.

Nader, L. (1990) *Harmony Ideology – Injustice and Control in a Zapotec Mountain Village*, Stanford, CA: Stanford University Press.

Pratt, Mary Louise (1992) *Imperial Eyes: Travel Writing and Transculturation*, London: Routledge.

Suggested viewing

Once Were Warriors
The Story of Joe and Elise

4 Cultures of silence – media denial of colonial oppression

Minority peoples find their voices silenced in many spheres. Until indigenous people started taking legal action in some of the more blatant and shocking instances of exploitation and abuse, their accounts of compulsory schooling were largely invisible in mainstream media. In Canada, Australia and elsewhere, 'stolen children' (whether actually kidnapped and coerced or merely 'persuaded' to attend residential schools) were twice marginalised to become a Diaspora within a Diaspora. Their parents and communities were removed from homelands or corralled within a tiny fragment of the land they had once occupied. Having acclimatised to these reduced circumstances, indigenous children were then removed from home again – sometimes for the duration of their school years, sometimes with the opportunity for occasional reunions with their parents.

The Australian National Inquiry into the Separation of Aboriginal and Torres Strait Islander Children from their Families (Wilson 1997) officially lifted the lid on Aboriginal experiences of being forcibly removed by police and welfare agencies from their families and homes in accordance with government policy (Bull and Alia 2004). According to Pilger:

> . . . up to a third of Aboriginal children were forcibly removed from their families between 1910 and 1970, making a total of 100, 000 stolen children. Placed in white missions, institutions and foster homes, the children were forced into a form of slavery, often physically and sexually abused and denied protection by the state. (Pilger 1998: 240)

In Canada more than 100, 000 indigenous children were taken from their homes and communities to government- and missionary-run residential schools, in which abuse of various kinds was common. Students were often malnourished, shorn and subjected to punishment for speaking their mother tongue. When they eventually did return to their communities, many had lost the ability to relate to their families. The disruption in family life and child-rearing practices has meant that many adult survivors do not have the requisite skills to care adequately for their own children. Thus the cycle of abuse continues (Sutherland 2002; Bull and Alia 2004).

Both sets of experiences lend themselves to dramatic and compelling viewing. The most recent media offering on the subject, Philip Noyce's 'outsider' feature film *Rabbit-Proof Fence* (2003) vividly depicts the plight of three Aboriginal girls stolen by the government from their home in Western Australia. Less dramatic but equally compelling is the landmark Canadian 'insider' television documentary, *The Mission School Syndrome* (1990), produced by Northern Native Broadcasting Yukon. In it, Ken Kane (broadcaster, policy maker and member of the Champaigne-Aisihik Southern Tutchone First Nation) talks passionately about his own mission school experience and the pain of losing parents, and parenting skills. Following broadcasts of the documentary the identity, cultural and familial crises experienced by Yukon First Nations people in Canada became known as the 'Mission School Syndrome'.

By contrast, in Aotearoa there was no forced removal, no dramatic imagery to project onto the silver screen. Instead, Maori men and women were criminalised for failing to send their children to school. Once there, the children received corporal punishment for speaking *te reo Maori* (Maori language). The identity, cultural and familial crises they have experienced in consequence are no less painful than those of Australia's 'stolen generations' or Canada's 'Mission School Syndrome' survivors. But where is the newsworthiness in someone being served a summons to appear in court? Or a child being disciplined for disobeying a teacher? Obviously such events are extremely compelling to the people concerned, and they ought to be compelling to those not directly involved. But in order to be compelled one must first be made aware, and imperialism has tended to silence the voices of minority peoples (Pilger 1998). The common tactic of outlawing 'native' languages has helped facilitate this silencing by compromising the ability of ethnic minorities to express themselves.

The media, as an allegedly independent arbiter of political relations, have the power to undo this silence, to give minorities a voice – or do they? In this chapter, the questions Spivak (1988) raised about the possibility of representing the subaltern in academic discourse are applied to ethnic minorities and the media. This gives rise to an analysis of the culture of silence surrounding 'outsider' representations of oppressive schooling policies imposed upon indigenous minorities in Australia, Canada and Aotearoa. Our analysis will draw broadly upon ethnocentrism, social psychology and Cohen's (1993) sociology of denial.

Breaking Spivak's silence

According to Spivak (1988), subjugated groups cannot speak for themselves because no solitary voice could adequately represent the diversity of experiences among the oppressed. The oppressed are simply too heterogeneous for any single member or group of members to speak for the whole. Thus she is dubious about the possibility that subjugated voices can ever be recovered without becoming essentialist fiction. But, in order for media representation to act as an evocative catalyst for social change, the fewer perspectives a story is told from the better. As Stalin is famously quoted as saying: the death of one man is a tragedy, the death of a million is a statistic. But it is precisely the plurality of voices that helps guard against the essentialising tendencies about which Spivak is concerned. Multiple 'truths' often suggest greater credibility – a point aptly illustrated by Akira Kurosawa's film *Rashomon* (1951), about the murder of a nobleman and the rape of his wife, told from four competing yet equally valid perspectives.

Jacques Derrida demonstrated in *Of Grammatology* that the question is no longer whether the oppressed can speak but whether the receiver can decode the messages uttered (Agozino 2004). In order for messages to be decoded in the first instance, they must reach a receptive audience. Too often, the messages of minority peoples fall on deaf ears. This is partly to do with 'Western' ethnocentric preoccupation with things that happen to 'Westerners' (Cohen 1993), and the propaganda fed to the masses over time that constructs minority peoples as criminals as opposed to survivors of systematic abuse (cf. Cunneen 1999). It also rests, in part, with the imperialism and ethnocentrism imbedded in the types of knowledge that are deemed to have high status; namely, rational, objective, scientific knowledge. Postmodern scepticism about truth claims derived from 'scientific knowledge' has led theorists such as Baudrillard to privilege cultural products (for example, storytelling, music, poetry, novels, biographical narratives, films, television) above official or academic discourse. Rationality, in the postmodern view, is merely an alibi concealing the desire to dominate and oppress marginalised sections of society.

The question should never have been, 'Can the subaltern speak?' but, 'Will the masters ever listen?' Oppressed peoples have been screaming for years through 'irrational' media. We have already mentioned *The Mission School Syndrome*. Toronto-based Cree director Pamela Matthews documented the experiences of one child in a residential school in her 2002 film, *Only the Devil Speaks Cree*. Bud White Eye's book, *Dark Legacy* (2004), recounts his experiences of physical, psychological and sexual abuse at a church-run residential school in Canada. On his 1996 album *Nendaä – Go Back*, Jerry Alfred, a songwriter from the Selkirk First Nation in Pelly Crossy, Yukon (Canada) and his band, The Medicine Beat, sing about the 'Residential School':

> Long ago my grandfather spoke
> Of the younger children
> Going off to learn new ways
> They are going to a big learning school,
> To learn about behaviour.

The Mi'kmaq poet, Rita Joe, describes her own school experience in the eastern Canadian province of Nova Scotia:

> I lost my talk
> The talk you took away
> When I was a little girl
> At Shubenacadie school (Joe 1996: 55)

Spivak's argument also holds that outsiders cannot speak for the marginalised because doing so perpetuates domination by creating a 'fictional' subaltern voice. While we accept that outsiders have presumed to speak for the marginalised before and frequently with a view to asserting their own superiority, we do not see outsider representation as inherently corrupt. Instead, it is our contention that outsiders can, and occasionally should, *borrow* the voices of ethnic minority peoples where it can facilitate constructive representation. Germaine Greer's (2004) *Whitefella Jump Up* borrows Aboriginal ways of speaking to serve up a scathing attack on the contemporary socio-political situation in Australia. In doing so, she retains her own outsider's voice as well, preventing the reader from misunderstanding her use of Aboriginal phrasing as cultural appropriation:

> What is there for whitefellas to cry about? In Australian literature, the Europeans'corrosive unease expresses itself in a curious distortion of the pathetic fallacy, which characterises the land as harsh, cruel, savage, relentless, the sky as implacable, pitiless and so forth. The heart of the country is called 'dead'. Vicissitudes of heat and cold are interpreted as a kind of punishment, and the physical world itself given the role of an avenging deity. The vegetation is described as 'stunted', 'warped', 'misshapen', another example of projection of a presentiment of evil within to the countryside without.
>
> It was not the country that was damned but the settler who felt in his heart that he was damned. His impotent cursing, which has left

a legacy in the unequalled degree of profanity in Australian speech, was a classic piece of transference. We hate this country because we cannot allow ourselves to love it. We know in our hearts' core that it is not ours.

The settlers did not mean to destroy the Aborigines, but they could not deny that the Aborigines were being destroyed. (Greer 2004: unpaginated)

In a similar fashion, writers and explorers have long used words like 'barren', 'desolate' and 'stunted' to describe the Arctic and by implication, in admiring but covertly racist tones, the lives of Inuit who live there.

Articulation theory holds that relationships between members of the dominant culture and ethnic minority peoples should involve positive alliances, hooking up and unhooking particular elements (Clifford 2001). In mid-1980s Aotearoa archival film footage painstakingly restored by the Film Archive was screened on *marae* (places to congregate) around the country:

To be present at showings of these early films on the marae among the people who are descendants of those appearing in them is a unique experience . . . This was acknowledged by the Archive and the remaining descendants as a way of returning images from a time past, back to the tribes and areas from which they were taken. No other film archive in the world has gone to such lengths to engage in dialogue or ensure that material with indigenous content is seen by those whose ancestors and lifestyle are in the subject matter . . . (Mita 1996: 50–1)

Borrowing voices may indeed be necessary in climates in which minority accounts must vie for acceptance against hegemonic narrative. To some extent ethnic minority voices are also more likely to be heard if channelled through outsiders. To an outsider audience, insiders may be too subjective, too biased, to tell their story. The same account told by an outsider has the appearance of objectivity, and is therefore more credible. While we must guard against careerist, profit-motivated and neo-colonial appropriation of culture, life and voice, we must also be open to acknowledging the different authenticity of respectful outsider observations. Insider audiences are also susceptible to seeing the accounts of fellow insiders as inauthentic or exaggerated, and themselves may prefer outsider accounts. Further, when the story is a particularly painful one, sometimes it is preferable to have an outsider tell it. It may be so painful and traumatising that an insider is unable to tell it. Alternatively, there are times when an insider–outsider team works best. As we demonstrate in the next section, not all articulations go far enough towards reversing the invisibility of ethnic minorities in the mainstream and breaking the legacy of denial.

'Propaganda of organised forgetting' (Pilger 1998: 330)

For the silenced Aboriginal 'stolen generations', a major media break-through came in the early 1980s with Alec Morgan's Australian Broad-casting Corporation (ABC) documentary *Lousy Little Sixpence* (1982). It retold the harrowing story of Aboriginal children who were forcibly re-moved from their homes and sent to mission schools. Several years later, Morgan teamed up with Alan Lowery and John Pilger to produce an ABC series, *The Last Dream* (1988), in which witnesses said that genocide had taken place in Australia – a view endorsed by the 1997 national inquiry (Wilson 1997; see also Cunneen 1999). Philip Noyce's (2003) feature film *Rabbit-Proof Fence* is the most recent instalment in the stolen generations saga.

Set in 1930s outback Western Australia, *Rabbit-Proof Fence* is the 'true story' of the abduction of sisters Molly and Daisy and their cousin Gracie, and their eventual reunion with their families. The Chief Protector of Aborigines authorised 'removal' of all three girls to the Moore River Native Settlement, where they were to be trained as domestic servants. He was empowered 'to remove any half-caste child' from their family – a policy emanating from the eugenics movement, which feared 'swamping' of the white races.

At a propitious moment Molly and her two younger companions make their escape. Searchers are marshalled, and quickly surmise that the girls are following the 1, 800 kilometre rabbit-proof fence (constructed in 1907 to prevent rabbits from destroying crops) back to Jigalong. Towards the end of their journey, the girls are deceived into altering their course and Gracie is captured. Molly and Daisy complete the nine-week journey on their own (Bull and Alia 2004).

Rabbit-Proof Fence provides a rare and memorable glimpse at injustices perpetrated against indigenous peoples during the process of colonisa-tion. It has done so for a large international audience. The dearth of main-stream attention to the issue makes this a 'must see' movie. Nonetheless, important opportunities to decolonise media representation of ethnic mi-norities have gone begging. Despite a strong cast of mainly Aboriginal ac-tors (Everlyn Sampi, Tianna Sansbury, Laura Monaghan, David Gulpilil, Ningali Lawford and Myarn Lawford) the cover art for the North American version of the video and DVD is dominated by the image of British actor Kenneth Branagh. Since the film goes to considerable lengths to include Aboriginal voices and images, it would have been more appropriate to leave the pictures of the girls on the front cover, as in the original Australasian release. That said, if the mere sight of Kenneth Branagh persuades more people to watch the film, then perhaps the decision is justifiable. Likewise, it seems a shame that Peter Gabriel was favoured to produce what turns out to be a forgettable soundtrack, over the growing list of talented Aboriginal musicians and composers. In commissioning a soundtrack from a British pop star, Philip Noyce missed an opportunity to enrich the film, and to expose a wider audience to Aboriginal 'voices' (Bull and Alia 2004). Even more importantly, in Noyce's outsider interpretation, the deeper implications of the 'stolen generations' debacle remain untouched. Instead:

> What appears on the screen are the symptoms of a deeper malaise represented as matters of the heart, acts of rebellion, insanity and misunderstood genius . . . this is not to say that they should never have been made, it is asking only that in future something deeper than the symptoms be probed and explored. (Mita 1996: 47–8)

This treatment reflects what has been called the 'sociology of denial' (Cohen 1993: 97). 'Aboriginal men and women of the Koori renaissance, the writers, teachers, elders, historians, broadcasters, artists and activists' (Pilger 1998: 246) have ensured that their peoples' history is known. And yet, despite 'an international media presence that insinuates itself over a fantastically wide range' (Said 1994: 352–3), it is simultaneously not known – the 'denial paradox'. At its most basic level, denial may result from a confirmation bias, a 'universal tendency to see only what it is convenient to see' (Cohen 1993: 103). For example, in former British colonies that have not gone 'republic', denial may preserve the glory days of the Empire that are deeply embedded in the collective British sub-conscious as one of few achievements of which to be proud. To borrow from Nietzsche: Memory says, 'I did that.' Pride replies, 'I could not have done that.' Eventually, memory yields. On the other hand, denial may represent the end result of governments negotiating the silencing of certain issues. Former colonial powers have been known to suppress information that threatens their preferred image. The 1896 *History of New Zealand and its Inhabitants*, by the missionary Dom Felice Vaggioli working in nineteenth-century Aotearoa, is one such example. When Vaggioli's observation that colonisation was an unmitigated disaster failed to accord with the image of colonisation British politicians were keen to promulgate, they pressured the Italian government into banning the book. Denial serves governments by protecting their public images, im-ages that dissociate the State from crimes against its people (Cohen 1993) and shield them from making potentially costly financial restitution.

'Past deeds illuminate present treacheries' (Ross 1998: 266) and 'victims of state crime are easy targets for repeated victimisation' (Kauzlarich et al. 2001: 187). Nonetheless, outsider accounts of minority oppression rarely explore the contemporary implications of previous government policies, preferring instead to consign them to the past and minimise their present relevance. This is just another manifestation of the anthropological hangover of synchronic essentialism – whereby colonised peoples are set as fixed, static and knowable in opposition to the forward moving, heterogeneous, colonising cultures (Asad 1973). Silencing accounts that legitimise claims of aggrieved minorities are essential to upholding the very foundations of bourgeois settlement and protecting its accumulated wealth. Moreover, dominant cultures use the media to project and defend images of themselves as competent, unblemished, and so on, often implicitly (and sometimes explicitly) at the expense of ethnic minorities (Ross 1998).

By contrast, the insider account on which *Rabbit-Proof Fence* is based, Doris Pilkington's novel, *The Long Walk Home* (1996), places the children's removal in wider socio-historical context. Pilkington shows what the arrival of settlers en masse meant for Aboriginal societies; namely, dispossession – of lands, cultures and identities. Foreshadowing this dispossession is one of the more vivid passages in the book, in which Captain Freemantle tells the Nyungar people in the most sincere terms that he will name their 'country' Western Australia on behalf of the British government. The scene is embarrassingly like that in the tables-turned 'conquest' of a white Australian settlement by an armada of Aboriginal 'colonials' in the biting television satire, *Babakiueria* (1986) ('What do you call this place?' the would-be colonist asks. 'It's a barbecue area', is the reply, respelled to fit the colonisers' understanding) (Bull and Alia 2004).

More akin to Pilkington's contextualised approach, Northern Native Broadcasting Yukon's documentary, *The Mission School Syndrome* (Istchenko 1988), and its sequel *Healing the Mission School Syndrome* (Istchenko 1994) have as their main theme the implications of mission schooling for adult survivors living in Canada today. The film's central thesis, supported by several of the survivors who are interviewed on camera, is that the dependency on institutional settings fostered by mission schooling may help explain why First Nations people in Canada (and similarly, Native Americans in the US) are believed to 'do time better' (Tarver, Walker and Wallace 2002). Some schools, such as the government-run school at Churchill, Manitoba featured a more enlightened and less damaging form of assimilation. Nevertheless, huge distances between communities like Igloolik, in the high Arctic, and the school were traumatic in themselves, and in the case of Canadian Inuit, were linked to the renaming programmes. As Elise Attagutaluk, her sister, Alexina Kublu, and others have explained, children went away to school with one name and returned home to another during the government-sponsored 'Project Surname'.

Mission schools were not run by any single faith, nor were their practices limited to North America. In 1987, the World Conference of Indigenous Peoples' Education held a conference in Canada. Indigenous peoples came from six continents. Among the participants were Coorg people from India. According to Randy Fred, their account of residential schools included all of the elements of mission school experiences in Canada. Randy Fred's father 'was physically tortured by his teachers for speaking Tseshaht: they pushed sewing needles through his tongue, a routine punishment for language offenders' (Haig-Brown 1988: 16). Fred reminds us that 'elimination of language has always been a primary stage in a process of cultural genocide' (Haig-Brown 1988: 15).

Gwendolyn Point, Education Manager of the Sto:lo Nation in British Columbia, writes: 'Ever since the Europeans first came, our children were stolen from our embrace ... First the priests took our children away, to churches, schools, even back to Europe. Then the residential schools took three or four generations away ... ' (Fournier and Crey 1997: 7–8). The social worker, activist and Executive Director of the Sto:lo Nation Fisheries Program, Ernie Crey says, 'Mine is the first generation of Aboriginal people to have the right before the law to parent our own children' (Fournier and Crey 1997: 10).

Making sense of media silence surrounding mission schooling and its derivatives can be difficult. Psychology may offer some insights.

Psychologies of communication: sitting on neutral ground?

The neutralisation techniques of Sykes and Matza (1957) may help explain how the media absolve themselves from any moral obligation to provide coverage of issues important to minorities. The first technique is denial of injury, in which wrongdoing is neutralised by claiming that victims exaggerate, have brought about their own harm, or some variant on this theme. The next technique involves denial of the victim – for example, by reconstructing victims with texts such as 'the Eskimo as a happy, childlike nomad' and images of smiling 'natives' – as was done in a photographic series distributed by the Canadian government. Third is denial of responsibility (I was following orders). The fourth technique involves condemnation of the condemners. Here, people claim they are being judged against double standards and things are worse elsewhere. In *Rabbit Proof Fence* the principal 'bad guy' – Mr Devil – is the quintessential

Englishman, suggesting that it was the British and not the Australian government who were responsible for Aboriginal oppression. Finally, appeal to higher loyalties rearticulates the idea that the ends justify the means (the 'ends' may be purity, state security, defence of the free world). Collectively these neutralisers represent a phase in the denial process, in which events are acknowledged, but there is no acknowledgement of responsibility for causing them, especially where negative labels such as 'genocide' have been applied (Cohen 1993: 107). Foucault would tell us that the vocabulary is crucial for propelling the spiral of denial forward.

Political discourses may contain evidence of neutralisation techniques employed to conceal and/or minimise State violence towards minorities (Cohen 1993, [our emphasis]). But we must question the willingness of media professionals to embrace this culture of silence and ask whether the mass media are passive recipients of neutralised events, or active neutralisers of potentially threatening accounts.

Cognitive dissonance versus social conflict: the battle for ideological supremacy

Still looking to psychology for answers, Festinger's cognitive dissonance theory describes a psychological mechanism underlying 'unwillingness to confront anomalous or disturbing information' (Cohen 1993: 102). Maintaining dissonant beliefs creates anxiety by compromising the need for consistency in our lives. We reduce discomfort by changing an inconsistent belief to a consistent one. For example, when a government claims to follow international human rights laws but violates those laws in its dealings with a group it wishes to suppress, an ugly inconsistency raises its head. Assuming the government experiences any discomfort at all, adopting a stance that questions whether methods of suppression really violate human rights legislation can reduce the uncomfortable dissonance: 'It doesn't happen here', or 'It is justified' (Cohen 1993). There is no particular reason why an observant media should be drawn in at this stage of the process. However, if media professionals see their role as that of watchdog yet fail to report government wrongdoing (for reasons we will discuss shortly), the reality of their failure to report will conflict with their self-image, resulting in dissonance. There are two possible ways of resolving this: adjust one's self-image, or reinterpret the reality of one's lack of action. Many people prefer the latter. Either way, those deploying the dominant message can sit back and watch as social psychological mechanisms help perpetuate their ideology.

Of course, in order for dissonance to occur in the first place, we need more than one source of information. But even where multiple sources exist, and there is a dissenting opinion, it is more likely to be the dissenting opinion that people alter to fit in with the dominant discourse. This is because it is the dominant discourse that they have had drummed into them. In such a scenario cognitive dissonance cannot work to the advantage of the oppressed. Yet history is replete with examples of the oppressed bringing about social change by converting others to their point of view. Such conversions have been possible, Moscovici and Lage (1976) claim, because we are driven not by the need to eliminate inconsistent beliefs (as per cognitive dissonance) but by the need to reduce social conflict. This we do by normalising and conforming. Minorities can, and have, converted others to their point of view by generating and maintaining social conflict until the majority change – a much more powerful result than mere compliance. Moscovici and Lage suggest that minorities wishing to bring about social change should disrupt established norms and introduce doubts into the minds of the majority; make themselves visible, draw attention; show that there is an alternative, coherent point of view; demonstrate certainty, confidence and commitment to this point of view; refuse to compromise.

Social conflict may counteract the effects of cognitive dissonance. But the ability of social psychology to help explain the culture of silence surrounding media representations of minority oppression does not necessarily end there.

Diffuse responsibilities and victim blaming

Several conditions associated with the 'bystander effect' may help to explain the culture of silence as well. The 'bystander effect' was originally used to explain how crime witnesses dissociate themselves from what is happening and thus defer intervention. The second condition, inability to conceive of effective intervention, explains that observers will only act if they know what to do, if they see reward rather than punishment in helping, if they do not feel powerless to intervene. The media seem to pride themselves on the fact that they can make quite an effective intervention in any situation where public scrutiny is unwelcome. Therefore, this notion of observer helplessness will not suffice as an explanation of media silence. In the first of these conditions, diffusion of responsibility, bystanders think that as so many others are watching there is no need for them to act. In so-called democratic societies numerous channels exist for expressing dissent. These include alerting the media, establishing a pressure group, organising a public demonstration, lobbying Members of Parliament, and, implicitly, voting for an opposition party at the next election. Because these avenues are supposedly universally available, perhaps the media are inclined to leave the dissenting to someone else.

Another condition of the bystander effect, inability to identify with the victim, recognises that helping behaviour is only extended to those who share the same moral universe as the bystanders. In *The Colonizer and the Colonized* (1965) Alberto Memmi paints a portrait of 'the Other', as described by the coloniser, in which 'the Others' are not seen as fellow individual members of the human community but rather as part of an anonymous collectivity quite separate from the colonisers (Bull 2004). Reasoning by analogy then, it is unlikely that media professionals see themselves as inhabiting the same moral universe as ethnic minority peoples. Thus, the media does not extend any helping behaviour and passively neutralises alternative accounts.

Ramifications of the bystander effect do not stop there. Those outside the bystander's moral universe may actually be blamed for their predicament. This can be explained, in part, by the fundamental error of attribution theory. The fundamental error refers to blaming 'others' for their own misfortunes. Since we have no knowledge of the circumstances that might have led to their misfortune, it must have been something they did. Blaming the victim in this way constitutes a positivist victimology that helps release the media from obligations to respond.

Given the high standards of reporting of human rights abuses elsewhere, it seems unlikely that most media professionals would support the ideology underlying the oppression of ethnic minority peoples, much less the methods employed to inflict same. The question then becomes, 'Does the event have to be contemporaneous in order for editors, and perhaps more importantly, owners, to view it as newsworthy and therefore of financial value to them?' And are media practitioners – like the general public – only comfortable with confronting atrocities not committed by their own governments? Undoubtedly there is a massive 'difference between reacting to your own government's actions as distinct from what might be happening in a distant country' (Cohen 1993: 104). Where domestic affairs are concerned, specifically in the realm of coloniser–colonised relations, the postcolonial consciousness of non-indigenous society appears to require a hiatus between gross violations of human rights (as well as other more mundane imperialist misdeeds) and the public acknowledgement of same. This is much like the decades-long delay between an event such as the Second World War and the time at which it becomes acceptable to joke about it. Such a hiatus serves the purpose of distancing from guilt over failure to do anything about it at the time. Or worse still, providing an indirect mandate for such action by voting in, or at least endorsing, the government responsible.

Priorities of the 'fourth estate'

Succumbing to a recognised psychological process would seem to suggest that the mass media are passive recipients of neutralised events. While there may be some truth in this, to credit psychological variables with greater power than organisational objectives in determining what gets silenced and what does not seems premature. Consider the time-honoured tradition of 'muckraking', a term once considered pejorative, which now is worn as a badge of honour. Investigative journalism, as it is described in more neutral terms, had its heyday in the US during the early years of the twentieth century thanks to writers like Ida Tarbell, Upton Sinclair and Lincoln Steffens, and publications like *McClure's Magazine*. These pioneer watchdogs provided critical discussion, analysis and information on corrupt business and political practices. For their persistence, they were stigmatised by Theodore Roosevelt whose famous rebuke about 'raking muck' gave them their title and who tried to thwart their crusade. While muckraking is alive and well today, it remains a marginalised activity in a sector obsessed with selling the public the sensational infotainment they seem to want.

Even heavyweights like John Pilger have their critical opinions drowned out – less by sheer weight of numbers than by political imperatives (Pilger 1998). Ownership, and therefore control, over the mass media is concentrated in a handful of people who have the power to block the formation of critical narratives (Said 1994). Where narratives are seen to conflict with the political interests of the powerful, they exercise that power to silence the narratives. From the initial stages of production, then, the mass media are active neutralisers of potentially threatening accounts.

In some respects, outsider media professionals are in a double bind. If they totally ignore, or merely pay lip service to important issues affecting ethnic minorities, they are perceived as neutralisers bowing to organisational and political pressure. On the other hand, if they seriously engage they can be seen as intruders seeking to assuage their guilt, or accrue some other benefit for themselves. Neither perspective is terribly conducive to improving media representations of ethnic minorities.

The danger is that if representation becomes too fraught, media professionals will shirk the task altogether, with potentially dire consequences for ethnic minorities. Foucault posits that memory is a site of resistance, and articulating it enables political self-recovery (hooks 1995). If we are prevented from articulating our memories, self-recovery cannot proceed. Without self-recovery there can be no sovereignty, and 'sovereignty is the border that shifts indigenous experience from a victimized stance to a strategic one. The recognition of this puts brains in our heads, and muscle on our bones' (Rickard 1995).

Land of the long white silence?

Writing in Sydney for *The Guardian* (2003) in a piece headlined 'The return of the native' (an unfortunate title that originated with Thomas Hardy's famous English novel) David Fickling asserts that, despite a resurgence in representations of minority peoples on the silver screen, Maori film making has been conspicuously absent. Fickling attributes this in part to a comparatively carefree history of colonial oppression:

> Maori represent one of the most vigorous and assertive indigenous cultures in the English-speaking world, but their impact on film has been relatively small. Australia's Aboriginal people endured a far more brutal history of oppression and exploitation under European colonialism, and continue to suffer levels of poverty and deprivation beyond anything suffered by the Maori. Their experience is also far more familiar to screen audiences, from Nic Roeg's 1970 classic *Walkabout* to *Rabbit-Proof Fence*, *Black and White*, and *The Tracker*, all released within the past 18 months. (Fickling 2003)

While the films Fickling mentions may be familiar to Australian audiences, none has approached *Once Were Warriors* in terms of global impact. Further, Fickling's hierarchy of suffering wherein Aboriginal people have suffered a much worse fate than Maori may represent an extension of Pilger's 'propaganda of organised forgetting'. If you cannot forget in your own country because those damned activists keep harping on it, you can still exercise a loss of memory in relation to other countries. Paradoxically, this marks out 'your natives' (in contrast to 'our natives') as more impressive because they have survived under much tougher circumstances – essentially progressing from 'noble savages' to 'resilient savages'. That resilience also offers an opportunity for neutralisation. If the 'natives' survived, their treatment cannot have been *that* bad.

Fickling's assertions do raise an important point. Namely, that silver screen portrayals are the *only* insight many outsiders have into minority peoples' experiences. If we stop to consider Maori experiences of oppressive schooling policies, it soon becomes clear that Fickling's 'oppression ranking' is misguided.

In the early to mid-nineteenth century missionaries of all flavours set out for Aotearoa with the intention of converting Maori to Christianity and 'civilised' living. In order to achieve this, they learnt Maori language, taught in Maori, and translated the Bible into Maori. However,

Pakeha officials came to see the continued use of Maori language – 'an imperfect medium of thought' (New Zealand Government 1867: 862–3) – as an obstacle to civilisation and enlightenment (Kirikiri and Wrighton 1990). English soon became the sole medium of instruction, reinforced by school subsidies under the Native Schools Act of 1867. There was some support for the English-only policy among Maori, who perhaps saw it as a way to access a share of power (Barrington and Beaglehole 1974: 116, 206; Kirikiri and Wrighton 1990; Walker 2001). By 1906, Maori language was completely banned at most schools, and frequently backed up by corporal punishment (Kirikiri and Wrighton 1990). Other Maori opposed the Pakeha education system entirely (Barrington and Beaglehole 1974; Kirikiri and Wrighton 1990). The prolific composer, Tuini Ngawai, expresses the mood thusly (Karetu 1975):

> Te matauranga o te Pakeha
> He mea whakato hei tinanatanga
> Mo wai ra?
> Mo hatana!
> Kia tupato i nga whakawai
> Kia kaha ra, kia kaha ra.

In English, this translates as:

> Pakeha education is propagated
> For whose benefit?
> For Satan's!
> Be wary of its temptations
> Be strong and firm.

By 1939 Sir Apirana Ngata, the great orator, politician and Maori leader who had originally supported the English-only policy, had changed his mind, arguing that 'nothing was worse than for one to be with Maori features but without his [sic] own language' (Barrington and Beaglehole 1974: 207; Walker 2001). By modern standards, Maori language embargoes violated the human rights of Maori to have their children taught in their mother tongue. The impact continues to be felt today, not least in the form of cultural-void theories of offending that seek to explain the apparent over-representation of Maori in the criminal justice system of Aotearoa.

Former educational policies directed at Maori also set out to criminalise in a more literal sense. To enforce conformity and obedience to colonial values, the colonial powers compelled Maori, under threat of criminalisation, to participate in formal Pakeha education systems. Beginning with the Education Act of 1908, successive legislation imposed strict regulations on Maori attendance at school. Previously, Native schools were not included with the ordinary public schools, coming under a ministerial regulation of 1903 instead. That regulation required every Maori child between the ages of 7 and 14 years, living within a three-mile radius of a Native school, to attend regularly unless exempted. Grounds for exemption included prior education, physical or mental disability, disease and geographical barriers to access. Children living beyond the three-mile radius were sent to State schools, where attendance was still governed by the 1903 ministerial regulations. The Maori Councils Act of 1900 empowered Maori Councils to enforce the regulations, where Maori parents or guardians lived outside the three-mile radius but could afford to live inside. Regular attendance was defined as:

> not less than four times in any week in which the school is open six times, six times in any week in which the school is open eight times, and eight times in any week in which the school is open ten times – morning and afternoon attendances being separately counted. (New Zealand Government – 1903, 20 April section 5)

Morning and afternoon attendances were defined respectively as, from 10 to 12 midday, and from 1 to 3 p.m. (New Zealand Government 1880). Appointed by the Minister of Education, Truant Officers were entitled to 'take steps to compel the regular attendance of any child' (New Zealand Government 1880, section 8). If the Truant Officer took no action, the School Committee or Education Secretary could 'take proceedings under these regulations to compel attendance' (New Zealand Government 1880, section 8).

A School Attendance Commission was established in each district. These consisted of several men appointed by the Minister of Education – members of the local Maori Council and a School Committee member; wholly Maori Councils/Village Committees; or wholly School Committees – to consider cases of irregular attendance and determine which 'if any, shall be brought before a Magistrate or a Justice of the Peace to be dealt with under the Act' (New Zealand Government 1880, section 12). School Attendance Commissions were empowered to 'lay an information, make a complaint, conduct a prosecution, or take any or all other proceedings specified in The School Attendance Act, 1901' (New Zealand Government 1880, section 15) if it determined that a child had failed to attend regularly. Any fines imposed went into school or Maori Council coffers. If they were not paid within two months, the Education Secretary was empowered to recover the money through The Justices of the Peace Act 1882.

Living in remote rural regions where they often comprised the vast majority, Maori found it difficult to solicit funds from the government or extract taxes from Pakeha in the same way that Councils in Pakeha territory could. It is therefore disturbing to see legislation that baited Maori into criminalising themselves in the guise of a revenue-generating exercise (Bull and Alia 2004). Parents or guardians could be prosecuted if they removed a child from a school district without sufficient reason, but only if the child did not regularly attend some other school. In cases where there was no Native school to attend, but a public school nearby, Maori children were expected to attend the public school, where they were subject to provisions of The School Attendance Act 1901. Indeed, all Maori or half-caste children were subject to the provisions of the 1901 Act, except insofar as those provisions were modified by the Ministerial Regulations of 1903 (Bull and Alia 2004).

By contrast, the Education Act 1908 required that parents whose children failed to attend school be served with written warnings. If the children did not attend within seven days of receiving the notice, the parents were liable to a fine of 5 shillings to £2, plus the prospect of further proceedings. Further proceedings might consist of a Magistrate ordering a parent or guardian to send the child to a truant school for at least six months, and if that failed, to an industrial school as per section 17 of The Industrial Schools Act 1908. Irregular attendance was punishable by a fine of 2 to 10 shillings for every week of unsatisfactory attendance. If a Truant Officer, Education Board Secretary, School Committee member or Clerk of a School Committee took legal proceedings, the onus was on the parent(s) to prove that the child had either attended or was exempt. Fines recovered went into School Committee or Education Board coffers; those arising out of failure to attend Native schools went into the Public Account (Bull and Alia 2004).

From 1897 to 1950, government harassment of Maori through educational legislation is readily discernible from official criminal justice statistics. The longitudinal *Statistics of New Zealand* series, published with some variations in title from 1853 to 1980, shows the first charges brought against Maori for breaches of education legislation in 1897, when a Maori man was charged and convicted of 'failing to send child to school'. The next cases appear in 1899 when a man and a woman are similarly charged and convicted. Out of several hundreds of convictions, a few cases may seem insignificant, but the number grew substantially in the early twentieth century when charges against Maori for breaches of school attendance laws became a regular feature of the 'offences against public welfare' category of crimes. Breaches of the School Attendance Act peak in 1914, accounting for just over 10 per cent of all charges against Maori: 161 charges (146 men, 15 women) of a total of 1, 599. Of these, 114 men and 14 women summarily convicted and fined. One woman had her case discharged (Bull 2004).

Clearly Maori have not had a relatively carefree experience of colonisation, at least insofar as their educational experiences are concerned. If history is to be prevented from repeating itself, and State crimes are to be exposed, it seems absolutely vital that outsiders borrow the voices of ethnic minorities. But no amount of borrowing voices will resolve the problems that arise when outsider representations contradict insider sources, as Fickling's commentary blatantly does.

Perhaps the hiatus in Maori film making to which Fickling refers actually reflects a residual fear about the liberating potential of the media that has resulted in a reluctance to support Maori media production. Insofar as film can act as a catalyst for change, it represents power (Mita 1996). The earliest signs of this fear emerged during the 1920s when the opening of movie theatres across Aotearoa ignited an acrimonious debate within the country's official culture as to the dangerous effects of American films on the behaviour of young Maori men in particular (Blythe 1994). Fickling also speculates that the 'assertiveness of Maori culture itself with an emphasis on Polynesian storytelling traditions at the expense of conventional plot-based imperatives that appeal to mainstream audiences, and a preference for juxtaposing scripts with Maori language instead of their English equivalents' is an obstacle to gaining entry into the mainstream activity of producing film (Fickling 2003). We do not see how these aspects can be considered inherently incompatible with successful film. Both *Once Were Warriors* and *Whale Rider* include elements of Maori language, and *Whale Rider*, at least, is based on a Polynesian oral tradition. But these are certainly good examples of the kind of excuses that can be invoked to deny minorities access to the medium.

Conclusion

The ways in which the media and ethnic minorities combine to further political goals can tell us a lot. Artists can embrace victim identity for its potential to mediate relations with dominant groups or they can use it to strive unashamedly for self-determination, though it is easier to make appeals that call for sympathy than to redress and reparations (hooks 1995: 58). The incidents depicted in *Rabbit-Proof Fence* and *The Mission School Syndrome* are not isolated. In all parts of the world, minority peoples have borne the brunt of contact, and are disadvantaged when it comes to making claims against the States that dispossessed them. They have endured decades of accommodation and resistance to oppressive policies (Bell 1998). Their protests are rarely heard. Hence, the lack of media representation concerning, for example, Maori educational experiences. Minority peoples continue to be revictimised by the culture of silence built up to protect their oppressors. Since media professionals are just as prone to the nuances of human psychology as anyone else, it is difficult to rule out the possibility that the particular ways in which ethnic minorities are represented in the media are due, in part, to psychological mechanisms. But to psychologise media practice in this way implies the media are 'mad not bad'. What must be taken into consideration is the organisational context that allows such phenomena to find expression. The power to narrate, or to block other narratives from forming and emerging, is very important to culture and imperialism (Said 1994).

Mass media have the power to undo this silence, to give minorities a voice, but that power rarely seems to be exercised. Even when it is exercised it is frequently with a view to deflecting responsibility away from the dominant culture. To answer Spivak's question, we believe that mass media can speak for the subalterns, if they borrow their voices. Perhaps the subaltern minority is too heterogeneous for simple portrayals to be adequate or balanced; but to deny the subaltern even that much, is to be complicit in the colonial enterprise that created the imbalance of power in the first place.

Exercises

4.1 The residential school experience

1. Watch the film *Rabbit-Proof Fence*. Then discuss:
2. Are there any aspects of the film that appear to deflect responsibility for the policy of forced removal away from the Australian government?
3. Now consider why a film like *Once Were Warriors* was made about Maori, but no film has been released on the colonial oppression endured by Maori through the combined forces of the education and justice systems.

4.2 Schools and the next generation: seeking redress

1. Each student should conduct an Internet search for media coverage of discussions, legal proceedings and other forums concerning grievances of indigenous people and other ethnic minorities against governments, churches and other bodies, in relation to their experiences of residential schools. There are current cases in the

courts, with governments, churches and others in Canada, the US, Australia and elsewhere. Bring some of the materials you have found to class.

2. In class or in small groups, share the materials you have found. Discuss the similarities and differences of people's experiences in different cultures and countries. Consider how those in power (church, government, and so on) are, or are not, dealing with their culpability and responsibility. How does that power and responsibility move from generation to generation? For example, how are today's religious leaders addressing the actions of their predecessors who ran the schools?

Further reading

Fournier, S. and Crey, E. (1997) *Stolen from our Embrace: The Abduction of First Nations Children and the Restoration of Aboriginal Communities*, Vancouver and Toronto: Douglas and McIntyre.

Haig-Brown, Celia (1988) *Resistance and Renewal: Surviving the Indian Residential School*, Vancouver: Arsenal Pulp Press.

Pilkington, Doris (1996) *The Long Walk Home*, Brisbane: University of Queensland Press.

Wilson, R. (1997) *Bringing Them Home: Report of the National Inquiry into the Separation of Aboriginal and Torres Strait Islander Children from their Families*, Sydney: Sterling Press.

Suggested viewing

The Learning Path
The Mission School Syndrome
Rabbit-Proof Fence

5 From colonisation to cultural revival: homeland, Diaspora, and the 'New Media Nation'

This chapter explores the progression from experiences of colonial domination to cultural revival and survival, and what we call the 'New Media Nation' (Alia 2004) – the international movement in which minority peoples, particularly indigenous peoples are creating and running their own media and programming and projecting their voices across cultural, political and geographical boundaries. Included is material on Sámi media in Arctic Norway, Sweden, Finland and Russia; *Iwi* (tribal) Radio and the Aotearoa Maori Television network in Aotearoa; Aboriginal programming in Australia and the Torres Strait Islands; and the emergence of indigenous radio, television, literary publications and a music industry under Greenland Home Rule. Also included is a case study of multiculturalism and Canadian media policy and its results, with particular attention to Inuit broadcasting and the Aboriginal People's Television Network (APTN). Founded in 1999, APTN is the world's first broadcast network developed, run and produced by minority people for a nationwide audience. Its founders lobbied successfully to include APTN in the regular cable television package, thereby making it available to all Canadians. It thus serves two main functions: to provide programming by and for indigenous people in several indigenous languages plus French and English; and to enhance cross– and multicultural understanding among minority peoples, and between minority and majority peoples.

Homeland and Diaspora

Concepts of homeland and Diaspora are not straightforward. Cultures are fluid and people mobile, across distances and times. Below, we explore the experiences and media representations of people from several cultures and regions, in relation to 'homeland' and 'Diaspora' and to their own cultural *re*appropriation and media creations and interventions. We include indigenous people in discussions of Diaspora because, although culturally distinct, the world's indigenous communities collectively experience many of the elements of Diaspora. Small numbers of people are scattered over great distances, some far from their homelands, as in Oklahoma – where survivors of forced relocation landed at the end of the 'Trail of Tears', the most infamous of mass relocations and genocide resulting from the Indian Removal Act of 1830. In Canada, Inuit were relocated from the milder climate and greener lands of northern Québec to the rocky lands and waters of the high Arctic. The degree to which their relocation was 'voluntary' and extent of government responsibility are still debated fifty years later. It is also the case that some people reside in ancestral homelands newly 'legitimated' by dominant governments – as in Nunavut Territory and Greenland under home rule. The following cameos focus on experiences of Diaspora and homeland in four cultural groups: Roma, Sámi, Maori and Inuit.

Roma experiences

Media representations of Roma tend to fall into one of three categories: Roma as victim; Roma as menace; or Roma as exotic exhibitionist Other. The news consumer is hard pressed to find links between these categories, or more nuanced representations. We are led to ask, 'Where is the opportunity for making art, or becoming an artist, in this embattled world?' And, 'Where are people's daily lives?' Audrey Gillan's respectful and detailed portrait of a Roma family and community, published in *The Guardian*, is one of the best pieces of journalism we have seen in the daily press. It is unfortunate that, as in so many other articles, its subject is brutality. 'People pick on us because of where we come from. As soon as they hear our voice, they say, "I am sorry, I am not serving you" ... They don't want to know you. It's just like being a racist against a black person ... It's not Johnny's fault that he was a Gypsy' (Gillan 2003).

According to Ian Hancock, a distinguished Romani scholar and international activist for Roma rights, the word 'Gypsy' (or 'Gipsy') comes from 'Egyptian', which in the sixteenth and seventeenth centuries was spelled (among other ways) 'gipcian' or 'gypcian' (Hancock 2002: xxi). The designations that are increasingly preferred, internationally, are Romani or Romany, Rom or Roma, sometimes spelled with a double R to help distinguish Roma from Romanians (Hancock 2002: xxi–xxii). Hancock's history of Romani experiences and representations in *We are the Romani People* is an excellent resource for journalists and scholars. Many fictional and journalistic representations ignore Romanies'

Indian origins, cultural and religious practices, and contemporary living conditions in the various countries they inhabit and visit. Claude Cahn challenges prevailing stereotypes, noting the persistence of the idea of Roma/Gypsies as a 'wandering people' despite the fact that today, far more are settled than travelling. British attitudes and policies date back to sixteenth-century portrayals of Roma as 'counterfeit' Egyptians (Cahn 2002: 10–24, 30).

As mentioned, depictions of exotic wanderers persist. The very people who ostracise actual Roma love to play at being 'Gypsies'. In a magazine supplement of *The Independent*, we were startled to come upon an advertisement featuring a photograph of 'white' children in white party dresses decorating a playhouse-sized, green-roofed caravan, under the heading: 'Hand made gypsy caravans for [children's] play' (Lavenders Blue Ltd 2004). The children pictured, the posh-looking construction, and the romantic and quintessentially English folk-songish company name of 'Lavenders Blue' suggest an intended clientèle of 'white', Anglo-Saxon, affluent children. The children's 'Gypsy' caravan has its parallels in adult play. In 2004, a four-page feature in Britain's *Mail on Sunday* headlined 'Romany Holiday' invited readers to 'Indulge your inner Gypsy' with bright patterns, styles and colours designed to 'bring out the wanderer in you'. An iconic (faceless) woman with long, black hair, photographed from the back, stands barefoot and housewifely beneath a clothesline hung with crocheted and patterned hippie-ish things, near a brightly painted 'Gypsy' caravan.

Accounts of systematic efforts to move, marginalise and decimate Roma populations reveal the lie that is deeply imbedded in such portrayals of Roma as fashion statement. Valeriu Nicolae describes what it feels like in the *real* world:

> Wherever I go, people ask me where I am from . . . I have to explain that although I am from Romania, I am a Gypsy . . . Gypsies are the people no one wants around: the thieves and the beggars . . . But I was the manager of a respectable company with partners all over the European continent. (Cahn 2002: 48)

In Europe Nicolae, a computer programmer, is met with fear and disdain; in North America, people assume he is 'a free spirit with some mystical ability to read their future in their palms'. Nowhere does he meet non-Roma who 'want to know that life for the majority of Roma in Romania is a daily struggle for survival . . .' (Cahn 2002: 48).

The cover of the 1990–1 edition of the *Berlitz Travel Guide to Ireland* is dominated by a photograph of a Roma-esque, horse-drawn caravan carrying a young blond-haired couple. Guiding the horse is a young man with long dark hair. No explanation is given, but on a back page under the heading 'Camping and Caravanning' is the following information:

> Horse-drawn caravans, in which tourists can live and travel like gypsies, may be hired by the week. They are most commonly found in the west and south-west of Ireland. Bookings should be made in advance through: Central Reservation Service, Irish Tourist Board... (Berlitz Guides 1990–1: 108)

Members of the Ácoma Pueblo (Native American) community in the US state of Arizona found a way around this. They permit no-one to enter their *mesa* (flat-topped mountain) village without an Ácoma guide. Tourists are welcomed to the Catholic chapel, but the traditional *kivas* (structures housing traditional, sacred ceremonies) are strictly off limits. Visitors are given information from and about the community; they are not invited to join it. The ability of Ácoma to control and limit tourism is facilitated by topography: it is virtually impossible to climb the *mesa* and enter the village without a guide. People living on the plains or in woodlands, or travelling from place to place, are unable to exercise such control over visitors to their lives and lands.

In the guise of enlightened pedagogy and touristic pleasure-seeking, the widespread phenomenon of romanticising minority peoples who are demonised in their daily lives perpetuates colonial programmes and essentialised images. The poet, Chrissie Ward, an Irish Traveller, explodes the myths imbedded in the Berlitz portrayal. Her poem, *The Stone*, describes 'the boulders blocking every traditional camping ground used by Travellers in the Republic of Ireland...'

> Take away the cruel stone
> longer and larger than life...
>
> Take away the stone
> that holds back our freedom
> killing the only life
> we've ever had...
> A chain of black stones
> around the green shamrock... (Ward 1998: 119)

Searching for media that 'make a difference', Beata Klimkiewicz considers two cases: an anti-Romani pogrom in Mlawa, Poland and the Stephen Lawrence case in Britain. She compares the role of *The Guardian* and its editor-in-chief, Peter Preston, in leading the public debate (Cahn 2002: 118) to racism-inflamed misreporting of events in Poland. From

1998 to 1999, Bulgaria brought in its Framework Programme for Equal Integration of Roma. Rumyan Russinov led the lobbying efforts by a coalition of Roma organisations, which pressured the Bulgarian government to develop and implement this landmark programme. Russinov explains: 'For the first time, Roma themselves initiated and actively took part in designing a policy that affects their lives' (Cahn 2002: 186). More than seventy organisations were involved. The down side is that in the years since the programme was established, its implementation remains frustratingly slow.

Sámi experiences

A cultural awakening emerged in the 1960s and 1970s as the first 'boarding house generation' of young Sámi began to rally against assimilationist policies. Not unlike the 1975 Maori Land March in Aotearoa, many Sámi were inspired by the Alta conflict over a proposed hydro-electric dam on the Alta River. Spanning fourteen years, from 1968 to 1982, this conflict, perhaps by virtue of its length, raised a multitude of issues relating to Sámi renaissance in ways that forced Scandinavian States to change their official policies and offer more recognition of Sámi rights (Lehtola 2002). The uncompromising position of the Norwegian State towards demonstrators only encouraged the politicisation of Sámi and awakened their identity. For those artists who participated in the struggle, or were liberated by it, the Alta conflict has been very influential in the work they have since produced. Even so, the increased awareness and appreciation of Sámi heritage has not resulted in all traces of assimilationist legacies being resolved (Lehtola 2002).

The Sámi journalist and academic, John T. Solbakk, emphasises the role of Sámi media in the Alta conflict and the cultural and political renaissance that followed. 'In 1980, the year before the Norwegian government sent a force of more than 600 police northwards to remove the demonstrators . . . the Sámi resistance had also begun to find stronger modes of expression . . . ' (Solbakk 1997: 172). Solbakk acknowledges the 'insider' practitioner's 'difficult double role as both defender and critic of Sámi society'. Minority media play a central role in the cultural, social and political worlds of minority and mainstream societies. Solbakk notes the differences in covering Sámi news for his own community and presenting it to those outside, as an alternative to mainstream coverage by non-Sámi Norwegians (and Finns, Swedes and Russians) (Solbakk 1997: 173–4).

Visual arts, literature, dance and music are essential to cultural renaissance everywhere. Some cultural revivals have legal support, an issue we will return to in Chapter 6. The revival of traditional handicrafts is protected under the Sámi Duodji trademark that identifies genuine Sámi work (Lehtola 2002: 78), much as Canada's government-supported artists' cooperatives developed the igloo trademark to identify and protect the work of Inuit artists.

Maori experiences

Between the early 1950s and late 1960s, 80 per cent of the Maori population migrated to cities, especially Auckland and Wellington, mostly in search of jobs (Walker 1975). The effects are captured brilliantly in the film, *Ngati* (1987). Once urbanised, Maori started attending university in greater numbers, though they remain seriously under-represented. At the same time, through television and other media, Maori were exposed to student political activism, the anti-war movement, the African American liberation movement, women's liberation and the gay and lesbian rights movements (Smith and Smith 1990; Poata-Smith 1996).

Whereas the capacity for media stereotyping is obvious, the media's liberating potential tends to be played down. Here, as in the Sámi countries, an explosion of journalistic and political activism accompanied the 'Maori Renaissance', led by new generations of increasingly politicised Maori attending university (Spoonley 1990; Walker 1992). Among its first creations was *Te Hokioi*, an underground newspaper that appeared in 1968, raising awareness of Maori oppression (Poata-Smith 1996). Out of *Te Hokioi* emerged the Maori Organisation on Human Rights (MOOHR). The inspiration and momentum that characterised *Te Hokioi* and MOOHR gradually declined in favour of the Black Power rhetoric (Poata-Smith 1996) voiced by Nga Tamatoa (Young Warriors), a group that had grown out of the leadership of young Maori living in Auckland, many of whom happened to be students (Te Awekotuku 2001).

During the 1990s, Maori opposition to State activities reignited (King 1997). A catalyst was the 'fiscal envelope' deal, proposed to settle all Maori resource claims by the year 2000 with a total budget of NZ $1 billion (King 1997). Waitangi Day celebrations in 1995 will be remembered for scenes of angry dissent, the culmination of months of protest action (Poata-Smith 1996). An Auckland landmark, the pine tree on One Tree Hill, was damaged with a chainsaw. A group invaded Television New Zealand's studio while *One Network News* was on air. The statue of former Premier John Ballance in Moutoa Gardens was beheaded (Poata-Smith 1996). Rather than seize this opportunity to highlight the legacy of Maori grievances and educate a largely ignorant general public, mainstream media bemoaned the passing of a 'racially' harmonious nation and revived stereotypes that associated Maori activism with a masculinised notion of criminal deviance (Wetherell and Potter 1992; Wall 1997).

Indeed, it is a key paradox of the Maori Renaissance that cultural efflorescence is accompanied by Maori social deterioration (Webster 1998). It is a paradox seen in many other parts of the world – for example, in present-day Siberia, where Chukotkan people are dying in unprecedented numbers but a cultural revival is in play; and in Inuit-dominated Nunavut and Greenland. Archer and Archer (1971) found that being Maori gradually became fashionable during the urbanisation process, expressed by unabashed expressions of Maoriness through hairstyles, dress, behaviour and name changing (Greenland 1984). Overnight, Stevens became Tipenes. Ethnicity itself was being politicised (Greenland 1984; Spoonley 1990a). Concomitant with the Maori Renaissance was a Maori reinvention of themselves, romanticised as 'everything Maori is good; everything Pakeha is bad'. Self-constructed images can be as flawed as those constructed by others. Although equally problematic, the indigenous constructions are more morally justifiable because they are self-imposed. We must ask whether the social deterioration that is being manufactured by mainstream media (and others) is a backlash to the cultural efflorescence, or whether it stems from another source. Either way, media continue to produce derogatory and misleading portrayals of Maori. Is it also the case that problems are exacerbated because Maori, by virtue of their social deterioration, have only recently secured sufficient resources to create their own media and counteract the negative images? Media are vital to the consciousness-raising process essential to decolonisation. The lifting of what Uruguayan author Eduardo Galeano terms 'collective amnesia' has been encouraged by oral history workshops, indigenous language radio stations and newspapers, and literature (Wearne 1996).

Following on from *iwi* radio developments, spurred by the 1986 Waitangi Tribunal claim discussed in the section on broadcasting later in this chapter, Maori demanded that 'their needs be met through the control and ownership of their own TV channel' (Mita 1996: 43). In addition to a separate Maori television channel, the continued presence of Maori language and culture on the mainstream networks and in prime time was seen as fundamental to the promotion and long-term revitalisation of *te reo Maori* (Maori language). It was considered that Maori have a unique perspective or 'world view' which should be seen as contributing to a wider 'national' culture, and portrayed on national television as a part of everyday life (Mill 1997: 15). Maori broadcasting is fundamental to the continued revitalisation of *te reo Maori*, and counteracting the disproportionately negative coverage devoted to issues affecting Maoridom.

Inuit experiences

At the same time that Maori were experiencing and creating these changes, Inuit in Greenland and the Canadian Arctic and sub-Arctic were experiencing political, cultural and media changes of their own. What might be called the Inuit Renaissance included reassertion of traditional ways of naming.

The French sociologist Pierre Bourdieu called official naming 'a symbolic act of imposition [that makes] the state the holder of the monopoly of legitimate symbolic violence' (Bourdieu 1991: 105). Nunavut educator Peesee Pitseolak explains that Inuit identity is tied to 'your Inuktitut name, because those are the names that are given to you when you're born by the people who love you' (Alia 2005: 252). Names are the heart and soul of Inuit culture. For centuries, visitors have studied and observed, praised and criticised, confused and distorted, regulated and registered, revised and amended Inuit names. In the 1920s, missionaries brought Christian names. In the 1940s, the government brought in 'disc numbers' – numbered identity tags that carried the label, 'Eskimo Identification Canada'. In the 1960s came 'Project Surname' – an assimilationist programme meant to 'normalise' Inuit in time for the 1970 Northwest Territories centennial (at the time, the eastern region that is now Nunavut Territory was part of the Northwest Territories). Many people predicted that the interference would mean the death of Inuit culture. They were mistaken; through it all, Inuit kept their traditions alive, and today, they are naming babies in the old ways and reclaiming names lost or changed by others. Cultural revival is a dominant theme in Nunavut, which in 1999 became Canada's newest territory.

The intricate naming system is based on *sauniq* – a powerful form of namesake commemoration some consider a form of reincarnation. Names are passed from one generation to the next, without regard for gender. The namesake, or *atiq*, can continue her or his life through many people. When a child is named, he or she becomes the *sauniq* or 'bone' of all those who have shared that name, and people linked by names are bound together in a complex and permanent set of relationships (Guemple 1965: 326–7). 'No child is only a child. If I give my grandfather's *atiq* to my baby daughter, she *is* my grandfather. I will call her *ataatassiaq*, grandfather. She is entitled to call me grandson' (Brody 1987: 139). The namesake ties are so strong that until puberty, kinship terms, dress and behaviour follow the relationship rather than the person's age or biological sex. Alexina Kublu is a linguist and educator from Igloolik – and a woman. Yet she and her husband and colleague, Mick Mallon, are also, as he puts it, 'fellow old men. I'm an old man because I've reached that stage all on my own. Kublu started life as an old man because she is her own great grandfather'. She explains:

> I am my *paniq's atatukulu*. My *paniq*'s my grandmother . . . My grand-mother is my *paniq*, which is daughter. I'm her *atatukulu* because I'm named after her stepfather. Her biological father was lost out at sea when she was a baby . . . The only father she knew was Kublu and so to her . . . he was her father. My younger daughter calls me *inni* (son), and I in turn, call her *atatta* (father). But first of all, I was always going to be Kublu because my *atiq* died before I was born . . . . My mother's midwife . . . the first person who held me . . . told my mother that she wanted her son [Kublu] to live with her . . . my mother by name [told] my mother by birth that she wanted . . . to have her son living with her. So that's how I became Kublu. (Alia 2005: 252)

That tangled constellation of identities is virtually impossible for an outsider to comprehend. Project Surname caused innumerable difficulties; thirty years later, Inuit are still sorting them out. In just over a year Abe Okpik travelled more than 45,000 miles, interviewing and renaming close to 17,000 people. For the colonial administrators, it was an opportunity to capture media (and public) attention. In April 1969, on the eve of Project Surname, the *New York Times* sent a reporter on an eighteen-stop, two-week tour of the eastern Arctic that had all the trappings of a public relations junket. It included a stop in Igloolik, Kublu's home town, where Inuit told the reporter they were concerned 'that they are losing their own culture'. Like so many others, he portrayed them as 'caught between two cultures' rather than as creating a new culture at the intersection. The reporter did not stay long enough to understand the errors in his story, which described the split between the Inuk's 'own leisurely [culture] of hunting, socializing and living by the season and the white man's structured style of schools, jobs and living by the clock' (Walz 1969). Only a person out of touch with what it takes to hunt in Arctic conditions would call the hunter's life 'leisurely'!

Euro-Canadian naming conventions got scrambled in the documentation process. Elise (Kunatuloitok) was stunned when, as an adult, she received a birth certificate with her *husband's* surname; her request for a correction was ignored. Renaming compounded the alienation of residential school experiences described in Chapter 4. Elise recalled that 'kids came back from school with new names. You go away and you come home, and suddenly, you're somebody else' (Alia 2005: 257). She was one of the first to challenge the government. In 1985, she presented a resolution to the Annual General Meeting of Pauktuutit (Inuit Women's Association).

It said Inuit 'now are forced to pay money to change their names as a result of government incompetence' and asked that government pay the costs of correcting the errors (Alia 2005: 257). Unlike the upbeat 'photo ops' organised by colonial administrators, Elise's ground-breaking efforts to improve conditions for Inuit received no media attention. Her resolution was passed but ignored by government and media alike. The cause was taken up by others, among them Peter Irniq, a distinguished leader and long-time advocate of cultural continuity and naming traditions, who changed his name legally from Ernerk to reflect its proper pronunciation.

Name changes did not just affect people. Over the centuries, visitors put their own names on places Inuit had known and named. They did not always welcome renaming of their ancestral lands. Today, they are correcting the record. Steve Kakfwi is a Dene (First Nation) political leader and writer living in the Northwest Territories. While his account of 'exploration' and naming refers specifically to Dene experiences, it parallels the experiences of his Inuit neighbours:

> Alexander Mackenzie came to our land. He described us in his Journal as a 'meagre, ill-made people . . . ' My people probably wondered at this strange, pale man in his ridiculous clothes, asking about some great waters he was searching for. He recorded his views on the people, but we'll never know exactly how my people saw him. I know they'd never understand why their river is named after such an insignificant fellow. (Kakfwi 1989)

Dene (Athabaskan language-speaking) peoples called the river Dehcho long before it became known to others as the Mackenzie. Similarly, the sixteenth-century explorer Martin Frobisher left his name on a body of water and a community that would later become the capital of Nunavut. In 1987 the official name of Frobisher Bay was changed to Iqaluit, reclaiming Inuit sovereignty and removing a visitor's name from the map and mental landscape. The impression given by older maps, of a north more *visited* than *lived in*, has changed. Today's multilingual maps reveal the diversity of linguistic and cultural influences – and people. It is a more accurate picture, placing Inuktitut (the Inuit language) front and centre as befits a region whose population is 85 per cent Inuit. Remapping is an integral part of the relationship between minorities and media; it filters into every aspect of public communication and communicates a non-colonialist world view. The same community has inhabited two 'worlds'. Readers who are informed about Iqaluit receive a very different understanding from those who once were informed about Frobisher Bay.

Canada has long been portrayed as a quintessentially *northern* nation. Imbedded in what some have called the 'idea of north' is the *reality* of north. While the northern 'idea' tends to focus on landscape, the northern reality is concerned with *people* and their relationship to the life-giving and life-challenging land – less the ''scape' of visiting painters and poets than the named and located home of its indigenous inhabitants. The north that permeates Canadian literature, identity and culture is a mix of 'idea' and lived experiences of northerners and visitors.

Inuit are said to be the world's most photographed people; except for the Inuk photographer, Peter Pitseolak and a few others, most photographers have been visitors. In 2000, Inuit started a project for young beneficiaries of the Nunavut Land Claim Agreement, who study Inuit history, the Nunavut agreements and current issues, and conduct research. One of their projects is to find the names of Inuit whose faces appear in hundreds of thousands of photographs taken in the early 1900s and stored for decades in Canada's National Archives. Students and elders are working together. Putting names to anonymous images is more than a research exercise – it is a way to reclaim images, families and communities while sharing them with Qallunaat and recording them for history.

Taking control: the development of minority media

Despite generations of alienation from media production, negative imagery and media mythologising, ethnic minority peoples have shown extraordinary resilience. The international movement of indigenous peoples has challenged prevailing media portrayals and fostered social, political and technological innovations. It has produced non-governmental organisations (NGOs) such as the Inuit Circumpolar Conference and World Council of Indigenous Peoples; regional, national and international media outlets; and organisations such as the Aboriginal Peoples' Television Network and the Native American Journalists' Association. Along with the NGOs that participate in some of its programmes, the UN and its subsidiary bodies, such as UNICEF and UNESCO, has also fostered positive discourses (Clifford 2001).

'Inuit are nomads . . . [who] rejoice in the ability to compare opinions abroad, as they did when travelling at will . . . the hamlet is the new iglu and the Internet is the new Land' (Alia 1999: 114). Thus the Nunavut journalist Rachel Qitsualik offers a cultural context for understanding the openness of Inuit to technological innovation and change. On a global scale, ethnic minority peoples are using radio, television, print and a range of new media to amplify their voices, extend the range of reception and

expand their collective power. Outsiders sometimes use such technological sophistication as evidence of inauthenticity, assuming that up-to-date
equipment represents a failure to maintain 'tradition' – a variation on the
idea that traditions cannot both change and remain authentic. As Étienne
and Leacock (1980) remind us, cultures are always in flux. To insist on
maintaining artificial boundaries constructs a false dichotomy between
static 'traditions' and the presumed enlightenment of modernity.

The Internet, for example, has heralded a new era in communications.
On the one hand, it has created unprecedented opportunities for ethnic minorities to communicate their world views, their cultural products,
their commerce, to a global audience. On the other hand, the Internet fa-
cilitates unauthorised reproduction and dissemination of digital images,
documents, and so on and thus enables the ongoing exploitation of ethnic minorities and undermines the control of knowledge and information
they have strived for – a point we will discuss in the next chapter. Earlier, we noted that the world's indigenous communities have experienced
many of the conditions identified with Diaspora. They have moved or
been moved, voluntarily or involuntarily, far from their original homelands. From the 1960s to the present day, indigenous peoples have created
connections across cultural, geographical and political boundaries. The
reasons are mainly strategic, to strengthen their power on the world stage.
At the centre of what is sometimes called a 'pan-indigenous' movement is
a burgeoning network of media and communications. The communications are directed towards both insider and outsider news consumers, and
to more generalised socio–political organisational and lobbying activities.

For example, during the Maori Renaissance in Aotearoa, Te Manu
Aute – a group concerned with cultural sovereignty in Maori communications – was formed in Wellington city. Their constitution begins:
'Every culture has a right and a responsibility to present its own culture
to its own people. That responsibility is so fundamental it cannot be left
in the hands of outsiders, nor be usurped by them' (Barclay 1996: 127).
Te Manu Aute promoted a Maori perspective on broadcasting to other
Maori communicators in an effort to secure control over Maori images,
songs, written and tape-recorded words (Barclay 1996). By the late 1980s,
audiences had benefited from:

> … a very determined and broadly–based effort by Maori communi-
> cators to take charge of their own affairs. Film and video training
> programmes by Maori for Maori sprang up here and there. Two fea-
> ture films with both significant Maori content and Maori production
> input – *Ngati* and *Mauri* – were completed. A Television New Zealand
> training programme (*Kimihia*) introduced some 50 Maori young

people to a range of television craft skills. A five-by-thirty-minute Maori drama series *E Tipu E Rea* was jointly funded by Television New Zealand and the New Zealand Film Commission. (Barclay 1996: 124, 126)

Consequently:

> . . . a certain degree of Maori self-determination in representing their community and culture has been achieved (for example in television programmes such as *Waka Huia* and *Marae*). Along the road an important way station was the six-part 1974 series *Tangata Whenua* produced by John O'Shea at Pacific Films. (Campbell 1996: 106)

But efforts to promote positive media representation of Maori continue to suffer setbacks. As noted in the Introduction, media are vital to the consciousness-raising process essential to decolonisation. This is a powerful position to be in – a point that does not appear to be lost on the mainstream who persist in assuming guardianship of minority efforts at media self-determination. Take, for example, the *Tangata Whenua* (people of the land; indigenes) series mentioned above, which was narrated by a Pakeha history scholar:

> If in a Tangata Whenua series you are obliged to include a Pakeha expert on Maori affairs . . . you are in bondage. How in heaven's name can a culture even begin to develop its own images of disquiet or playfulness, of the too-tender or too-harsh, when the landlords of every gully stare down from the ridges whispering, 'But I feel left out.' (Barclay 1996: 128)

Since planning for the Maori television service began in 2001, hot on the heels of the Aotearoa Television pilot project, Maori broadcasting efforts have in themselves been subject to negative coverage. Controversy has surrounded the alleged use of State funding for the personal expenses of some of the Maori male executives. Further controversy surrounded the bogus qualifications of the Canadian broadcaster appointed as Chief Executive.

The mainstream media have tended either to ignore or misrepresent ethnic minorities. In response, there are reactions of negation and affirmation. Negation comes in the form of legal challenges, formal complaints to media bodies such as Britain's Press Complaints Commission (PCC), and informal complaints such as published 'letters to the editor' or e-mails to media representatives and journalists. On the affirmation side, members of ethnic minorities have taken the media into their own hands, increasing their participation in the mainstream while developing their

own media outlets. They are using satellite, digital, cable and other technologies to strengthen their culturally and linguistically diverse voices and
disseminate information to a rapidly expanding global audience. They are
finding ways simultaneously to maintain or restore particular languages
and cultures, while working across cultural and linguistic boundaries to
promote common objectives and interests. Their progress is consistent
with Ien Ang's idea of the 'progressive transnationalization of media audiencehood' (Ang 1996: 81). However, 'transnationalisation' implies a
unidirectional crossing of national boundaries. We have extended it to
account for internal colonialism and boundaries between ethnicities and
regions. We call this fluid, constantly changing crossing from boundary to boundary and place to place – the *inter*nationalisation of media
audiencehood and media production – the New Media Nation.

Starting from Arjun Appadurai's idea of 'mediascapes' and
'ethnoscapes', new flow patterns of media and people, John Sinclair and
Stuart Cunningham observe that whereas flows of people often tend to
be from the periphery to the 'centre', 'media flows historically have travelled in the other direction' (Sinclair and Cunningham 2000: 2). This is
not always the case with respect to indigenous peoples and their media.
Although dominant-society media made early incursions into indigenous
communities, the main movement in Canada, for example, has been from
'periphery' to 'core' – with indigenous media originating in the remote
Arctic and sub-Arctic communities and moving gradually towards the urban centres. The most recent example is the transformation of Television
Northern Canada, based in the minimally populated northern regions, to
the Aboriginal People's Television Network, which covers all of Canada
and is gradually internationalising its programming and audience. A similar pattern is evident in Aotearoa, where *iwi* (tribal) radio is fostering
urban Maori radio programming.

While we refer here to pan-indigenous projects, the process of creating and running self-defining media organisations is seen in many cultural communities. It reflects a trend towards both culturally specific
self–representation and transcultural and global coalition-building. Our
comparative research on indigenous media in Canada and Maori media
in Aotearoa and their roles in forming the global 'New Media Nation' is
a case study, which can illuminate the broader picture of minority media,
internationally.

The experience of indigenous peoples reflects the conditions and developments in a number of ethnic minority communities and border-
crossing coalitions, such as those in emerging regional and international
Roma communications, media and socio-political networks. Ethnic minorities are developing their own news outlets using a range of technologies and formats. Many of the radio stations begin (and sometimes

continue) outside the legal bounds of broadcasting. Roth gives an example from the Inuit community of Pond Inlet in what is now Nunavut. In 1964:

> ...a local Inuit group within the small community on northern Baffin Island innocently put together an inexpensive radio station and began to broadcast culturally-relevant programming without going through the conventional regulatory channels of the Canadian Radio-television and Telecommunications Commission (CRTC). Its existence was discovered, years later, when two pilots flying over Dorval airport in Montreal heard the Inuktitut programming and could not identify the language. Thinking it was Russian, but knowing that no Russian plane was in the vicinity, they had the air traffic control tower employees research the source. They discovered that the voices originated from the tiny community radio station in Pond Inlet. Apparently, the sound waves had travelled unusual distances due to atmospheric abnormalities on that particular day. The radio station was contacted by the CRTC and procedures were normalized in accordance with Canadian broadcasting regulations. (Roth 1993: unpaginated)

Broadcasting

The first indigenous broadcasts in North America were on Alaskan radio in the 1930s, but despite Alaska's nearly thirty-year head start, Canada is the world leader in indigenous broadcasting. The US has moved all too slowly to support indigenous and other ethnic minority media. There are about thirty Native American radio stations nationwide as compared to several hundred in Canada. In 1991 Canada's 1976 Broadcasting Act was updated to enshrine Aboriginal and multicultural broadcasting.

In 1985 Australia's first exclusively Aboriginal station began broadcasting at Alice Springs. There are now stations at Brisbane and Townsville and a community television station at Alice Springs. The National Indigenous Media Association of Australia (NIMAA) has a membership of 136 community broadcasting groups.

Indigenous broadcasting is more recently arrived in Aotearoa, where twenty-one Maori radio stations are linked to Ruia Mai – the national Maori radio service founded in 1990. For Maori, self-representation has stemmed from recent legal decisions obliging the Crown to promote *te reo Maori* (Maori language). Indirectly, Maori broadcasting was the subject of a 1986 claim to the Waitangi Tribunal lodged by Huirangi Waikerepuru and Nga Kaiwhakapumau i te Reo (Inc.) asking that the Maori language receive official recognition. In reference to Article 2 of the 1840 Treaty of Waitangi, the tribunal established that the Maori language is a *taonga* (valued possession). As such, the government is obliged actively to assist Maori to protect it. With regard to broadcasting, the tribunal concluded that by allowing English language to dominate radio and television broadcasting, the Minister of Broadcasting had failed to live up to treaty-based obligations. Further, the tribunal urged broadcasters to remove any obstacles to any matters of Maori interest finding a secure place in broadcasting (Waitangi Tribunal 1986).

With funding from New Zealand on Air, *iwi* radio stations were first established across Aotearoa between 1990 and 1994. In response to a separate recommendation from the tribunal in respect of a claim on the radio spectrum (Waitangi Tribunal 1990), the government reserved frequencies for the promotion of Maori language and culture to enable full coverage of *iwi* areas. When the funding body, Te Mangai Paho, was established in 1994 it assumed responsibility for funding all stations. Remaining coverage deficiencies were alleviated by the launch of Irirangi.net in Wellington on 11 November 2003 (New Zealand Government 2003). It enabled listeners to tune in to *iwi* radio stations on the Internet, improving access for existing listeners (particularly those dispersed away from home) as well as attracting potentially vast new audiences.

Conway Jocks is the founder, talk-show host and former station manager of CKRK-FM in the Mohawk First Nation of Kahnawake, in the Canadian province of Québec, which First Nations people identify as Mohawk Territory. Jocks emphasises the empowering role of talk-back radio – within indigenous communities, between and among communities, between indigenous and other ethnic minorities, and between ethnic minorities and members of dominant ethnic groups such as Anglo- and Franco-Canadians. It also fosters pan-indigenous and other international communications, activities and movements. Talk-back radio 'forges the communication links in ethnic neighbourhoods, small towns and aboriginal communities from the farthest Arctic coasts to the outskirts of major Canadian cities, sending hundreds of languages through the air' (Jocks 1996: 174). As minority recording industries expand, the impact of music radio increasingly parallels that of talk radio. Indeed, in Aotearoa, Maori Radio has pioneered the use of quotas to allocate local artists higher airplay priority. On mainstream radio, local artists struggle to get any airplay (New Zealand Government 2003).

Radio is a medium of linguistic and cultural continuity, and sometimes of survival. During the Kanehsatake-Oka crisis of 1990, outlined on page 117, Conway Jocks' station, CKRK-FM, in blockaded Kahnawake, was the sole connection with society outside Mohawk Territory and an essential link between the two main Mohawk communities of Kahnawake and Kanehsatake. At the same time as CKRK-FM broadcasters maintained the two-way link with Canadian and international listeners, two young Mohawk Kanehsatake broadcasters were literally trapped inside their own station. Marie David and Bev Nelson provided on-the-spot news and commentary for CKHQ, keeping the community informed and helping to maintain morale.

Bev Nelson, Marie David and the academic (outside observer) Lorna Roth describe the events in a format that exemplifies the multilayered nature of the account. 'Three Women, a Mouse, a Microphone, and a Telephone: Information (Mis)Management during the Mohawk/Canadian Governments' Conflict of 1990' is printed in three columns, with the women's narratives running side by side (Roth et al. 1995). Incidentally, the 'mouse' in the title refers to a small, squeaking mammal rather than to the kind attached to your computer. Roth's involvement was more than academic. She helped develop CKRK and CKHQ. When the Kanehsatake-Oka crisis erupted, she had just completed a training course for the volunteers who ran CKHQ.

Québec has a number of minority ethnocultural communities and First Nations (Mohawk, Cree, Inuit, Attikamek-Montagnais, Algonquin, Mi'kmaq). Because their range and budgets are limited, most local media outlets are little known outside these communities. In 1990, the relative anonymity of Mohawk radio changed sharply and abruptly. The range of a station's reception depends on the level of power of its transmitter and antenna. Kanehsatake's low-power transmitter limited the station's reception to the local community and a few members of the wider public. The transmitter at Kahnawake allows CKRK to reach a much broader range of listeners:

> CKRK's audience also includes the listeners of CKHQ, weather permitting. The station directs its antenna towards Kanehsatake, in the hope that atmospheric conditions will carry their signal to the other Mohawk community . . . During the conflict, both communities used their radio stations as public address systems to provide . . . daily information of a strategic nature necessary to survive their ordeals . . . (Roth 1993)

CKRK was founded in 1978 'as the communication voice of the Kanienkehaka Raotitiohkwa Cultural Center, a local institution dedicated to the promotion and reinforcement of Mohawk culture and language'. Its primary goal was to circulate information and promote discussion within Kahnawake. It has helped to reinforce Mohawk cultural beliefs and facilitate discussions relevant to the community (for example, on land claims and traditional practices). The secondary objective was to inform the non-Mohawk public, the reason CKRK extended its listening range by installing a larger antenna. The extended range was to play an important part in maintaining morale within the Mohawk communities and informing the wider public of perspectives and realities not provided by mainstream media outlets. For its part, CKHQ became the sustaining voice of Kanehsatake. As Roth explains, not all of the developments were planned:

> CKHQ is located on a road that was occupied and regularly surveyed by Canadian security officials during the conflict. If CKHQ staff had left the station, there would have been no guarantee that they could have returned. For this reason, two dedicated Mohawk broadcasters, Marie David and Bev Nelson, decided not to risk the closure of the station. They made the difficult decision to live there, instead, not knowing how long they would be away from their homes and families. They ate minimally because of food shortages, and slept at the community radio station from July 11 until the very end of the crisis on September 26, 1990. (Roth 1993: unpaginated)

Their heroic broadcasts resonated far beyond the confines of their community and its particular struggle to become part of the iconography of the New Media Nation. Down the road at CKRK, the station maintained a policy of keeping things 'normal', though music play lists 'tended to have high message value, e.g., *Give Peace a Chance* by John Lennon or *The Freedom Song* by Frosty, a well-known resident of Kahnawake' and there were regular transmissions of:

> ... surveillance information; survival tips ... public service announcements regarding military and police manoeuvres ... political negotiations [and] news updates ... The station became one of the most important vehicles for keeping the town informed in a fairly calm manner and for retaining open channels to outside communities. Talk-back radio programming was the most effective way of encouraging and promoting communication with outsiders. (Roth 1993: unpaginated)

CKRK's phone-in programme, *The Party Line*, was a major force in forging Mohawk solidarity. 'It also became the point of cross-cultural exchange with the outside world' (Roth 1993: unpaginated).

The Mohawk–Québec–Canada conflict recalls an earlier conflict between government and First Nations (in this case, a clash between the Lakota Nation and the US government). In 1973, Lakota people were involved in the siege at Wounded Knee, in the US state of South Dakota. As at Kanehsatake, where Marie David and Bev Nelson moved into the radio station to be sure of continuing their daily broadcasts, at Wounded Knee, Lakota women kept the local radio station going under tense and sometimes life-threatening circumstances (Crow Dog 1992).

In the Sámi world, the period from the 1970s to the 1990s saw 'a quiet revolution' in Norwegian Sámi radio (NRK), broadcasting from studios at Karasjok. In 1992 the radio outlet issued a mission statement saying, 'NRK shall in the coming years be one of the most important tools in the preservation and development of Sámi society' and would encourage Sámi 'to want to be Sámi' (Solbakk 1997: 190–1). Sámi in other countries are equally involved in a range of media projects. In Finland, Norway, and Sweden they are represented by a Finland-based service which broadcasts in three languages – North Sámi, Inari Sámi and Skolt Sámi.

In Greenland, Danish broadcasters sent and controlled the early radio broadcasts, but Kalaallit (Greenlandic people) were soon involved, and by the 1950s programmes were broadcast in both Danish and Greenlandic. In 1978, a year before the launch of Greenland Home Rule, Kalaallit-Nunaata Radioa (KNR, Greenland's national public broadcaster) became an associate member of the European Broadcasting Union, establishing exchange programmes with Faroe Islands Radio, Radio Iceland and Canadian Broadcasting Corporation (CBC) Northern Service. Today, KNR has its own television building and news departments in Nuuk, North Greenland, South Greenland and Copenhagen, with a daily radio newscast in Copenhagen for Greenlanders living in Denmark. It hopes eventually to provide most of its programming in Greenlandic, while Greenlandic language television programming doubled in the past decade. Greenland also has a handful of privately owned radio and television stations.

The first Native American-owned and operated radio station in the US, KYUK radio in Bethel, Alaska, began broadcasting in 1971. It is the only station broadcasting in the Yup'ik language and the only Inuit (Alaskan Eskimo) television news service in the US (Alia 1999). Its television service, KYUK-TV, was launched in 1973, followed by the newspaper, the *Tundra Drum*. KYUK originated in the conditions of the Alaskan bush. Perrot (1993: 150) laments the scarcity of indigenous media in Chukotka in the Russian north, seeing the post-Soviet shift as 'le passage de la propagande à l'anomie' (the passage from propaganda to anomie). After years of having their places marked by a symbolic empty chair and flag, Siberian Inuit were finally permitted (by the Soviet government) to attend the 1989 ICC General Assembly in Sisimiut, Greenland; they became full ICC members three years later. In 1998, the ICC passed Resolution 98–14 establishing an ICC Communications Commission with a global and pan-indigenous mandate of improving communications 'between Inuit and other Aboriginal and non-Aboriginal peoples' as well as among Inuit of ICC's member regions in Siberia, Alaska, Greenland and northern Canada (ICC website).

Media, culture and technological change

The arrival of satellite-transmitted television in the 1970s marked an international breakthrough: using Telesat's Hermes Anik satellites, Canada became the first country to develop a domestic telecommunications satellite system, and indigenous people were among its first creative users. Early projects included crossovers such as the experimental interactive audio project carried by satellite across northern Québec (Nunavik) which linked eight radio stations, run by the Aboriginal Communications Society Taqramiut Nipingat Incorporated (TNI), then affiliated with a land claims lobby group, the Northern Québec Inuit Association.

The 1977 document *Ikarut Silakkut: Bridges-Over-the-Air*, 'described a new cross-cultural contact space' for Inuktitut-speakers of the circumpolar countries, a circumpolar cross-border short-wave radio service (Roth 2000: 251–2). In 1978, the Anik B satellite carried programmes developed by Project Inukshuk – the start of Inuit-produced television. In 1980 the CRTC appointed a committee to consider proposals for satellite television services in northern and remote communities. It included John Amagoalik, the first indigenous leader in Canada to help set national communications policy. The committee emphasised the role of broadcasting in preserving and maintaining Aboriginal languages and cultures and sought nothing less than a 'New Broadcasting Universe' (CRTC 1980: 1)

The government responded by funding Inuktitut programming in northern Québec and the Inuit Broadcasting Corporation (IBC) in what is now Nunavut, and licensed the private satellite distribution service Canadian Satellite Communications Inc. (CANCOM), with the stipulation that it make a substantial contribution to indigenous programming. Lobbying by indigenous communities and their supporters led to the 1983 launch of the Northern Broadcasting Policy and Northern Native Broadcast Access Program with a commitment to fund thirteen Aboriginal Communications Societies. Linked to an umbrella organisation, the National Aboriginal Communications Society, they would become regional centres for radio, television and print media services. In 1991, out of this series of programmes and events came the world's largest indigenous television network, the multilingual Television Northern Canada (TVNC). Along with television, the Anik satellite system brought high-quality telephone service to 25,000 Inuit in fifty-seven communities and initially transmitted sixteen hours a day of English-language television programming over the national broadcaster, CBC.

By contrast, television in the Sámi countries is more a dream than a reality. 'What should one say about something that doesn't exist?'

(Solbakk 1997: 195). Solbakk considers the monthly half-hour for adults and weekly half-hour for children scarcely a beginning. Despite many advances and slowly increasing government support, indigenous broadcasting in Australia also remains far behind that of Canada. Nevertheless, indigenous media are the fastest growing in Australia and include print, radio, film, video and television, multimedia and online services. As elsewhere, radio is the most advanced. In 1998 more than 1,000 hours of indigenous radio went out weekly over indigenous and non-indigenous community stations the Australian Broadcasting Corporation (ABC) and the Special Broadcasting Service (SBS); of ninety-four licensed stations, eighty were in remote communities. Australia's equivalent to Canada's Northern Native Broadcasting Access Plan (NBAP) and National Aboriginal Communications Society (NACS) is the Broadcasting for Remote Aboriginal Communities Scheme (BRACS), developed in 1987 to deliver satellite radio and television to 28,000 people. BRACS serves about fifty indigenous media associations, broadcasting on non-indigenous community radio in the language of each community's choice. In 1993, ten years after its conception, the National Indigenous Media Association of Australia (NIMAA) was officially recognised and incorporated, representing 'the collective of Indigenous media bodies Australia-wide' with a goal of increasing 'availability of culturally appropriate and effective media service for Aboriginal and Torres Strait Islander peoples' (http://www.nimaa.org.au).

In 1996 Australia established the National Indigenous Radio Service (NIRS), a satellite service somewhat akin to TVNC in Canada. ABC also produces two national indigenous programmes. Relatively belatedly, in March 2004, the Maori Television Service in Aotearoa went live to air with a dedicated Maori television channel. The station is being broadcast on Channel 6 of Sky Television's UHF network and Channel 33 of its digital network. Previously, Maori programmes such as *Waka Huia* and *Marae* were consigned to the anathema of prime time – Sunday mid-morning, or in the case of Maori news segment *Te Karere*, weekday early evening. Only in the case of popular music video shows hosted by young Maori presenters, often speaking in Maori, were the programming slots close to what you would expect to see in mainstream programming. The culmination of several decades of efforts to revive their language and culture, this latest Maori broadcasting initiative is seen as a cornerstone.

Ethnic minorities on film

In Chapter 2 we looked at Robert Flaherty's iconic portrait of Hudson's Bay (northern Québec) Inuit, *Nanook of the North* and other instances of filmed representations of ethnic minorities. In recent years, cinema–goers have witnessed a resurgence in representations of minority peoples on the silver screen (Fickling 2003). Fickling asserted that Maori film was conspicuous by its absence, at a time when the film industry in Aotearoa was burgeoning; but this was unreasonable given the then imminent release of Oscar contender *Whale Rider*, based on a Maori story and with Maori actors (also see commentary in Chapter 4). Fickling assigns part of the blame for the supposed hiatus in Maori film making to a relatively youthful written literary culture among Maori. This also seems incorrect. Fickling places the genesis of published Maori literature in the early 1970s, with Witi Ihimaera's short story collection *Pounamu Pounamu* (1972); but in the 1950s, the Maori Affairs Department sought out and published short stories by Maori authors in the hope of encouraging more creative writing. Judging from the subsequent writing of Ngahuia Te Awekotuku, Patricia Grace, Apirana Taylor and others, the strategy has met with some success (Blythe 1994). Maori media practitioners agree that more Maori filming could have been undertaken, but provide more compelling reasons for its absence. First, there is money. Finding overseas producers and investors prepared to fund such projects is difficult. The cottage film industry in Aotearoa is simply too cash strapped. Second, and perhaps more difficult to overcome, is the sense that Maori stories are too complex to be presented in the simplified medium of cinema, and too important to be stripped down for the sake of international tastes. The same can be said of most media representations, but is insufficient reason for avoiding representations altogether.

Fickling thinks '. . . few Maori films have the easy relationship with their heritage seen in Australian Aboriginal films such as *Rabbit-Proof Fence* or the recent Canadian Inuit film *Atanarjuat (The Fast Runner)*.' We disagree with that analysis. Those in Nunavut know of the long and sometimes uneasy relationship between Inuit film makers, community members and media outlets. The makers of *Atanarjuat* had conflicts and disagreements with the Inuit Broadcasting Corporation. In their community of Igloolik, they found countless variations on the ancient Inuit legend of Atanarjuat. They interviewed a number of elders, recorded several versions of the story, which the writer, Paul Apak, then distilled into a single script.

Conclusion

In recent decades, a series of movements have arisen within ethnic minority communities in a number of Western countries. These movements revolve around media production under the control of ethnic minority groups, often emphasising 'talk' or transmission of local information. Frequently formed by the unification of many local initiatives in a 'periphery-to-core' process, such movements result in a product that is capable of surviving and even competing with mainstream media outlets on a large-scale commercial basis. When the local movements form coalitions, such as the pan-Arctic news bureau created by the Inuit Circumpolar Conference, those coalitions constitute what we refer to as the 'New Media Nation' – a movement that spans ethnic and geographical boundaries.

A key catalyst to the development of the New Media Nation is the availability of telecommunication systems such as satellite, cable, digital radio and television, and the Internet. These technologies can achieve coverage over huge geographical areas, and can be used by many broadcasters simultaneously, so that minority interests (including ethnic minorities) are able to obtain access. Canadian Inuit were among the first to benefit, as Canada was the first country to institute satellite-based domestic telecommunications.

The New Media Nation serves its communities in many ways. Local stations form a 'sustaining voice' in times of trouble, such as conflict with agents of the majority government. Where ethnic minorities have been scattered by Diaspora or the processes of colonisation, sometimes across political boundaries, they can be brought together by their own media networks. By these means, ethnic minorities can develop the 'critical mass' necessary to preserve languages, foster artists including film makers and musicians, and strengthen cultural identity.

'Insider'-controlled networks also provide a means of disseminating information to any 'outsiders' who happen to 'listen in'. As we have discussed in previous chapters, majority mass media typically misrepresent ethnic minorities, generally in a denigrating way, and often to a gratuitous extent. Thus, the information flow from the New Media Nation is likely to be quite new to outsiders. Any consequent improvement in majority understanding of ethnic minorities must be greatly to the benefit of society at large.

Exercises

5.1 Creating New Media Outlets

1. As a class, or in smaller working groups, outline a plan for creating a cross-cultural media organisation.
2. Using the first exercise as a starting point, write a code of ethics or statement of principles to guide your new media organisation.

5.2 'Slanting' the story

Below is a table reproduced from Stuart (2002: 51) applying Todorov's five stages of a narrative to a news story about the 1995 occupation of Pakaitore Marae (Moutoa Gardens) by a group of Maori protesters. The table interrogates the structure of the narrative from both Pakeha (main-stream) media and Maori media perspectives. Examine closely the different slant that each perspective puts on the story.

	Pakeha narrative	Maori narrative
1. Status quo	Council controls gardens	Maori control Pakaitore
2. Disruption	Maori protesters move on	Council takes it over as a gardens – rename it Moutoa Gardens
3. Deterioration	Protest continues – confrontations with the police/City Council	Maori excluded from management of ancestral lands
4. Work through the issues	Court case/police inter-vention/discussion	Protest – discussions with settler government and Pakeha city authorities
5. Restoration of status quo/new status quo	Maori leave gardens	Council/Maori become partners in management of gardens

Using this model, construct a similar table based on the land dispute in Canada. The events described below are distilled from Alanis Obom-sawin's documentary, *Kanehsatake: 270 Years of Resistance* (1993). This 'insider' account should help you complete the Mohawk side of the table. For the mainstream media side simply construct a hypothetical scenario. If you have access to Canadian media sources from the early 1990s, you may want to see how closely your hypothetical scenarios match reality.

The Kanehsatake story

Obomsawin's film surveys the history of the gradual appropriation of Mohawk land by the government of the Canadian province of Québec. Kanehsatake is a Mohawk community near the predominantly

French-Canadian town of Oka, where planned expansion of a golf course threatened to encroach on a sacred Mohawk burial site known as The Pines. On 11 July, 1990, armed police arrived to evict Mohawk from their land, resulting in an armed standoff in which one officer was killed (whether by Mohawk or police bullets remains uncertain). The notoriously militaristic 'SQ' (Sureté Québecois), Québec provincial police, sent 1,000 heavily armed police. Mohawk from nearby Kahnawake helped block major roads, stirring up public contempt for a protest seen as an 'inconvenience' to townspeople and commuters. Police, in turn, restricted delivery of food and medical supplies to Kanehsatake. The Prime Minister appointed a judge as mediator and called in the army to replace the Québec police. Mohawk warriors reinforced their barricades. Communities were divided, physically and politically. Across the country, multicultural and Aboriginal support groups and individuals organised activities and blocked roads in a show of solidarity.

In Oka, townspeople and their supporters marched, chanting for Mohawk to leave. Anti-Mohawk riots escalated; one night of rioting involved more than 7,000 people. Subsequently, 2,600 troops were deployed. Eventually, talks between federal and Mohawk representatives led to a government ultimatum: Mohawk must open the bridge in three days or the army would move in. On 23 August 1990, a bus carrying negotiators was intercepted and the army advanced, contravening an initial agreement to engage in dialogue. Police tactics shifted to assaults on civilians, public strip-searching, and intimidation of Mohawk representatives who signed official documents under duress. Finally, Mohawk warriors and the army agreed to open the bridge, leaving the people of Kanehsatake feeling shocked and abandoned. Despite the agreement, the army invaded The Pines, forcing warriors to retreat from bunkers to a treatment centre where they made a last stand. On 2 September 1990, the army broke another promise by invading a longhouse and severely beating a point guard who had fallen asleep. Army manoeuvres escalated and attendees at protest-related peace camps were forced to leave. People were stopped and questioned, asked for their names, addresses and other personal details. Thus, Mohawk were symbolically criminalised, all on account of a golf course!

On 26 September, seventy-eight days after the siege began, the remaining thirty warriors, nineteen women, seven children, and two community leader elders decided to pack up and return home. Soldiers attacked the men; a 14-year-old girl was bayoneted in the chest trying to protect her 4-year-old sister. All were loaded onto a bus and taken to court for arraignment. In July 1992, a jury acquitted all but three of the defendants in the Oka trial, tacitly endorsing the original protest and highlighting the idiocy of spending over $ 155 million defending a golf course. Numerous social and financial issues have yet to be resolved since the Oka crisis.

Further reading

Aboriginal Peoples Television Network (APTN) website, http://www. aptn.ca/en/CRTCJan5-01.htm

Alia, Valerie (1999) *Un/Covering the North: News, Media, and Aboriginal People*, Vancouver: University of British Columbia Press.

Alia, Valerie (2003) 'Scattered Voices, Global Vision: Indigenous peoples and the New Media Nation', in Karim, Karim H. (ed.), *The Media of Diaspora*, London and New York: Routledge, 36–50.

Appadurai, Arjun (1996) *Modernity at Large: Cultural Dimensions of Globalization*, Minneapolis, MN: University of Minnesota Press.

Basso, Keith H. (1996) *Wisdom Sits in Places: Landscape and Language among the Western Apache*, Albuquerque, NM: University of New Mexico.

Clifford, James (1997) *Routes: Travel and Translation in the Late Twentieth Century*, Cambridge and London: Harvard University Press.

Gaski, Harald (1997) 'Voice in the Margin: A Suitable Place for a Minority Literature?', in Gaski, Harald (ed.), *Sámi Culture in a New Era: The Norwegian Sámi Experience*, Karasjok: Davvi Girji, OS, 199–220.

Suggested listening

Nunavut: Where Names Never Die

Suggested viewing

Aboriginal People's Television Network promotional video or any of APTN's programming (available from APTN)
Babakiueria
Magic in the Sky

6 Reciprocal seeing

Cross-cultural communication, the ethics of representation, and the nature of 'authenticity' are the key themes of this chapter. To this end, we examine the mutual cultural appropriation that is often a by-product of representation, and discuss specific examples in detail. These include academic appropriations such as what scholars in Aotearoa have called 'Smithing', and more commercial appropriations of art and intellectual property, explored in the case study of indigenous art in Canada.

We consider the cultural history of colonial image-making and the complexities of reciprocal influences – minority–minority and minority–majority. We look in new ways at cultural appropriation and reappropriation, for example, in the work of Jane Ash Poitras, who 'appropriates' images of indigenous people from all parts of the planet and 'steals' images made by Aboriginal and non-Aboriginal photographers from the early days of photography to the present. Artists are central figures in the indigenous cultural renaissance that is taking place in Canada, represented by documented exhibitions such as the 'Indian Princesses and Cowgirls' show curated by Gail Guthrie Valaskakis and Marilyn Burgess; Gerald McMaster's and Lee-Ann Martin's 'Indigena' and McMaster's 'Reservation X'.

Identity and appropriation

According to Black Elk, an Oglala Sioux who for a time joined Buffalo Bill's Wild West Show, 'Wherever you are can be the centre of the world. Your world has a centre you carry with you' (Clifford 1989: 200). The Sámi writer and academic, Harald Gaski, finds that having 'a more or less traditional' upbringing in a contemporary society leaves one 'standing with both legs in both cultures'. In the end, he finds the experience more positive than negative because standing with two legs in two cultures ends up giving a person 'more than two legs to stand on', as the intercultural fusions and intersections create new, hybrid cultures (Gaski 1997: 199–200).

Canadian videographer and writer Richard Fung finds that 'most of what we think of as culture involves some degree of appropriation...'

(Fung 1993: 17). In Nunavut, we have seen young Inuit in *parkas* and *kamiks* (sealskin boots) perform traditional Scottish *ceilidh* dances, which their ancestors learned from Scottish whalers and traders who visited and sometimes settled in the Canadian Arctic. At community gatherings, we have heard Inuit elders play fine Scottish-style accordion and fiddle. We have seen photographs, sculptures and paintings of Inuit playing Scottish instruments. In Yukon, we have heard fiddling inspired by Scottish and French styles, reworked and filtred through Métis, Cree, Anishnabe and various Dene cultures. All of these hybrids and fusions are *authentic* expressions of the people who enjoy and share them as they fluidly make and remake culture and 'tradition'.

'Smithing'

Unlike cultural fusions and transformations, the sinister side of appropriation is always about unequal power and carries a legacy of defining, objectifying and categorising 'inferior' or subjugated others (Fforde et al. 2002). From the 1850s onwards, Pakeha with a scholarly bent became an important source of Maori mythology (Belich 1997). Men such as George Grey, John White, S. Percy Smith and Elsdon Best encouraged Maori to write their history (Salmond 1983; Jenkins 1991), and kept them supplied with writing materials for this purpose. While the interest of Pakeha did help to preserve Maori knowledge for future generations, their inclination to see much of Maori mythology as worthless babble meant that many of the stories were distorted; nowadays these versions are regarded as reliably biased at best (Belich 1996). Because Smith led the key group, the whole process of forging a picture of the Maori past for Pakeha ideological purposes has come to be known as 'Smithing' (Belich 1997).

In the mid-1840s, Sir George Grey paid Aotearoa's first professional historian, Te Arawa scholar Te Rangikaheke (Belich 1997), to write about the traditions and heritage of his forebears as well as his contemporaries. According to Curnow (1983) Te Rangikaheke was criticised by his elders for writing on points of Maori doctrine and lore when he had not been schooled in the *whare wananga* (house of learning). Not only was he disadvantaged by his lack of formal education, it also seems likely that he was not an authority on the things he wrote about. According to Smith (1900) many old men of Te Arawa said that Te Rangikaheke's work was *pokanoa* (unauthorised proceeding); it left out much detail, and frequently credited actions to the wrong individuals. Apart from giving his own tribe precedence, Te Rangikaheke deliberately tailored legend to a form he considered digestible for a Pakeha audience (Belich 1997). Grey subsumed and further laundered the work, along with that of other sources, and published it under his own name in *Polynesian Mythology* (1855), magnifying its effect (Jenkins 1991; Belich 1997).

Grey often drew on a number of sources for the same tradition, thereby homogenising a varied cultural heritage and misrepresenting the traditions of particular regions (Heim 1998). In some cases, Grey's editing – which amounted to censorship – significantly altered the stories' meaning (Thornton 1985; Jenkins 1991). Nonetheless, because *Nga Mahinga a Nga Tupuna Maori* (1854) and Grey's own translation, *Polynesian Mythology*, are some of the earliest published collections of Maori material, both texts have become important sources for those studying Maori traditions (Simmons 1966). Elsdon Best, another prominent Smithian, adopted an elaborate pretence of respect for the traditions of elders he interviewed and disrespect for his European readers. His real attitude and methods show the extent to which colonial subjugation and acquisition of knowledge are closely intertwined. During Best's service with the Armed Constabulary (a paramilitary arm of the Police) and later with the Native Contingent of the Armed Constabulary, he collected ethnographic material from captured Maori. To his literally captive subjects, Best provided food and money in exchange for Maori knowledge. He ridiculed the resultant texts through demeaning references, censorship, and belittling comments that often wilfully misrepresented the cultural meanings of the narratives (Reilly 1995).

John White's most significant work, the *Ancient History of the Maori*, was intended to be the definitive account of the various tribal histories, from the creation myths to the early nineteenth century. White's 'editorial' and 'research' methods have been heavily criticised. They included having his wife and daughters write papers for him. As well, he constructed entirely new accounts and was known to plagiarise from other published sources, with no regard for authenticity. He was far from the only person to do this (Reilly 1995; Smithyman 1979). White's informants were paid to write down their stories, a practice that resulted in an emphasis on quantity rather than quality of material (Reilly 1990; Belich 1996). Despite the financial incentives, many potential informants objected to his requests to record their historical knowledge (Reilly 1985). Those who were prepared to fulfil White's requests tended to be younger men with little, if any, real knowledge of their own and insufficient authority to overcome older people's deeply-rooted feelings of distrust of the writing down of their words (Pere 1991). White did use a wide variety of other sources, and accepted the place of varying or contradictory versions of tradition. He even went so far as to draw attention to disparities. Nonetheless, like many of his contemporaries, he treated different traditions as part of a unitary Maori history (Reilly 1985).

Smith, in particular, has been cited (Simmons 1976) for using traditions of questionable authenticity, and for uncritical acceptance of traditional accounts (Hanson and Hanson 1983). However, many Maori still embrace his demonstrably fictional 'Great Migration' concept as their authentic heritage (Hanson 1989). Smith arrived at his 'Great Migration' thesis by comparing a large number of genealogies; he found that, on average, twenty-two generations separated various notable canoe ancestors and their descendants of 1900. Allowing twenty-five years to a generation, he deduced that in about 1350 a single great fleet had arrived in Aotearoa from Tahiti (Simmons 1976). However, in this case the end does not justify the means! Simmons' (1963) thesis, 'The Great New Zealand Myth', showed that Smith had merged several distinct tribal traditions, and the various canoes actually made landfall over a time span of several hundred years (Simmons 1969). The 'Great Fleet' myth and its precursors gave Maori a heroic and European-like history of exploration and settlement (Belich 1997). If Maori were willing to accept any qualities of racial greatness that Pakeha scholars might want to attribute to them, it was probably to bolster a sense of their own ethnic distinctiveness and value (Hanson 1989).

Maori were not always naïve victims of the Smithing process (Belich 1996). Based on his experiences researching the biography of Te Puea, Michael King (1978) discovered that matters involving sex, alcohol or money were particularly prone to censorship. Ngoi Pewhairangi, the famous Ngati Porou composer, in particular made it clear to him that some things might be appropriate for oral transmission among Maori but were not appropriate for preservation on the written record for anyone to see (King 1978). Similarly, when writing a booklet on Sir Apirana Ngata for the Department of Education in 1982, King (1985) was confronted with the Ngata family's objection to the mention of the 'Ngatapa Incident', in which Ngata's uncle Ropata Wahawaha had executed more than 100 prisoners. Given the corruption of Maori sources by previous Pakeha researchers, it is hardly surprising that Maori would be wary of relinquishing control over the dissemination of their history.

In addition to exploiting minorities for their knowledge systems, and the kudos such revelations can garner, there is an obvious financial incentive to appropriation.

Colonisation, commerce and icons of dispossession

The vast British Empire 'began as a primarily economic phenomenon, its growth powered by commerce and consumerism' (Ferguson 2003: xxiii). Those colonies not exploited for their sugar (in the Caribbean) or their spices, teas and textiles (in Asia) were exploited for their land and the opportunities it afforded for primary production. That is not to say that all those who voyaged from Britain to the colonies had profit motives in mind. 'Some quit the British Isles in pursuit of religious freedom, some in pursuit of political liberty, some ... went as slaves or as convicted criminals' (Ferguson 2003: xxiv). Nonetheless, the predominance of commercial interests cannot be denied. Many British nationals emigrated under the auspices of commercial enterprises such as the Hudson's Bay Company, East India Company and New Zealand Company. The hurdle of indigenous resistance was overcome through epidemics, intermittent warfare, conversion to Christianity and criminalisation. The resulting general demoralisation saw the indigenous population succumb to alcohol and even suicide. Whether through indigenous misfortune or by colonial design, colonists were keen to help themselves (Ferguson 2003; Loewen 1995). The mass media constituted another product of the age of Empire (Ferguson 2003).

Just as 'entrepreneurship' is often associated with 'deviant' business activities (Muncie and McLaughlin 2001), the pioneering spirit associated with colonisation is also associated with innovative methods of generating wealth. Many of those methods are considered deviant by the indigenous peoples on the receiving end. The appropriation and commodification of minority peoples' 'cultural capital' is 'doubly deviant' in that it seeks to extract commercial value from cultural decimation. In a cruel twist of postcolonial fate, the dispossession of ethnic minority peoples has created a new status for them as rare and unique icons for white commerce. Consider, for example, the dollar value of 'Indian' culture to the American tourist industry and the appearance of Native Americans in movies, on television, on coins, and as wooden 'cigar store Indians'.

In Canada before 1951, the Royal Canadian Mounted Police had federal orders to seize indigenous people's ceremonial art. Some items were hidden away and survived intact. Others, many of great spiritual significance, went into non-indigenous public and private museum collections. Cultural appropriation encompasses theft of (intangible) intellectual property as much as physical possessions, making it easier to conceal and more difficult to quantify. As a branding tool, the appropriation of language has indirect economic benefits for owners of sports clubs and various businesses. Consider, for example, the Atlanta 'Braves', the Washington 'Redskins', 'Eskimo' Pie ice cream products (created in the wake of the stunning worldwide success of Robert Flaherty's film, *Nanook of the North*) and the ubiquitous *anoraks* whose European and British wearers seldom realise the garment's name is Inuktitut and the origin of its (un-copyrighted) design, Inuit. The Atlanta Braves baseball team routinely peddles plastic foam 'tomahawks' and implores fans to perform the 'tomahawk chop', offensive to many Native Americans (and anyone else who understands its derogatory nature). Native Americans are widely used as logos for several major US corporations all without adequate consideration for their intellectual and cultural property rights. By contrast, appropriation of Te Raupraha's *haka* (performed by Aotearoa sports teams such as the All Blacks rugby team immediately before international fixtures) by the BBC was perhaps less of a revenue-generating exercise and more of an attempt to imbue BBC imagery with exoticism.

The power dynamic is not solely inter-racial. A swimwear manufacturer in Aotearoa, Moontide, used the Maori *koru* (a type of spiral design) motif in one of their product lines debuting at Sydney Fashion Week in 1998, and were congratulated for their 'ethical' handling of the 'indigenous designs issue' (Shand 2000). The owner of the business and the firm's designers developed this swimwear line in conjunction with Buddy Mikaere, a Maori entrepreneur of standing in his rural Aotearoa community (Shand 2000). In recognition of their dual aims of commercial viability and cultural respect, part of the royalty from sales goes to the Pirirakau *hapu* (sub-tribe) of the Ngati Ranginui people (Shand 2000). The ability of an individual, *hapu* or *iwi* (tribe) to sanction independently the use of a motif or to register some sort of interest in it that might exclude both indigenous and non-indigenous use is highly questionable (Shand 2000). That said, is it better to do this and ensure continuity of specific cultural skills, or risk losing them altogether?

Nor is the power dynamic necessarily gender neutral. From Malinowski's failure to acknowledge women's wealth in banana leaves to Lévi-Strauss' tacit endorsement of women as commodities, resistance to recognition of women's contributions to production (not *re*production) in a variety of settings continues to limit the scope of our understanding of the impacts of appropriation. In many societies, women played valuable economic roles. Hence the importance of looking specifically at their experiences of appropriation:

> Ethnohistorical research has shown that early trade with Europeans, and the exchange of furs, skins, or other local goods for metal tools, concentrated foods, guns, and clothing undercut the interdependence of cooperatively organized bands and villages. This did not mean the disappearance of egalitarian traditions, but it did mean unequal access to important resources that undermined the economic structure of egalitarianism. (Étienne and Leacock 1980: 13)

By virtue of their own misogyny, colonists resorted to trade with men by default, thus undermining women's positions in the long term: 'In

Tlingit society . . . women's labor was important to the production of trade goods and . . . they directly engaged in distribution and exchange, often guiding or even controlling the trading transactions of men' (Étienne and Leacock 1980: 15). In transforming colonised peoples into producers and consumers of commodities, colonisers addressed their demands and innovations to men and encouraged the economic dependency of women: 'The imposition of capitalist exploitation linked the subjugation of people generally with the special subjugation of women' (Étienne and Leacock 1980: 16). These changes were compounded by the transition from group land rights to private property rights, which also worked to men's advantage.

Continuing appropriations

It would be convenient to be able to show a chronological progression from inaccurate and irresponsible 'outsider' representations to accurate and responsible self-representations of minority peoples. To do so would be grossly to misrepresent the history and nature of indigenous art; the complex experiences, motivations and explorations of indigenous artists, and indeed, of artists in general. The exhibition, 'Indian Princesses and Cowgirls: Stereotypes from the Frontier' organised by Marilyn Burgess and Gail Guthrie Valaskakis (1995), featured 1920s images of Native American 'pinup girls'. Pale, white- and male-identified damsels were portrayed for decoration, or to promote and market an array of services and products. 'Sakaka-wea (Bird Woman)' advertised the Oriental Dyeing and Cleaning Works (Valaskakis 1995: 11). Another porcelain, feathered woman furthered the cause of Chippewa's Pride Beer (Valaskakis 1995: 18).

More than eighty years later, indigenous people are equally exoticised, though the gendering and implicit gaze have shifted somewhat. A blatantly blond boy sporting a generic 'Indian' headdress promotes the virtues of a Japanese car with 'Room for the tribe' (Suzuki 2002). '. . . there's ample space for *braves* and *big chiefs* . . . the tall cabin means *young Hiawatha here* needn't leave *his headdress* behind, which could avoid some ruffled *feathers* [ours italics] (Suzuki 2002)'. The puns indicate an attitude of fun, ostensibly at no-one's expense.

A Swedish designer features clothing inspired by 'wild, colourful Native Americans', modelled by Nordic women in her spring 2003 collection (Sjöden 2003: 50–5). The ubiquitous feathers are there, but the bodies are more athletic and less naked than those of the 1920s, and T-shirts suggest utility and comfort, but the garments are as unrelated to anything Native American as those in the 1920s ads. 'Squaw, Pawnee and a little Kickapoo. Sometimes you just feel like doing something wild . . . It's probably my rebellious artistic soul that loves the unexpected and surprising...And so the Native American theme was born...It's so exciting, don't you think? Yee-haa!' (Sjöden 2003: 50). Thus, Native Americans are linked to 'rebellion', 'excitement', and an expression (Yee-haa!) generally associated with white people's country and western dances. The collection features fringes, beads and geometric patterns. 'Squaw Hanna dances wild in a native American-inspired tunic...and pretty ikat-weave silk scarf...' The text (in the designer's own voice) has a self-congratulatory air; footnotes imply the author has done a little research...very little. 'Red Indians prefer to be called "Native Americans"'...'Chippewa' is 'The highest leader (Chief) in the Algonquian tribe'; 'Squaw' is 'A Native American woman' (Sjöden 2003: 50). All of this is misinformation, presented in an authoritative voice. *Ikat* is an Indonesian weaving technique. Its origins are thousands of miles and several cultures removed from anything Native American. 'Chippewa' is one name for a culture whose people reside in parts of Canada and the US and are sometimes called Ojibway, Ojibwa, Anishnabe and other variations of the name (see, for example, Valaskakis' essay, 'The Chippewa and the Other'). There is no 'Algonquian tribe' – the word refers to a group of Native American/First Nations languages. A great number of indigenous people consider the word 'squaw' derogatory and offensive. What is especially frustrating about this is that the designer's own heritage is Sámi, and her catalogues are notable for including models of all colours, sizes and ages, who travel to locations around the world. The catalogues often include interesting and respectful information about the people and regions visited, though the 'inspiration' for the collections, which comes from an array of cultures, straddles the line between inspiration and appropriation.

Such appropriation is common in the fashion world and is usually reconstructed as 'inspiration' or 'influence'. The 2001 Dior collection featured a European-looking woman showing more feathers, and leg, than her 1920s counterpart, though with midriff rather than shoulders bared (Dior 2001).

Appropriating humans

Examples of colonial and postcolonial appropriations are not in short supply. Abduction of Native American men, women and children was not uncommon. Many were sold into slavery, or simply shipped far away and interrogated for all sorts of knowledge that generated fame, prestige and wealth for their 'captors'. One of the most ignominious examples is the sponsored abduction of the 'live Eskimo specimen', Minik Wallace, from his home in north-western Greenland by the reputedly ruthless explorer, Robert Peary. In 1897 Peary brought Minik to the American Museum of Natural History in New York, which was presided over by the distinguished anthropologist, Frans Boas. It is an ugly chapter in Boas' history, as his research broke much new ground and his teaching influenced generations of anthropologists. In many ways, his work and perspective was notable for its humanity and respect – a fact that makes his role in the Minik case especially deplorable. He was not a crass, commercial colonialist. Of all people, Boas should have known better. When he was prodded to consciousness, it was too late.

During his twelve years in the US, Minik lost his language, hunting skills and health. In the most shocking moment, he discovered his father's remains among the collection of bones kept for study and displayed in the museum. After a brief, largely unsuccessful stint back in Greenland Minik returned to the US, where he died of Spanish flu at the age of twenty-eight. While Boas finally relented, the relentless Peary used his association with Minik's people to acquire the asteroid now named after him (Harper 2000).

On the opposite coast, in California, another live 'specimen' emerged, in 1911. The case of 'Ishi' is far less clear-cut than that of Minik. While Minik was taken from his homeland to a new country by an explorer whose objectives were transparently profit-motivated, the man known as Ishi was 'discovered', 'rescued' and 'adopted' by the anthropologist, A. L. Kroeber for a number of different and sometimes contradictory reasons. The man others called Ishi was the last surviving member of the Yahi tribe who inhabited the Mount Lassen Foothills of northern California. They were originally driven out of their valley homeland by other tribes, and forced to change in order to survive. This raises a point we have made before: that human history is made up of transformations and transmutations; all cultures evolve; and there is no such thing as a 'pure' culture or tradition. The mountain-centred Yahi culture of Ishi's time was not the Yahi valley culture of 1,000 years before. In the late 1840s came the California Gold Rush and immigration. In search of gold and land for ranching, the immigrants were not inclined to peaceful coexistence. Faced with deliberate killings and rampant disease, the Yahi disappeared. In 1908 Oro Light and Power Company surveyors discovered a man fishing, and a village, which they ransacked. An old man and a younger woman fled, never to be seen again. 'Ishi' and his mother remained until she died in 1911. Facing starvation, Ishi left his homeland. He was found near the town of Oroville and jailed, turned into a criminalised and exoticised celebrity. His 'discovery' was widely reported; two University of California anthropology professors 'rescued' him and became his legal guardians. He stayed with them until 1916, when he died of tuberculosis. Two years before his death, he took them to his homeland, where they recorded Yahi place names, visited key places in his life, and photographed him making traditional tools.

Motivated at once by concern for Ishi's welfare and his own self-interested careerism and quest for knowledge, Kroeber gave him a 'home' with his own family, and in the university museum Kroeber was able to engage in rudimentary conversations – the only person in the world with whom Ishi could speak his own language. Kroeber dubbed him Ishi – the Yahi word for 'man' – out of respect, because according to Yahi tradition his true name could not be spoken or revealed to strangers (Kroeber 1961 and 1964). Their relationship evolved into a complex mix of appropriation and exploitation, colleagueship and genuine friendship. When Kroeber's first wife, Henriette, was dying, Ishi was a compassionate and understanding friend. There is no denying Kroeber's scientific obsessions and anthropological ambitions, or the criminalisation and paternalism that led to legal guardianship; neither can we ignore his humanity.

The placing of Ishi in a museum was equally complex and contradictory. On the sinister side, it made him a 'living exhibit' to be stared at and exoticised. On the constructive side, it made him a recognised and appreciated expert on his own culture – which he was able to teach to others. Living in a preserved 'collection' of the sacred and everyday objects of his people, Ishi was able to maintain some fragile connection to his past. There was no way to undo the brutality he had experienced – the genocide of his tribe at the hands of early settlers. It can be argued that he and the 'collection' should have been returned to the mountains. There is a patronising side to that position as well – first, because he himself had left his homeland; second, because it would have disconnected him from other humans, whose language and culture he was also learning. Having lost all of his family and community, there was no way he could live a fair and human existence anywhere. The story was eventually told by Kroeber's second wife, Theodora, in *Ishi: The Last of his Tribe* and *Ishi in Two Worlds*, published in 1961 with the unfortunate subtitle of '*the Last Wild Indian in North America*; and also in the film *The Last of his Tribe* (1992) with Hollywood's ubiquitous generic 'Indian', Graham Greene, in the title role. In the film, Kroeber expresses respect and mourning by singing the Yahi death song, which Ishi has taught him. It is ironic that the depopulated Yahi homeland in the mountains of northern California now is designated the 'Ishi Wilderness Preserve'.

Minik's discovery of his father's bones in a New York museum was far from unique. Appropriation of human remains loomed large in colonial life. Mariners often described their purchase and exchange; the crudest profiteering involved theft, pillage and grave robbery (Te Awekotuku 1996). Many collectors, both private and institutional, are intractable when it comes to returning such remains. When Ishi died in 1916 his earlier requests that an autopsy not be performed on his body were never respected. Not until 8 August 2000 did the Smithsonian Institution return Ishi's brain to northern California tribes now believed to have close ancestral links to him (Gunnison 1999; see also Starn 2004). While many *moko mokai* (tattooed heads of Maori anecstors) have been returned, most remain in the US. The Robley collection of thirty-nine *moko mokai* at New York's Museum of Natural History is a case in point.

Appropriating Maori art

It is not only human remains that collectors are reluctant to return, even if the work was acquired by questionable, perhaps illegal means. *Pataka* (carved storehouse panels) from Motunui near New Plymouth were smuggled out of Aotearoa and sold to Bolivian tin millionaire George Oritz. In 1978 he offered these for auction; the government of Aotearoa obtained an injunction preventing their sale, and sued for their return. After a protracted legal battle in the English courts, Oritz prevailed, despite evidence that these unique carved panels had been illegally sold and secretly exported (Te Awekotuku 1996). Other wood, stone and fibre artefacts are finding their way back home. One notable example is the huge, 18- centimetre *hei tiki* (a particular type of pendant worn around the neck), returned with the quiet ceremony to Te Arikinui Te Atairangikaahu, the Maori Queen, by Count Carlo di Marchi of Switzerland in 1984. Another is the bequest of a rare red parrot feather bag by the widow of a land court judge to the great-great-granddaughter of the weaver (Te Awekotuku 1996).

Visual arts of indigenous peoples were looted, stolen, traded and bought by colonials of every status – from Governors General to itinerant sealers (Shand 2000: 3). From 1769, Maori weaponry, textiles, ornaments and carved items were eagerly acquired by travellers and curiosity hunters in the Northern Hemisphere (Te Awekotuku 1996). Some objects were studied and admired; others never saw the light of day again (Shand 2000). Major collections were accumulated and eventually housed in the museums of London, Salem, Rome, Leningrad, Dublin, Stockholm, Philadelphia and elsewhere (Te Awekotuku 1996). Once displayed, these items of great value became available for appropriation by the very colonisers who had initially dislocated them (Shand 2000).

According to Te Awekotuku (1996), when Maori parted with *taonga* (treasured possessions) such as personal jewellery they did so on the understanding that those items would be returned at some future point, having been enriched by the experience.

Interestingly, Hans Neleman's (1999) book *Moko: Maori Tattoos* contains an image of a *moko* styled after Native American design, by bringing black lines close to the eyes and thereby emphasising the whites, chosen by the bearer for impact (Kassem 2003). Here is another example of one minority culture appropriating imagery from another. We wonder which Native American tribe inspired the *moko* design, and how its members would feel about sharing their own imagery without prior consultation. Attitudes vary considerably among different tribes. Hopi, for example, are extremely careful to protect the privacy of their sacred ceremonies and images and rarely share them with outsiders. Certain designs are given or sold, in jewellery, for instance; but they are made, and made available, by Hopi. It would seem that ethnic minority people should be particularly sensitive to the borrowing or stealing of other people's images. The difference between respectful sharing and inappropriate acquisition lies in conscious communication and equity of power. It is possible that some Native Americans would feel honoured to have their imagery carried across the cultural divide, to Maori traditions, while others might take offence unless the designs were willingly and consciously given.

Selling Sámi

The many strands of Sámi culture can be seen with particular clarity in traditional clothing. The design and decoration distinguishes Sámi from different regions. There are at least five main designs among Finnish Sámi alone, and a comparable range of designs in Norway and Sweden. The highly coloured men's tunic characteristic of the 'Eanodat style' is the one most commonly featured on postcards and in tourist brochures. To dress inappropriately is to run the risk of being labeled *rivgu* (not a Sámi). Because of the intricate connection with identity and the subtler cultural and linguistic codes, many Sámi find it offensive when outsiders wear Sámi garments without appreciating the symbolism with which they are imbued (Lehtola 2002).

It is also the case, in our own encounters and work with Sámi scholars, journalists and politicians, that our Sámi colleagues most often wear European dress – though frequently accompanied by a small item of traditional clothing or jewellery. Traditional clothes are worn on festive or ceremonial occasions, or for political purposes. We see this in other cultures as well. When Mary Simon was President of ICC, she wore a *parka* for the opening of the assembly and other special occasions, donning Western-style business clothes for daily meetings. In similar fashion, Greenlandic leaders wear *anoraks* for special occasions and Western-style business or casual clothes more generally, and First Nations leaders who normally wear everyday 'street clothes' wear special garments and carry eagle feathers and other spiritually important items for important occasions.

Awakenings: indigenous art in Canada

The Canadian Métis leader, Louis Riel said: 'My people will sleep for 100 years, and when they awake it will be the artists who give them back their spirit' (Mattes and Racette 2001: 3). Artists are central figures in the indigenous renaissance that is taking place in Canada, represented by exhibitions such as Gerald McMaster's and Lee-Ann Martin's 'Indigena' and McMaster's 'Reservation X':

> Individual expression has been pitted against 'collective identity' ... artists are encouraged to identify with movements such as the avant-garde ... But what of our own theories of art, our own philosophies of life, our own purposes for representation? By reducing our cultural expression to simply the question of modernism or postmodernism, art or anthropology ... contemporary or traditional, we are placed on the edges of the dominant culture ... When we assert our own meanings and philosophies of representation we render the divisions irrelevant, and maintain our Aboriginal right to name ourselves. (Todd in McMaster and Martin 1992: 75)

A number of themes and subjects recur across the works of many indigenous artists. These include:

- Christianity, church, and missionary experiences
- Residential schools (government- and missionary-run)
- Treaties (absent, signed, broken)
- Land (wild, rural, urban)
- Border crossings (US–Canadian, international, pan-indigenous)
- Emotion and experience (sadness/depression, anger/outrage, humour/hilarity/satire)
- Links between art, politics and society
- Links between visual and textual representations.

School and missionary experiences permeate the works of Jane Ash Poitras, Jim Logan and many others. Jim Logan is Cree, Sioux and Scottish, born in New Westminster, British Columbia. For many years, he has lived and worked in Yukon, and has become known as a Yukon artist. His painting, *National Pastimes*, features the deep pink sky and other colours familiar in his work. Canada's favourite sport, ice hockey, is the 'national pastime' that dominates the painting. Other pastimes are shown or hinted at – an Aboriginal fiddler; an ice-white, black-suited and -hatted man taking a photograph of a trio of Aboriginal ice hockey players, the figure of a priest standing paternally over them; a couple embracing; others playing, walking, drinking. Logan writes:

> I see myself as a social commentator. I paint my life the way I see it lived. I...paint Native society in its relation to the mainstream for a number of personal reasons...many of my pieces reflect poverty, oppression, alcoholism and abuse in the native community...there is a time to laugh and a time to weep. I always attempt to balance reality in my shows...(Logan in McMaster and Martin 1992: 142)

Father Image I and *Father Image II* are part of a series done in black, white and shades of grey, like stills from an old movie. Clearly, these are portraits of two very different fathers. *Father Image I* repeats an image from the highly coloured *National Pastimes* painting – as if a black-and-white close-up lens were fixed on the same scene. In close-up, we see discomfort and unhappiness in the boys' faces, a stern and rigid look on the face of the priest, whose large hands sit possessively on slim shoulders, one thumb reaching with barely contained, inappropriate intimacy toward a boy's throat. Behind the uncomfortable group is the mission school, with black, blind windows and a white crucifix.

Father Image II is a warm, family scene. A father and son sit, watching television, while another family member sits nearby, fiddling. Behind them we can see smoke curling from the houses just beyond the window. A mysterious, shadowy figure appears amidst the wallpaper flowers on the cabin wall. Like the priest 'father', this father also has his hand on a boy's shoulder. Positioned almost identically, it is subtly different – here, the spread fingers look affectionate instead of sinister.

Luke Simon's painting, *Columbus Decelebration Series: Past, Present and Future*, echoes the irony of Jane Ash Poitras' *Bonne Fête Canada* and the missionary images in Jim Logan's work. Simon is a Mi'kmaq, born on the Big Cover Reserve in New Brunswick. He studied in Toronto and Santa Fe, New Mexico; the influence of New Mexico pueblo cultures is evident in his work – again raising the question of what is 'authentic', and who is authorised to represent whom.

Mary Longman was born on the Gordon Indian Reserve in Saskatchewan and sent out to foster parents. After being reunited with her original family, she pursued formal art studies in Vancouver, Montreal and Victoria. She spent several years on the Shackan Indian Reserve, ancestral home of the Nle?kepmx people known for their pictographs (McMaster 1998: 67). Her sculpture, *Reservations*, features a rusty birdcage atop a formal-looking metal column; caught in the locked cage is a 'tree of life' (McMaster 1998: 69). A very different tree features in the installation, *Strata and Routes*. Smooth stones arranged in 'strata' ring a tree trunk that has been stripped of its bark and glazed. The strata contain 'layers of memories and experiences entangled in the delicate branches; near the top of the tree is a large rock' with photographic images of the artist's family.

The artists draw attention to the links between history and contemporary society (for example, juxtaposition of historical texts with historical and contemporary images). While some people pressure indigenous artists to identify with Western 'schools', others complain about 'inauthenticity' of contemporary works. Some of the Inuit artist Pudlo Pudlat's drawings contain helicopters; some Inuit sculptors work in marble instead of soapstone. Declaring a work invalid because its maker has abandoned a fictional 'tradition' is based on the colonialist view of an essentialised indigenous artist who is expected to produce retroactively traditional works ad infinitum.

Élitism and ethnocentrism are imbedded in art history and criticism. Among the received myths: 'serious' artists must receive formal training in professional institutions; 'authentic' indigenous art is 'naïve', 'untrained' and 'primitive' (Alia 1991: 99). Mainstream art history and criticism relegate indigenous art and artists to margins, footnotes and appendices. Galleries devote special exhibitions, floors, wings and catalogues to 'Native' art, in opposition to 'Canadian' or 'American' or 'Australian' art. Much of indigenous art remains in museums of natural history. Even the McMichael Canadian Collection, which treats indigenous artists with great respect, presents the Group of Seven painters as Canada's artistic core. Its front galleries show Group of Seven landscapes without reference to indigenous Canadian art, while the permanent collection of First Nations and Inuit works resides in the upper galleries.

The distinction between 'art' and 'craft' has often turned on the association of objects and skills with women's and men's social roles. Men are most often designated artists and women craftspeople. In the European tradition, women artists receive secondary treatment, if they appear at all. Women have been in the front ranks of indigenous art all along. Although at the outermost extremes of the art–craft continuum, utilitarian craft and aesthetically motivated art can at least theoretically be separated, we would challenge the conventional definitions and distinctions. Art–craft crossovers are numerous and complex, especially where historical evidence is concerned. We do not, therefore, separate 'art' and 'craft'.

In subsistence societies, art is tied to livelihood and work roles. Practical first and beautiful second, it is usually called 'craft'. Utility-free, or utility-secondary art appears when there is surplus production. But art in some form is there all along, no matter how scarce the resources or how basic the economy. While early Aboriginal art emerged in the form of homes, tools, utensils and clothing, it was never strictly utilitarian. Spiritual objects might be kept separate from daily use, but daily-use objects often had spiritual as well as aesthetic and utilitarian attributes. It is not *necessary* to add elaborate beadwork or fringe to a pair of moccasins or a caribou jacket, or intricate figures to the handle of a knife or spear. There is art in form itself – the gracefully curved and much-imitated *ulu* (Inuit woman's knife) whose curve works a thousand practical wonders; the beautiful and practical *kayak* or canoe. No people produces utilitarian objects without considering form and colour (Alia 1991: 100).

Who's right? Whose rights?

The United Nations Draft Declaration on the Rights of Indigenous Peoples (1993) includes rights: affirming the practice and revitalising of cultural traditions and customs (Art. 12); affirming the maintenance and development of distinct identities (Art. 8); and recognition and full ownership, control and protection of cultural and intellectual property (Art. 29).

The unauthorised appropriation of indigenous cultural heritage brings real harm. Appropriation of cultural forms effectively dislocates them from their intended context. In so doing, specific meanings are erased (Shand 2000).

Research has tended to emphasise local appropriation of global material. However, the Bionicle product range (which includes a Website and a movie) highlights the equally significant global appropriation of local material. The designer of Bionicle drew inspiration from television programmes about indigenous communities (see further discussion on pages 140 and 150). The resultant virtual community draws conceptually on many of the components of ethnic communities, and derives its communication from *te reo Maori* (the Maori language). The case points to the fluid nature of culture which belongs to no single location or people. Media interventions contribute importantly to the transformation of cultures rooted in distinct communities to fluid, mobile, diasporic cultures. We are placed at the centre of the relationship between local communities and globalising tendencies (Brincker undated).

Appropriate culture; cultural appropriation

'Appropriation occurs when . . . someone else becomes the expert on your experience' writes Métis film maker Loretta Todd (Fung 1993: 18).

In Richard Fung's view, cultural appropriation is not self-evident. The free exchange of foods, religions, languages and other cultural attributes means that most cultures experience appropriation and 'there are no clear boundaries where one culture ends and another begins' (Fung 1993: 17). Fung says that appropriating someone else's voice, sound, imagery, movement or stories 'can represent sharing or exploitation, mutual learning or silencing, collaboration or unfair gain, and, more often than not, both aspects simultaneously'.

The cutting up and combining of cultural elements – when done ethically, with appropriate acknowledgement and/or permission of the original source – can be considered positive, an example of articulation. There are many examples of this type of cross-cultural borrowing. For example, innumerable renditions of Shakespeare's plays have been performed around the world for centuries. Recent examples include *The Maori Merchant of Venice*, and the world premiere of *Hamlet* in the Sámi language, performed in 2003 in a scaled-down replica of the original Globe Theatre constructed out of ice (*Nunatsiaq News* 2003). Consider also the articulation of reggae with indigenous projects in the Pacific and elsewhere helping to propel 'globalization from below' (Brecher et al. 2000).

Examples of the tensions surrounding mutual appropriation include the work of Jane Ash Poitras. Raised in a non-Aboriginal home in Edmonton and educated in microbiology, she worked for a time as a microbiologist before studying printmaking and design at Yale and Columbia. In 1981 she returned to Fort Chipewyan, Alberta.

Poitras' works emphasise commonality while focusing on individuals – individual character and cultural specificity imbedded in a pan-indigenous politics and art. Her paintings and mixed collages 'incorporate traditional Cree iconography with text and imagery referring to Western instruments of oppression' (McMaster and Martin 1992: 165). Perhaps her complex outsider–insider experience has contributed to her pan-indigenous sensibility. She has 'appropriated' not only a multiplicity of images – of indigenous people from all parts of the planet – but also has 'stolen' images made by Aboriginal and non-Aboriginal photographers from the early days of photography to the present. How are we to understand 'authenticity' in the light of works by this Chipewyan-Cree woman who persists in painting and collaging images of Inuit, Kayapo, Ute and other Aboriginal people amidst a range of colours, texts and figures that make passing (and often inaccurate) reference to the subjects' original cultures? Many of the images were taken by the Euro-American photographer, Edward Curtis – with people redressed and posed in 'traditional' costumes. Does such multilayered 'inauthenticity' diminish or enhance Poitras' magnificent opus, and how does this case study contribute to our

understanding of acceptable and unacceptable media/cultural appropriation and representation?

Resistance and repatriation

In 1997, a prominent Maori protester sought to 'teach Pakeha what it
feels like to have taonga stolen' (District Court 1998; *60 Minutes* 1998).
His target was the *McCahon Triptych*: a well-known painting displayed
in the Department of Conservation headquarters in Urewera National
Park. Eventually, he and a fellow protester were arrested and charged
with eighteen assorted offences, for which he claimed the right of *utu*
(reciprocity) as his defence. The court rejected the argument, handing
him a 15-month suspended sentence, a NZ$15,000 fine, and 200 hours'
community service (*60 Minutes* 1998). It is ironic that this man had no
objection to carrying out his community service in the Auckland City
Art Gallery, a repository of Pakeha *taonga* (treasured possessions) and
fine arts which includes 'stolen' images of Maori ancestral portraits (Te
Awekotuku, personal communication 1999). In a *60 Minutes* television interview (1998) after the trial, both protesters insisted they were not guilty
under their tribal rules. They likened their plight to that of Rua Kenana,
the Tuhoe prophet. However, the circumstances involving Kenana were
rather different (Bull 2004). The Tuhoe prophet was not seeking to 'teach
Pakeha a lesson'; his beliefs were merely a pretext for Pakeha authorities
to suppress Maori independence.

In the 1990 Aotearoa box office flop, *Te Rua*, Maori film maker Barry
Barclay addressed the question of repatriation of indigenous artefacts.
The film's central characters, Rewi Marangai (Wi Kuki Kaa) and his
relative Peter Huaka (Peter Kaa) are shown in Germany conspiring to
retrieve a set of carvings stolen from a meeting-house more than a century
earlier (Peter Calder 1991; Te Awekotuku 1996).

Despite the many pressing issues that demand their attention, ethnic minority peoples have mustered the resolve to resist appropriations.
More often than not, they do so in the absence of legal sanctions. Three
main platforms tend to be used in discussions about protecting cultural
heritage: international documents, national *sui generis* legislation, and re-
vision of existing intellectual property legislation (Shand 2000) – none of
which imposes criminal sanctions (with the stigma they carry) on trans-
gressors. Another solution is adherence to the 1970 UNESCO Conven-
tion on the Illicit Import, Export and Transfer of Ownership of Cultural
Property (Te Awekotuku 1996). The Australian Copyright Council suggests the Aboriginal and Torres Strait Islander Heritage Protection Act
1984, as a means of protecting indigenous intellectual property in ways

which are satisfactory for the indigenous community. Mind you, copyright is commonly rejected as the most unpalatable form of protection available (Shand 2000). In Aotearoa, the Taonga Maori Protection Bill was introduced in 1995, with an impressive Maori consultative record, and as a distinctly Maori initiative (Te Awekotuku 1996).

While rampant criminalisation should be opposed, it is important to recognise the double standard exercised when we are intolerant of 'typical' white collar crimes but do not treat appropriations of cultural heritage as criminal violations. It is also important to remember that ethnic minorities have experienced several hundred years of treaty violations and are likely to view the idea of signing more treaties as merely more hollow gestures. The difficult challenge is to find ways to strike an appropriate balance between criminalisation and cynical avoidance of criminal sanctions.

Not every effort to protect indigenous culture is premised on the latter, or is misplaced. Early in the 1990s, the New Zealand Film Archive and the Museum of New Zealand worked together to separate material from the Taonga Maori collection into *iwi*-specific collections. They then worked with *iwi* representatives to hold screenings for their respective communities. Known as Te Hokinga Mai o Nga Taonga Whitiāhua (The Returning of Treasured Images), the project was launched in February 1996 among the Ngati Tūwharetoa *iwi*. Protocols and procedures were formalised into a Memorandum of Understanding, which is available from taonga@nzfa.org.nz (New Zealand Film Archive 2003).

It is abundantly clear that self-determination is a vital part of protecting indigenous cultural interests. For example, the New South Wales Ministry of the Arts (Indigenous Arts Reference Group 1998) has enumerated five principles (haphazardly) observed by non-indigenous people but nonetheless important guides as to appropriate behaviour: respect for the culture of the indigenous peoples of Australia; the recognition that Aboriginal cultural heritage, including cultural expression, is the intellectual property of Aboriginal people; the protection and correct management of cultural heritage is crucial; the benefits of that heritage ought to go to its first owners; government support is required with respect to these issues.

Indeed, 'repatriation and reburial are loci for processes which both construct and reaffirm Aboriginality, empowering its participants by enabling them to assert, define (and thus take control over) their own identity' (Fforde et al. 2002: 38).

At grass-roots level, 'fish-ins' and 'sit-ins' have been staged (in the US states of Oregon and Maine during the 1980s) to protest against fishing quotas and lumber company activities on sacred ground. The 1990s witnessed consumer and sporting event boycotts protesting against the application of Native American imagery and words to products and athletic teams. There have also been direct repatriations. In 1990, the US government signed the Native American Graves Protection and Repatriation Act (NAGPRA). It gave federally funded institutions five years to document all Native American human remains and associated funerary objects, and then to offer them repatriation (Appleton 2002). Likewise, in the UK, Glasgow museums repatriated a Ghost Dance Shirt taken from the body of a Sioux after the Battle of Wounded Knee in 1890 (Appleton 2002).

Since the signing of NAGPRA, a group called Hui Malama I Na Kupuna o Hawai'i Nei (Caring for the Elders of Hawai'i), has successfully repatriated Hawai'ian remains stored in the Smithsonian Institution, Yale University, Harvard University, and Berkeley University's Hearst Museum (Fullard-Leo 1998). Hui Malama members have been instrumental in burying these bones according to Hawai'ian custom, hence the boat journey from Hawai'i to the Smithsonian to claim back the bones of Native Hawai'ian ancestors (Fforde et al. 2002) and the maintenance of strict secrecy during transportation. Kanaka Maoli waged another 'Battle of the bones' in the 1980s when a Ritz-Carlton hotel was proposed on a burial ground at Honokahua. Protests resulted in the shifting of the site to preserve the burial ground. Alutiiq people of Larsen Bay, Alaska, discovered the remains of their ancestors at the Smithsonian. Museum officials resisted repatriation on the grounds that the skeletons could not be reliably traced to present-day Alutiiq. In 1991, after two years of legal wrangling and more than $100,000 in expenses the Alutiiq were able to rebury the remains (Daes 1993). Goods confiscated when the *potlatch* ritual was criminalised eventually found their way into museum collections (see www.umista.org/potlatch/potlatch.asp). Repatriation of the entire *Potlatch* collection began (slowly) in the 1960s, and continues today through the U'mista Cultural Society. In Canada, the Nisga'a Treaty ratified in 2000 provides for the return of artefacts belonging to the Nisga'a Nation, taken in the nineteenth and early twentieth centuries for collections throughout Canada and across the globe.

Indigenous resistance is nothing new. Commentators are at pains to stress that the very institutions who did the appropriating have pioneered repatriation, often despite apparent lack of interest from indigenous groups (*The Independent on Sunday* 2002; Thornton 1998; Fforde, et al. 2002; Thomas 2000; Appleton 2002). The media do not always mention that those groups have too many issues competing for their attention and insufficient resources to address them all. 'In classic colonial style, the victim of an atrocity is presented as the enemy' (Ramamurthy 2003: 43), a convenient device for those reluctant to acknowledge their complicity.

Conclusion

It is too soon to applaud a few years of reluctant repatriation, following centuries of pillaging. Cultural appropriation is more than a mere relic from the past. It is a key feature of modernity, with its emphasis on consumption and ironic attraction for 'otherness' as evidenced by non-indigenous fascination with Maori *ta moko*, Native American symbols, Inuit *parkas* and the like. Power is central to deciding whether appropriation is innocuous, constructive, or damaging and unacceptable. Things are clear cut where the appropriator is in a position of colonial dominance and authority. Where people co-appropriate, or where those once colonised turn the tables and reappropriate or appropriate artefacts and imagery *from* the colonisers, things are complicated indeed. Consider this example:

The artist and film maker, Shelley Niro, is Mohawk from Six Nations Reserve, a large community of member nations in the Iroquois Confederacy, which today is located on two sides of a border imposed on the Iroquois peoples, bridging the Canadian province of Ontario and New York State in the US. Niro's whimsical use of tinted photographs plays with issues of power, identity and First Nation – 'white' relations. Looking at her playfully titled works, *Mohawks in Beehives* (self-satisfied-looking Mohawk women sporting 1950s Caucasian-style 'big hair') and *The Iroquois is a Matriarchal Society* (Mohawk women at the hairdresser's, sitting under old-fashioned hair dryers) we might well ask, 'Who has colonised whom?'

Exercises

6.1 Naming products for people

1. Look through your local newspaper; wander through your local supermarket and community. Collect all the examples you can find where products are named for people. Collect all the examples you can find where product logos, drawings, photographs and other imagery are taken from the faces, artefacts, traditions and lives of minority peoples. Look especially at sports teams, tyres, cars, butter, children's toys.
2. Discuss the nature of the products and advertising you have found. Are any products named for white, English-speaking people? Do white people's faces appear as logos? Who are the objects of these appropriation exercises? What is being sold? What is the ratio of females to males and adults to children in the advertisements and marketing campaigns, and on the labels of the products? What ethnic minorities appear most often, linked with marketing and products?

6.2 Law, ethics and cultural appropriation

1. You have graduated from university. Curiously, you and all of your former classmates are now analysts working for the Office of the Ombudsman of Intellectual Property Rights. Part of your remit is to monitor the commercial use of the cultural heritage of ethnic minority peoples. Your office has received a complaint from Maui Solomon, a lawyer representing a group of Maori who wish to register a case against the Danish toy manufacturer, Lego.

2. Conduct a preliminary desk-study of Internet sources on Lego's Bionicle product line. There should be numerous hits pertaining to the range, which includes toys, a film (jointly promoted by Burger King), video games and a dedicated Website <www.bionicle.com>, as well as the clash with Maori over appropriation of Polynesian mythology and names.

3. Having conducted your preliminary research, meet in small groups and consolidate the main points of contention between Lego and Maori, as represented by Mr Solomon.

4. Each group should report its findings back to the class as a whole, which should then engage in a general discussion about whether or not it is thought that Lego has a case to answer. The discussion should include the complexities of appropriation. If you like, organise this final discussion into a structured debate, 'for' and 'against'.

Further reading

Burgess, Marilyn and Valaskakis, Gail (1995) *Indian Princesses and Cowgirls Stereotypes from the Frontier*, Montreal: OBORO.

Harper, Kenn (2000) *Give me my Father's Body : The Life of Minik, the New York Eskimo*, South Royalton, VT: Steerforth Press.

McMaster, Gerald (1998) *Reservation X: The Power of Place in Contemporary Aboriginal Art*, Seattle, WA: University of Washington Press.

McMaster, Gerald and Martin, Lee-Ann (eds) (1992) *Indigena: Contemporary Native Perspectives*, Vancouver: Douglas and McIntyre.

Suggested viewing

The Last of His Tribe
Nanook of the North

7 Ethnic roots, diasporic routes, and resistance from below

Gone are the days of the Golliwog, Sambo, fearsome Injuns, and Poly-nesian dancing girls. Or are they? It seems that the more things change the more they remain the same. The mass media continue to operate along racist lines without acknowledging or even recognising it, even in the face of a political climate that is at least superficially intolerant of discrimination.

At the same time, the media position is not consistent. Sometimes journalists challenge negative social behaviour and stereotyping, as well as promote and perpetuate it. A case in point is the episode in which a number of the British royal family, the 20-year old Prince Harry, was photographed wearing Nazi regalia to a social event, and splashed on the front page of a major tabloid, *The Sun*, along with a huge headline: HARRY THE NAZI (*The Sun* 2005). In this case, the media fuelled public outrage, reminding readers, viewers and listeners that the prince's insensitivity was compounded by the event's proximity to the 60th an-niversary of the liberation of the Auschwitz death camp (CBC News online 2005). It took journalists a couple of days to consider the wider implications: the prince's costume was only one of many worn by the nation's 'finest' young adults, to a 'colonial and native' themed party. So much for the death of racist labels. Mark Lawson's column in Britain's venerable daily, *The Guardian*, headlined 'The very nasty party', brought all of the issues under one roof. As we have complained loudly about media coverage that sends us backwards to the worst of colonial times, we must also laud the exemplary journalists who keep working to make things better. As a good journalist should, Lawson went to the source(s), interviewing the owner of Maud's Cotswold Costumes, from whom many of the party-goers had rented their garb. The shop has not one, but many Nazi costumes, rented on countless occasions by people less prominent than Harry. Decrying journalists and others who dismissed the young royal's clothing choice as simply a youthful indiscretion, Lawson wrote his column in a state of righteous rage:

> Every so often, something happens – an investigative documentary,
> a social worker's report into the murder of a child – that lifts up the
> British carpet to show the stamped-down filth. This is such a moment.
> While Harry's costume was shocking, it seems equally shocking that, in
> 2005, there is a section of society in which it is not considered odd for
> a teenager to throw a party with the theme of 'colonial or native' and at
> which, according to some reports, young male guests blacked up their
> faces. The implication of much coverage is that Harry misjudged the
> party mood, but perhaps he merely took the nasty theme to its logical
> conclusion. (Lawson 2005: 19)

Yasmin Alibhai-Brown, a columnist for the national British daily newspaper, *The Independent*, observes that 'I am, at present, apparently one of
only two non-white regular newspaper columnists in Europe' (Alibhai-
Brown 2004: 1). Alibhai-Brown is known for her take-no-prisoners approach to critical journalism and her insistence on transparency where
her own identity and experiences are concerned:

> Few of us have a single, all-defining identity which you can use for
> all seasons. When the [Stephen] Lawrence case was so much in the
> news, I felt black. This was our battle – whether Asian, Muslim, Hindu,
> African – against racism. On forced marriages, I react as an angry Asian
> woman. Watching ripe young Palestinian boys dying, my emotional
> response comes out of feeling with them as a Muslim but more out
> of a burning belief in basic human rights and self-determination. But
> when Palestinian men carry out honour killings...I condemn them
> absolutely...
>   All of us – black and white Britons – feel [a] multitude of allegiances,
> some connected to an ethnic past, some not. (Alibhai-Brown 2004:
> 8–9)

It is the job of the media to communicate that multitude of identities to
the public. Such coverage is an antidote to the essentialism that encourages physical and structural violence. Readers will recall the discussion of
Diaspora in the introductory chapter and snippets throughout the book.
Mirroring the cyclical nature of ethnic minority oppression, we return to
the changing complexion of Diaspora now. Following on from the previous chapter, we begin with some consideration of the tensions between
Diaspora, appropriation, and self-determination.

Ethnic roots: clinging to the remaining vestiges
of the power to define

In her article for an academic journal, the anthropologist, Leslie Conton, seemed perplexed at some of the responses she received to the classes she was offering at Fairhaven College, Western Washington University. Along with other projects, programmes and positions, her teaching sparked a controversy that reportedly threatened to split the college. 'The challenges I have encountered in my several years of teaching experiential shamanism include . . . critique from some Native Americans and ethnic minorities who raise issues of cultural and spiritual misappropriation . . .' (Conton 1996: 43). In subsequent years, the issues were addressed in two ways: by broadening Conton's course to make it an international study of what is now titled 'Cross-Cultural Shamanism' and by adding classes in a range of subjects, taught by Native Americans. Conton's new course explains that shamanism:

> is an ancient and worldwide method for personal learning and healing, a paradigm or way of life concerned with the healing of the individual, family, community, and environment. We explore the relationship be-tween shamanic healing, visions, mythic consciousness, and alternate states of consciousness in cultural and historical context, including the modern western revival of shamanic practices. (Fairhaven College 2005)

That description is a little disingenuous, because many people consider the 'modern western revival' no revival at all, but appropriation of Native American practices by descendants of European immigrants to North America. Around the same time, in another part of the world, the annual Inuit Studies conference was held in an Inuit community (Iqaluit) for the first time. Inuit townspeople, leaders and scholars had access to a conference that had long been 'about' them but had included few of their number. The event received little attention in the wider media universe, but was widely covered in northern and indigenous press and broadcast outlets. One session, on Inuit names and Project Surname, was recorded for CBC (Alia 1995). Another session featured a presentation by then Nunavut Implementation Commissioner, Peter Irniq (at the time spelled Ernerk). That session was reported in the Nunavut weekly newspaper, *Nunatsiaq News*. Surrounded by Qallunaat 'experts' on Inuit shamanism (and the controversy their work had engendered) Peter Irniq told the participants: 'It's Inuit who should be invited to talk about shamanism at an Inuit Studies conference' (George 1996: 11). Because it was held in the Inuit homeland, the conference was well attended and well covered by local and regional media. There were news broadcasts over IBC (Inuit Broadcasting Corporation) and CBC northern service, and a string of newspaper stories, opinion columns and letters to the editor.

In an altogether different vein from the studies of shamanism, Dan First Scout Rowe teaches a course at Fairhaven College on 'American Indian Resistance and Activism'. It 'examines historical and contemporary American Indian resistance to European and United States settler-state colonialism'. Because Rowe considers the attempts at military resistance 'futile', he focuses on religious and social revitalisation movements of the eighteenth and nineteenth centuries; early twentieth-century pan-Indian reform movements and organisations such as the Society of American Indians and the National Congress of American Indians; and post Second World War 'tribally based activism' (Fairhaven College 2005). The main emphasis is 'on the resistance and activism of the Red Power movement and related organisations', including the 'National Indian Youth Council, American Indian Movement, Indians of All Tribes, International Indian Treaty Council, Women of All Red Nations, Indigenous Women's Network, and Indigenous Environmental Network' – demonstrating the scope and depth of Native American activism and resistance. To encourage students to work across cultures and disciplines, 'Great latitude will be allowed in the choice of individual projects that might include dance, stand-up comedy, art, oratory, music, film, photography, interviews, or an academic research paper' (Fairhaven College 2005).

There is increasing attention to a need for greater complexity in framing questions, constructing media portrayals of multi-ethnic communities, and developing a research agenda. Lorna Roth (1991: 5) warns that identifying people according to their 'ethnicity' may not be a sign of progress, but a way of reinforcing 'divide and rule' colonialism and ethnic elites. The Native American writers, Joy Harjo and Gloria Bird, call the use of the 'colonizer's tongue' by new people, in new ways, 'reinventing the enemy's language' (Harjo and Bird 1997: 19, 22). The Sámi scholar, Vigdis Stordahl cautions that the signs and symbols indigenous people sometimes adopt to help mobilise 'group spirit and joint political action' are too 'symbolically simple' and narrow – for example, the binary construction of 'traditional' versus 'modern' practices or the labelling of practices and events as representing a 'Sami way of life' (Stordahl 1993: 128–9). To move forward, we must stop portraying 'cultural appropriation' simply as stealing by the ill-intentioned, from the well-intentioned; look more deeply at the nature of 'race', ethnicity, the politics and economics of colonisation; and create opportunities for cross-cultural dialogue, ethnic minority participation in media production, and improved media representations of ethnic minorities and indigenous peoples.

'Tribe challenges American origins' – so the headline goes. The story concerns the research of Dr Silvia Gonzalez who believes she has found the remains of a tribe of people who pre-date Native Americans (Rincon 2004). The headline writer's labelling of this story creates the distorted and unhelpful impression that the controversy is between two Native American groups vying for the title of 'indigenous'. This kind of binary approach to people, groups and events is a familiar journalistic trick, taken, perhaps from drama and the movies. The operating principle is that readers, watchers or listeners need opposition and conflict to hold their interest. Too often, that means skewing or even changing the story. In reality, the battle for supremacy in this particular news story is not between different ethnic minorities but between indigenous peoples and academia, which remains firmly imbedded in imperialist rhetoric.

Gonzalez' claim is interesting. What is more interesting and far more important is the politics, the history behind the claim, its implications – a point clearly wasted on this particular news source, which saw fit to reproduce pictures of human remains on the accompanying WebPages. Broadcasting images of dead ancestors hardly suggests any sensitivity to the broader issues at stake. The prize for 'most offensive', given the legacy of stolen human remains and the grief such theft entails, goes to Professor Clive Gamble of Southampton University who is reported as saying, 'We want to make headlines from heads.' Well, why not? Science has made plenty of money from them. A headline or too won't hurt! The report quotes Gamble as saying, 'DNA will give us a completely new map of the world and how we peopled it.' It is with trepidation that we contemplate exactly who the 'we' represents; to whom Gamble refers. In case he has forgotten, the 'how' in many colonial contexts frequently involved rape and other forms of gross exploitation.

The story made the usual rounds of the world's media, courtesy of Reuters. According to a related online article the research is 'one of 11 different projects in America, Asia and the Middle East being funded over a four-year period by Britain's Natural Environment Council. The projects – focusing on diet, dating and dispersal of people down the millennia in the face of climate change – aim to rewrite anthropology' (www.msnbc.msn.com 2004). On the surface this may seem a worthy ambition. Anthropology has certainly espoused its fair share of dubious ideas and unethical methods. It is also true that much of history has recently undergone a similar rewriting, with the result that the voices of 'the subalterns' (to borrow from Spivak) have reached more receptive ears. That said, the ardent disregard for indigenous peoples' identity and right to define themselves, which is characteristic of anthropology's own identity crisis, is a depressing indication that imperialism continues to wear away at the (sometimes fragile) foundations of minority peoples' existence.

The issues of settlement and Diaspora are fundamental to the self-image of minority peoples. Recognition of the 'Smithing' activities of researchers aiming to refute minority knowledge bases has led the United Nations to reject outright the necessity to define the term, 'indigenous peoples'. Instead, the UN has endorsed the view articulated by Jose R. Martinez Cobo, Special Rapporteur of the Sub-Commission on Prevention of Discrimination and Protection of Minorities, in his famous *Study on the Problem of Discrimination against Indigenous Populations*, that 'indigenous communities, peoples and nations' preserve 'the sovereign right and power to decide who belongs to them, without external interference' (Martinez Cobo 1986).

The fervour for defining ethnic minority peoples, manifest in current scientific research on origins and migration patterns, is matched by a determination on the part of minority peoples to control their own dispersal, and shift the meaning of Diaspora.

Diasporic routes...

Ordinarily when we think of indigeneity and Diaspora, we imagine opposite ends of the spectrum. However, there is such a thing as a specifically indigenous kind of Diaspora that combines rural and urban, island and mainland, on-reservation and off-reservation (Clifford 2001). Binary oppositions between 'home' and 'away', or a linear and chronological 'before–after' progression from rural to urban settings, do not reflect the realities of 'circulation' (Chapman 1978). To suggest otherwise is to fall into the essentialist trap discussed throughout the book, in which each distinct group of people is fixed to a specific location. Contrary to the assumptions underlying such fictional fixity, there is evidence that most people(s) have a wide range of attachments to land and place, dwelling and travelling. Indigeneity and Diaspora combine to produce liminal identities of people who live out their lives in 'composite worlds' but who nonetheless exhibit characteristic patterns of visiting and return, of lived connections across distances. When people move, or are moved, they are able to take their roots with them, as 'rooted cosmopolitans' (Appiah 1998: 91). Black Elk's statement, quoted earlier, bears repeating: 'Your world has a centre you carry with you' (Clifford 1989: 178). We return, as well, to Harald Gaski's praise of cultural multiplicity: 'one stands with both legs in both cultures' (Gaski 1997: 199–200).

One of the outstanding films in recent years is a perfect example of the sort of travelling Clifford, Appiah, Black Elk and Gaski have described.

Grand Avenue was produced as a pilot for a US Home Box Office series. It is based on short stories by Greg Sarris, a Pomo-Miwok Native American from Santa Rosa, California. Shot mostly in an urban neighbourhood, the film counters stereotypes while allowing a range of actors to create subtly drawn and finely nuanced characters. A mix of voluntary and involuntary exiles from 'the res', they hold on to tradition and each other within the Diaspora of a multi-ethnic city. Although it was warmly received, and won the Best Feature award at the American Indian Film Festival, *Grand Avenue* has had limited distribution since its release in 1996 and was shown in theatres only in Europe.

Diaspora may benefit representations of minorities by reinforcing the ideal of the cosmopolitan critic unanchored by territorial confines. Inasmuch as diasporic existence is perceived as a means of acquainting oneself with alternative outlooks, mindsets and experiences, 'dispersed' insiders may appear more 'objective'. It is one of the reasons the experiences of minorities are so often given greater credence when depicted by cultural outsiders. While under-representation of minorities in the film industry and intense competition for funding also play significant roles, depictions produced by respected outsiders frequently dominate public understanding of particular issues, even though earlier or more original accounts are available. Whether this is good or bad is open to question. Faced with a choice between an outsider depiction that reaches a wider audience or an insider depiction accessible mainly to insiders, it is difficult to know which to favour. Neither is ideal. In an ideal world, there would be a perfect balance of insider, outsider and collaborative representations. What is disturbing about the outsider depiction is that often it is regarded as 'truth', while insider accounts are considered bombastic, melodramatic or exaggerated. As Primo Levi said of Holocaust survivors, 'only they, by their unique experience, are immersed in the truth' (Pilger 1998: 246).

It is not always easy deciding who gets to represent whom. In recent years, the Royal Shakespeare Company has adopted a position of 'colour-blind' casting, while at the same time, indigenous actors are finally being hired for (sometimes) culturally appropriate parts on stage and screen. Both developments are important. In the 1980s, the distinguished broadcaster, actor and scholar, Rita Shelton Deverell, who is African American by birth, won an out of court settlement but not the television role she sought when she auditioned for a docudrama about farmers in the Canadian prairie province of Saskatchewan:

[I] made an appointment to audition...went to the studio and the producer said, 'Rita I would have you audition for this, but these people are white', and I said 'Are you sure?'... The image that [the producer] had in his head of the character was that of a white person. I'm not white . . .

One reason given for the casting conflict 'was that a typical Saska[t]chewan farmer was white and therefore to put a typical Saska[t]chewan farmer on the air as not being white would just befuddle everyone . . . (Roth 1996: 86–7)

Contrary to the producer's assumptions and mental image, there are black farmers in Saskatchewan:

There are black farmers all over the Prairies. The historic concentration of black people in Saska[t]chewan is around Maidstone . . . There was a wave of immigration from the early part of the century. These people are farmers, not to mention all of the Native [First Nations] farmers . . . and the sort of dark farmers of Slav origin. There is a whole group of people who are not white. (Roth 1996: 88)

Audiences have become accustomed to seeing people of many colours playing many types of roles. It can be argued that there are times when a role is so culturally or 'racially' specific, it must be cast according to colour. It is hard to imagine a white actor playing the part of Paul Robeson or a black actor as Princess Diana. Perhaps one criterion is whether a film or play is biographical or fictional. In Rita Deverell's case, research revealed that the problem was with the producer's imagination, and not with historical reality. It would not be surprising to find that twenty years later, many white Canadians would still 'see white' when they hear the word 'farmer'. Let us complicate the matter further.

While it is cause for celebration that talented indigenous actors are finally playing a range of roles (including those cast without reference to colour or culture), it would be a mistake to assume inherent 'authenticity'. In the decades following his performance in the 1990 Hollywood film, *Dances with Wolves*, Graham Greene has become one of several 'hot properties'. Along with benefiting from culturally neutral casting in several films and television shows, he has become one of the new generic 'Indians' playing a range of roles once given to non-indigenous actors such as Anthony Quinn. Greene, who is Oneida from Ontario's Six Nations Reserve, has featured as the last surviving member of the Yahi tribe in *The Last of His Tribe* (1992) (discussed in Chapter 6), as a generic 'local tribesman' in *Clearcut* (1992), as Lakota, and as a member of several unidentified indigenous cultures. Similarly diverse roles are given to Tantoo Cardinal (who, after years of distinguished work in Canada, also got 'discovered' in *Dances with Wolves*), Gordon Tootoosis and Floyd Red Crow Westerman – an American Indian Movement activist and musician whose bitingly funny song, 'Here Come the Anthros' is a classic portrayal of 'Indian'–white relations:

And the Anthros keep on diggin'
in our sacred ceremonial sites.
As if there was nothing wrong,
and their education gives them the right.
...
coming like death and taxes to our land. (Westerman 1991)

There is no universal rule about how to avoid misrepresentation and discrimination. However, there is a clear need to distinguish between cultural authenticity (a construct of questionable credibility) and fair and accurate representation and equality of opportunity. A Gwich'in First Nations actor from northern Yukon is likely to consider the lands of Oklahoma Cherokee, or the Santa Clara Pueblo in New Mexico 'Diaspora'. Still, perhaps it is better to cast that actor in a 'foreign' Native American setting than an actor of Italian or Anglo-American descent. The rules are not clear cut, and are further complicated by multicultural identities. What of the First Nations actor who also is European-Jewish? Is she equally at home in both cultures? Do we decide according to her cultural or political preferences? Her facial features?

Hau'ofa suggests that an element of 'diasporism' is part of the act of escaping belittlement – of increasing stature, becoming global and sufficient. While he stresses the importance of remaining rooted and maintaining connections he does not deny the liberating aspects of diasporic existence, which in turn can facilitate resistance (Hau'ofa 1993, 2000).

Resistance from below

Wherever there are ethnic minority peoples, there is resistance. Although we must take care not to assume that people who share a legacy of oppression will necessarily respond to it in the same deterministic ways, a number of commonly used tactics and strategies are apparent.

For centuries, minorities have used articulations of one sort or another as a means of passive resistance. Maori appropriated Pakeha religious concepts and principles and adapted them to suit. Hence the *Ringatu* (upraised hand) faith, which combines elements of Christianity with Maori cultural concepts. Active resistance continues today in Maori reinventing themselves via the King Movement, modelled on what Maori knew about English royal lineage. Subversive tactics are in also evidence. In his monograph, *Eskimo Underground*, the anthropologist Robert Williamson used the term 'underground naming' to refer to the maintenance of traditional

Inuit names in private, while publicly complying with dominant-society naming practice.

Another form of active resistance is the legal or legislative approach – a fraught path given the traditional exclusion of ethnic minorities from the voting franchise out of which legislation arises. Since the Second World War, greater recognition has been given to the varying forms of oppression experienced by minority peoples and the need to reaffirm their rights. The UN Declaration on the Rights of Indigenous Peoples (1994), for example, protects rights in a number of spheres, such as the revitalising of cultural traditions and customs, the maintaining and developing of distinct identities, and the ownership, control and protection of cultural and intellectual property. UN declarations are notoriously difficult to enforce. Other legal approaches can secure some measure of redress. A class action is being taken against the government of Canada, the New England Company and the Diocese of Huron, by former students of the Mohawk Institute Residential School in Brantford, Ontario. The plaintiffs seek damages in excess of $1 billion for breach of fiduciary duty, negligence and breach of Aboriginal rights. Litigation of this sort obviously serves a cathartic function, as well as compensating victims and eliciting official acknowledgement of oppression. But we might well ask if it is merely an imitation of the litigation-obsessed sick Euro-American model (Ross 1998). Fanon exhorts us to:

> not pay tribute to Europe by creating states, institutions, and societies which draw their inspiration from her. Humanity is waiting for something from us other than such an imitation, which would be almost an obscene caricature . . . if we want humanity to advance a step further, if we want to bring it up to a different level than that which Europe has shown it, then we must invent and we must make discoveries. (Fanon 1963: 315)

While we recognise that indigenous peoples possess their own systems of justice, we see legal intervention as more characteristic of Euro-America. Nonetheless, because this is the default context in which mainstream media operate, the language of litigation is sometimes the only language that is understood, and this can work to the advantage of ethnic minorities. Maori claimants represented by Mr Maui Solomon initiated legal proceedings in response to Lego Company's Bionicle toy range. Bolstered by a Website and a movie, the range includes characters with distinctly Polynesian names, and a plot and setting that borrow heavily from blended Polynesian mythology. The appropriation involved no consultation or dialogue with the custodians of that culture. Out of court, the Lego Company agreed to make changes (such as altering characters' names) to dilute the Polynesian influence.

Litigation can also backfire. The skeletal remains of 'The Ancient One' (Kennewick Man) became the subject of a court battle between Native Americans and scientists. That court case was important for two reasons. Primarily, it was about determining who has rights over human remains, and to what uses those remains should be put. The second and obviously related reason is that the court's decision cannot be entirely separated from broader efforts to dispossess Native Americans of their claim to indigeneity, through the potential of those remains to show that contemporary Native Americans are not descended from the people who first settled the Americas. In the end, the federal appeals court found in favour of the scientists. The court ruled that the tribes had not clearly shown they were related to Kennewick Man, which they were obliged to do in order for their rights enshrined in the NAGPRA legislation to prevail (Hecht 2004).

Resistance tactics are not universally successful. Chapter 3 outlined a pertinent threat to strategies for resisting oppression, taking the novel and film versions of *Once Were Warriors* as a case in point. That threat is known as 'passing' (for white, or for a dominant group) or 'covering' as Goffman (1959) prefers to call it. By trying to 'pass', ethnic minorities seek to rid themselves of the stigma of being minority, and thereby win the approval of the majority by covering their identity and acculturating to the status quo. Alberto Memmi considers imitating our oppressors in this way indicative of the 'colonized mentality' (Memmi 1965). The need to decolonise takes on new significance and a new urgency in the light of lingering effects of colonialism. Edward Said (1994) used the term 'decolonisation' to refer to the mass devolution of Empire and the concomitant upsurge in sovereignty movements in the mid-twentieth century. There is more to it than this. As Linda Tuhiwai Smith explains, in *Decolonizing Methodologies* (1999), decolonisation is about fundamental shifts in perception and action. For example, Maori custodians of the main site of the annual ceremonies commemorating the signing of the 1840 Treaty of Waitangi have refused access to Pakeha mainstream media because the media tend to present negative images of Maori.

Less akin to assimilation is the notion of subtle, invisible resistance. This is the age-old strategy wherein ethnic minority peoples behave in stereotypical ways in the presence of the majority but drop the front in each other's presence (Ross 1998). The sociologist Erving Goffman calls this 'front stage' and 'back stage' behaviour and applies his theory to a study of restaurant workers – not all of them members of ethnic minorities. His view is that such behaviour reflects dominant and sub-ordinate, or powerful and less powerful groups, rather than specifically culture or colour. He finds that when members of the group in question (in this case, the employees) are 'backstage' (Goffman 1959), they poke fun at the customers (the dominant group) whom they teasingly depict as naïve and gullible. Their behaviour echoes in the Ethiopian proverb, 'When the great lord passes, the wise peasant bows deeply and farts silently.'

As discussed in Chapter 3, there is a risk that minority peoples may lose sight of the political foreplay that underpins this type of resistance and internalise the image intended for the edification of outsiders. If such is the case, it is difficult to see how this kind of 'invisible resistance' meets the requirements of decolonisation. It can be argued that it must therefore be rejected as the way forward. However, we must take care not to make blanket assumptions. There are cultural as well as personal differences in the ways people resist colonisation and maintain ethnic identity. Inuit, for example, have a long tradition of cooperation and non-confrontation. This has sometimes been misunderstood as complicity, and explains why Qallunaat journalists and academics who predicted the demise of Inuit culture are surprised at its resilience. At its most sinister, the pressure to go underground can be a life-or-death matter. The so-called 'hidden children' survived the Holocaust because they were given non-Jewish names and Christian identities. Some lost their religious, cultural and personal identities, but others remained fully aware, and reclaimed their names and affiliations as soon as it was safe. In a conversation with the Inuk leader, Jose Kusugak, we referred to cultural revival, and were corrected: 'It's not revival; it's respect – the traditions were never lost' (Alia 1995).

There are times when going quietly underground saves lives and cul-tures, and open confrontation can mean death. The effectiveness of one strategy over another varies according to people, places and circum-stances. Our research in the Canadian Arctic, over the past three decades, shows that Inuit who took their naming and other traditions underground continued the central practices – along with developing their own media outlets – through all of the various colonial interventions and disrup-tions. In 1999, Nunavut became an official Territory with its own gov-ernment and infrastructure, and powers akin to those of the Canadian provinces. Since then, Inuit have brought their still-living culture back above ground, and from a position of greater confidence and strength, are more openly challenging Qallunaat governments and programmes. It is also important to note that, while Inuit took some aspects of their culture underground, at the same time they were engaged in an array of activist enterprises which were entirely above ground. Many of these focused on media projects, such as creation of the Inuit Broadcasting Corporation and development of local and regional radio and television. Inuit became broadcasters on regional and national television and radio, created the pan-Arctic Inuit Circumpolar Conference and its regular General Assemblies, Arctic Communications Policy and emerging international news bureau. In Greenland, they created a major recording industry featuring music of the cultural renaissance, sung in Greenlandic, and a publishing industry featuring Greenlandic language books. They lobbied to persuade governments to settle land claims and legalise self-government in their own homeland (in Canada, Nunavut; in Greenland, home rule separate from Denmark). At the same time, sensing danger, they shielded their names and traditional practices from the public eye, surfacing only when they deemed it safe. Such tactics cannot be dismissed as 'passivity'; they are components of a carefully constructed and highly effective socio-political strategy.

Moscovici thinks that social conflict is a necessary component of persuasion and social change. While much of Inuit activism can be seen as engendering 'social conflict', the simultaneous underground–above ground project does not fit Moscovici's model. Similarly, Fanon's belief that 'decolonization is always a violent phenomenon' (1963: 35) does not apply equally to all ethnic minority struggles. In the Inuit ca⸗ ⸗here is experience of structural violence, but not of violence born of p. confrontation. However, if we extend Fanon's notion of 'violent' decolonisation to encompass Galtung's idea of structural violence, we can see that Nunavut did indeed emerge from the conditions Fanon describes:

> . . . the proof of success lies in a whole social structure being changed from the bottom up. The need for this change exists . . . in the consciousness and in the lives of the men and women who are colonized . . . But the possibility of this change is equally experienced in the form of a terrifying future in the consciousness of another 'species' of men and women: the colonizers. Decolonization [is] . . . a program of complete disorder. (Fanon 1963: 35)

In the Inuit case, perhaps less 'disorder' than multiple sites of struggle.

Educating the colonials: pathways to cultural reappropriation

Provocative statements can be used to draw attention, which in turn provides opportunities to debunk the myriad stereotypes flourishing in mainstream media representation of ethnic minorities. Maori artist Lisa Reihana, for example, produced a video called *Wog Features* (1990) in which she 'subverted the tradition of children's television programmes with a macabre dance of sexist and racist stereotypes – golliwogs, dolls, tourist souvenirs, minstrels in black face, and coloured skeletons, moving to a hip-hop beat' (Horrocks 1996: 78).

To take another example, African American performance artist damali ayo's *Negro for Hire* spoof, advertised on her Website, www.rent-a-negro. com, involves offering her services as a conversation partner to answer the myriad ridiculous questions people have about African Americans. 'Questions like: "Do black people get tanned?" And: "When you wear black, can anyone see you?" And: "Why are you always talking about racism? Can't you just relax?"' (Gumbel 2003: 20). If you doubt that anybody still thinks like this, perhaps you should reconsider your initial assessment of the excerpt on 'Black crime' that appears at the beginning of Chapter 1. In her *Negro for Hire* project:

> ayo has marketed herself as the ultimate chic accessory to take along to gatherings of would-be trendies who wished they weren't so unrelentingly white . . . For a price, she offers added extras such as the opportunity to touch her hair – apparently a constant source of fascination to whites – and 'dance lessons for the rhythm-challenged'. 'Challenging racist family members' costs $500 a time. The rental form asks whether the customer has 'used black people before' (the 'yes' box is ticked in advance) and if so, whether the services were paid for (the 'I did not pay' box is also ticked in advance). She has not yet decided whether she will follow through on this, and really hire herself out. (Gumbel 2003: 20)

A comparable use of humour appeared in Canada in 1991. Abe Okpik, the man who conducted 'Project Surname' in the late 1960s and early 1970s and renamed more than 15,000 Inuit, used humour to turn things around. Before Project Surname, the government gave Inuit 'disc numbers'. Though few people did, all were expected to wear the numbered discs. Prefixed 'W' for western Arctic and 'E' for eastern Arctic (where they were nicknamed 'E numbers') they were recorded in a national registry. Disc numbers started at a time when Inuit were not full citizens and, among other things, could not yet vote in Canadian elections. The Nunavut newspaper, *Nunatsiaq News*, reported Abe's spoof programme:

ALL YOU QALLUNAAT, GET REGISTERED!

What do radio host Peter Gzowski, actress Cynthia Dale, blues singer Colin James and former Edmonton Oilers defenceman Randy Gregg have in common? They're all official members of a unique club called the Iqaluit Qallunaat Registry, a fund-raising project started by the

Iqaluit Elders Society. It's a gentle parody of the E-number system by which Inuit were once registered by the Canadian government...

Abe Okpik, who was awarded the Order of Canada for organizing Operation [sic] Surname, helped Iqaluit's elders create a 'Q' number system... they have sold registration certificates and mock Q-number disks, bearing a striking resemblance to the original E-numbers, to Qallunaat... at a cost of $10... The idea has been a big hit with southern visitors. When Gzowski, Dale, James, Gregg and other southern celebrities passed through Iqaluit last May enroute to Pond Inlet for a celebrity golf tournament to promote literacy, one of the first places they headed for was the Iqaluit Elders Centre where they all enrolled in the Qallunaat Registry. (*Arctic Circle* 1991: 13)

Humour is a problematic method for challenging stereotypes. While there are those for whom damali ayo's and Abe Okpik's stunts are demeaning, many people find such satirical approaches to challenging hackneyed representations of ethnic minorities useful catalysts for debate. Abe Okpik and damali ayo have effectively reappropriated the right of Inuit and African Americans to define their own cultures.

Insiders and outsiders can work together to contest 'folk devil' representations of ethnic minorities. In 2002, a group of Native American students at the University of Northern Colorado urged Eaton High School to change its mascot from the offensively named 'Fighting Reds'. When the school refused, Native American and white members of the university's basketball team rebranded themselves the 'Fightin' Whites'. When their campaign attracted national media attention, the team began selling T-shirts bearing the slogan (spoofing the song, 'Everything's gonna be all right') 'Everythang's going to be all white' from their dedicated Website (www.fightingwhites.org). The more than $100,000 they raised went to scholarships for Native American university students.

In the 1990s, a First Nations journalist and a Euro-Canadian academic created a cross-cultural programme aimed at educating the next generation of journalists. Distressed by the poor quality of media coverage of indigenous people and issues, Enos 'Bud' White Eye, a newspaper and television journalist from Moraviantown Delaware First Nation, and Valerie Alia, a Hungarian-Jewish-Anglo-Canadian academic, organised an annual seminar called the First Nations Intensive, for students in the University of Western Ontario Graduate School of Journalism. Most of the students were Caucasian; over a five-year period, only four of about 200 were from ethnic minorities. The students met journalists and leaders from several nearby First Nations communities and cultures. Each year, they expressed surprise at the range of people, ideas, politics, professions, colours and cultures. They said things like, 'We thought everyone would have the same political agenda and the same attitudes.' Encouraged to visit First Nations communities and look for news and feature stories there, they returned in shock. They said, 'We expected something exotic; we never expected to see stores and [petrol] stations, schools and libraries; it looked just like a town.'

The seminar was a continuing success, no thanks to the university, which never acknowledged its value, and gradually decreased its minimal funding. Nevertheless, it had a noticeable effect on media coverage. Several of the students who took that seminar now have prominent jobs in Canadian print and broadcast media. The Intensive experience is reflected in their work; years later, some of them continue to work with people they met there. The seminar's founders collaborated on other projects as well. They helped to found Native News Network of Canada, on whose behalf they authored a brief. It was presented in 1992 to the Royal Commission on Aboriginal Peoples, organised in the wake of the Kanehsatake-Oka 'Crisis' described in Chapter 5. In 1990, scarcely a year after the founding of Television Northern Canada, the government had cancelled the Native Communication Programme, cutting support to thirteen indigenous newspapers. In response to this and other conditions, the brief stated:

> Communication is at the core of First Nations concerns. In a democratic society, news media ensure that information is communicated to the public. Many of the myths and misperceptions which persist among non-Aboriginal people are perpetuated by non-communication, poor communication, or one-sided communication... Aboriginal people remain underrepresented in these media, both in accurate coverage and in employment. Where they are hired, they are often subject to the last-hired, first-fired syndrome, leaving employment statistics at the status quo. Ethnic minority newspapers, magazines, radio and television provide an effective training ground for journalists... promoting programs which facilitate entrance of minority students into university, as well as those which exist outside the college or university system. It is more urgent than ever that minority perspectives reach a wider public. (White Eye and Alia 1992: 1)

In addition to developing programmes aimed at communicating across cultures, there is a need to provide 'insider' options for those who need and want them. In 2003, the first university run entirely by indigenous people opened in Regina, Saskatchewan, in Canada. The First Nations University of Canada grew out of a smaller institution, Saskatchewan

Indian Federated College, founded in 1976 with a handful of students, and housed within the University of Regina. Today's independent university serves about 1,200 students in a building designed by Douglas Cardinal. At the opening ceremonies, the university's President, Eber Hampton, said, 'My heart is so full I can feel the tears in my eyes; no one did it for us, but we certainly didn't do it alone' (CBC 2003a).

Two faces of media representation

Media representation has two faces. It has the power to raise awareness. It also raises the status of minority imagery, thus exacerbating the existing tendency of outsiders to appropriate that imagery. Often, it is this latter 'face' that dominates, and often, the appropriation is profit-motivated. In the aftermath of the film version of *Once Were Warriors* (1994), for example, advertising agencies were quick to recognise the marketability of *moko*. Campaigns for the New Zealand Army and the All Blacks (a reference to the colour of uniform worn by the New Zealand rugby team) have used the imagery. Former France and Manchester United football legend, and exponent of the karate kick (directed at spectators), Eric Cantona, adorned the cover of *GQ Magazine* wearing a *moko*. In turn, these military and sporting appropriations of *moko* have reinforced the masculine stereotypes of Maori as fierce, hostile, aggressive and belligerent – hardly a decolonised stance.

Similarly, in the frequently asked questions section of their WebPages (http://www.boneart.co.nz), the artists at The Boneart Place warn that:

> Traditional Maori bone carvings have become very popular in recent years which has resulted in a lot of people now making knock-offs. Unfortunately most of the carvings offered on the internet (and even in shops in New Zealand) these days are in fact very poor quality fakes...Much of the work being sold as 'Genuine Maori Carving' has in fact been factory made in Malaysia, India or China and a lot of it is not even carved but is stamped out by machines from a bone and resin paste. To add insult to injury these same people have stolen their designs from the real artists, including one company in China that stole over 60 of our designs along with photos from our site for their brochure. They were offering them to retailers at $1.95 each for orders of 5000 or more!!! (Boneart Place 2005)

A quick scan of items for sale on the worldwide on-line auction site, eBay (2003) reveals the extent of the commodification of indigenous culture. Items available to purchasers in the United Kingdom include a multitude of historical postcards featuring Maori subject matter, auctioned for US $3–5 each, as well as:

> Maori Rotorua New Zealand Photo 1895, US $9.95; Maori Belles, N.Z. Very Early Real Photo, US $3.00; New Zealand Maori Fertility God Tiki Charm, US $4.99; MAORI POI, US $5.00; N.Z. MAORI FAMILY STANDING OUTSIDE WHARE 1910, US $4.00; Maori Ceremonial Adze With Green Stone Blade, US $30.00 ... (eBay 2003)

The list goes on for many pages. Particularly coveted items included a Royal Doulton cup, saucer and plate set bearing the 'Maori Art' design, and finally selling for £103. 'This stunning trio was made by Royal Doulton probably between 1920–1930. It is the very collectable design called "Maori Art" ... This stylish trio, in good condition, is a must for your collection' (eBay 2003).

Despite the gloomy picture of appropriation created by the examples here and in Chapter 6, ethnic minority peoples are equalising power differentials that, given this kind of virtual diasporism, do not work in their favour. Edward Said (1994) sees the threat to independence posed by new electronics, at the disposal of the international media, as greater than that of colonialism itself. However, ethnic minority peoples can harness the very same electronic media to facilitate resistance. A *panui* (notice) on Winson's WebPages (http://winson.artist.maori.nz/) reads: 'Use of Graphix. Once again, it's Free for Non Commercial use. And for those users that need to cover their butt, I have written out a permission Form for you.' In the spirit in which the site is presented, we reproduce Winson's 'Use of Graphix' permission form here, without permission, and encourage readers to visit the website.

Winson's *panui* and 'Use of Graphix' form suggest that many browsers are trying to be responsible in their use of images – to the point where the artist is getting *hoha* (fed up) with people seeking permission. The tone of the WebPages is carefree. The artist may have discovered a useful tactic for minimising unauthorised appropriation: start by offering people something unfettered by restrictions on use. It is much more difficult to steal from someone who has effectively given you an unrequested gift, and when it becomes necessary to impose restrictions, people are perhaps more likely to respect them.

The examples of colonial and postcolonial appropriation in this book can only begin to show the extent of appropriation experienced by minority peoples. Pakeha scholars invented Maori history in a way that reflected their views of the world rather than those of Maori. Tribal myths and traditions were amalgamated to form new pan-Maori versions that drew heavily on both European tradition and the Old Testament.

Maori Flava'd
Version 1.01 6/19/2004
http://winson.artist.maori.nz

PERMISSION FOR USE OF COOL MAORI DESIGNS SLIP

Terms & Conditions:
- You the user may not use them for commercial use, unless otherwise stated or agreed upon.
- You must show them off to your Whanau
- You can use them in your Webpage
- You can use em in your Power-Point presentation or Word Documents in Company meetings
- You can print them out and hang them on the wall next to your Britney Spears posters
- Use them for whatever you like

Who Can Use Them?
- Anyone
- Anyone in Commercial or Business who is willing to give me some "Koha" for the use of them.
- Any Educational or Health Departments (Koha, only if you can afford it)

Non-Commercial users:
- Anyone, i.e.: Nana, Koro, Te Kohanga Reo, Kura Kaupapa, Kura, and Wananga or Marae.
- Anyone getting W.I.N.Z assistance and wants to flash his or her Resume up.

Obligations:
- On your Webpage, could you just mention where you got them from?
- On printed Documents no need for any links.
- On you Power Point can you put in an acknowledgment aye? Up to you.
- If you win Lotto, using the Lotto number picker on my Webpage, we split 50-50?
- Don't Vote for the National Party.

Permission Acknowledgement:
I, WINSON, (*Maori fulla who made them cool as Maori graphics*) SAID, "Yep"! "EE's Kool"

Note: This Document and earlier versions are neither legal nor binding but acknowledged by artist of the graphics as proof of permission
In case I see you selling T-Shirts or Postcards with my graphics on them, at the Flea Market
I make NOT all the graphics on my site, TUTU GRAPHICS made some, therefore I have
NO rights to sell them. They have been acknowledge and mentioned as made by other artist/s.

Figure 7.1 Winson's permission slip.

It was part of a colonising process that brought Maori history and culture into a regimented framework, so it could readily be understood and controlled by the colonisers (Durie 1998). It is obvious that the power to narrate, or to block other narratives from forming and emerging, is very important to culture and imperialism (Said 1994).

Colonial and postcolonial misdeeds are not isolated instances of government wrongdoing but represent a pattern of behaviour characteristic of State interactions with indigenous peoples the world over. The wholesale vandalism and theft of cultural artefacts during the war on Iraq provides further indication of the contemporary relevance of confronting appropriation. The Greek government has requested the return of the Parthenon Marbles (friezes from Athens) from the British Museum on many occasions, most recently for the Olympics, and been steadfastly denied every time. The museum usually takes the line that they are better at looking after antiquities than the Greek government, but the economic objective to retaining them cannot be denied.

Having set a precedent for exploiting minority peoples and their resources, colonists established a code of conduct which contemporary producers of various media emulate and similarly justify. We have seen the continuity of appropriation from colonial times up to the present day, looking beyond actual artefacts to the commodification of art and iconography.

It is difficult to reconcile our ambivalence about minority representation in *Once Were Warriors* with our suggestion that students read the novel and watch the film. Our ambivalence is compounded by the knowledge that 'protection discourses' abound, shielding the film from accusations that it perpetuates negative stereotypes, and from claims that it is more appropriate to locate Maori domestic violence in the context of colonial oppression. 'Protection discourses' are achieved by constructing critics as politically correct ranters, or people in denial (Pihama 1996). However, to understand the ways these portrayals continue to reflect colonial stereotypes, one must see for oneself. The critical interpretation offered in Chapter 3 aims to contextualise the film and novel because, according to Pihama (1996: 192), 'Until the images and stories presented in *Once Were Warriors* can be seen as only one aspect of a wider context, they will continue to contribute to the "so that's how the other half lives" mentality.'

We hope readers will make use of the case studies, as examples of particular experiences of Maori in Aotearoa and Inuit in Canada with parallels and similarities to those of ethnic minorities in many parts of the world. While each group is distinct and unique, some experiences are strikingly common. Both differences and similarities can be instructive.

There is no ultimate solution to continuing exploitation and oppression. The stereotype of the inferior savage is alive and well, in the form of media criminalisation of ethnic minorities who are portrayed as at once insufficiently 'white', and, living in contemporary society, insufficiently 'native'. Assertions of the moral superiority of outsiders are allowed to run rampant (Ross 1998), and incentives to continue 'passing' (for white) linger. Ethnic minority media professionals encounter additional obstacles. For example, Maori film makers must:

> ... satisfy the demands of the cinema, the demands of their own people, the criteria of a white male-dominated value and funding structure, and somehow be accountable to all. As well, their projects have to show what Americans call 'crossover potential', and the film maker has to raise about one third of the projected budget. Worse still is the

knowledge that the Maori film maker carries the burden of having to correct the past and will therefore be concerned with demystifying and decolonising the screen. The expectation of positive imaging means destroying the stereotypes that come from cultural appropriation, and clearing the colonial refuse out of oneself in order to make a fresh new start... (Mita 1996: 49)

Magic in the Sky: Inuit resistance and reappropriation of the airwaves

As we saw in Chapter 5, the New Media Nation has placed control of some of today's news media in the hands of ethnic minority people. It was a long time coming, and the movement is still growing. Inuit were at the forefront of this movement, under the leadership of people like John Amagoalik, 'father of Nunavut', who insisted all along that Inuit culture would survive colonial onslaughts. One of the prime movers in indigenous broadcasting is the Inuk broadcaster and political leader, Rosemarie Kuptana. In a famous speech delivered in various locations during the 1980s, she compared non-indigenous television to the neutron bomb, which destroys the soul of a people while leaving them physically intact. She was one of a number of ethnic minority leaders who spoke out against colonisation through television.

The incursions of dominant media into small, isolated communities meant intense exposure to the programming and values of southern Canadian and American TV. People who still relied on subsistence hunting, fishing and gathering for a good deal of their livelihood were suddenly inundated with advertisements for products they could neither see nor afford, and which in many cases were simply irrelevant. Try using a lawn-mower on the tundra and you will immediately understand this point. Inuit objected especially to the message of acquisition and greed that permeated American television programmes sent north by satellite. For this reason, some communities refused for many years to accept southern television. Peter Raymont's 1981 film, *Magic in the Sky*, documents this period in Canadian broadcasting history. Focused on the community of Igloolik, which would later produce the first full length Inuktitut-language feature film, *Atanarjuat* (2000), the documentary depicts the last hold-out against southern television. Year after the year, community members continued to vote against allowing mainstream television into Igloolik. *Magic in the Sky* records yet another ballot against commercial television, but this time the vote is closer. It would not be long before Igloolik said yes, but not without conditions. The position was that first, there would have to be television programming by and for Inuit. Once the Inuit Broadcasting Corporation (IBC) was in place, Igloolik voted to accept the rest of the broadcasting universe.

Such decisions and developments are essential to the process of decolonising and reappropriating media and cultures.

Exercises

7.1 Kennewick Man: who 'owns' our ancestors?

1. Do an Internet search and survey the media coverage of this case. It is essential that you read different media representations of the case: from Native American media; mainstream media, such as daily newspapers; and alternative non-Native American media (for example, alternative weeklies and publications of other ethnic minority communities).
2. Review the legal arguments and the responses from Native American, scientific and broader communities as represented on the Websites you find on the Internet, and in the various media.
3. Outline the main issues raised in the media – not the court's arguments, but the public and media arguments. Consider the tendency of media to set up binary structures of opposing categories; in the light of this tendency, consider that some of the scientists concerned may themselves have been Native Americans, and some Native Americans may have been lawyers and judges. Consider as well the separate interests and cultural differences of different Native American communities.
4. Note *who* is interviewed in which media, and how Native Americans are represented.
5. In small groups then, report back to the whole class, discuss your findings, with particular reference to representation and self-representation in the context of this case.

7.2 Consider the case of Rita Shelton Deverell and the descriptions of indigenous actors and casting. Write a set of guidelines for the fair and equal treatment of actors, and the fair and accurate portrayal of ethnic minorities on stage and screen.

Further reading

Alibhai-Brown, Yasmin (2004) *Some of my Best Friends are . . . Collected Writings 1989–2004*, London: Politico's.
Clifford, James (1997) *Routes: Travel and Translation in the Late Twentieth Century*, Cambridge and London: Harvard University Press.

Harjo, Joy and Bird, Gloria (1997) *Reinventing the Enemy's Language: Contemporary Native Women's Writings of North America*, New York and London: W. W. Norton.

Suggested listening

Westerman, Floyd (Red Crow) (1991) *The Land is Your Mother; Custer Died for Your Sins* (2-album set); Germany: Trikont. Includes 'Here Come the Anthros'.

Suggested viewing

Dances with Wolves
Grand Avenue
Magic in the Sky
Ngati

Bibliography – references and recommended reading

Abel, S. (1997) *Shaping the News – Waitangi Day on Television*, Auckland: Auckland University Press.

Aboriginal People's Television Network (APTN) (2001) press release, website, http://www.aptn.ca/en/CRTCJan5-01.htm.

Aboriginal Voices (1999) Cover photograph and caption, October/November.

Adams, R. (2004) 'Beyond the foreshore', *The Guardian*, 6 April, http://www.guardian.co.uk/comment/story/0,3604,1193151,00.html.

Agozino, Biko (2003) *Counter-Colonial Criminology: A Critique of Imperialist Reason*, London: Pluto Press.

Agozino, Biko (2004) personal communication.

Alia, Valerie (1989) 'Closing the Circle', *Up Here*, Sept./Oct., 18–20.

Alia, Valerie (1991) 'Native Art and Craft', in Boden, Jurgen (ed.), *Canada North of Sixty*, Toronto: McClelland and Stewart.

Alia, V. (1992) 'Seeing racism from the inside', *Globe and Mail*, Facts & Arguments, 24 March, A20.

Alia, Valerie (1994) *Names, Numbers and Northern Policy: Inuit, Project Surname and the Politics of Identity*, Halifax: Fernwood.

Alia, Valerie (1994–6) personal communications.

Alia, V. (1995) *Nunavut: Where Names Never Die* [radio documentary], transcript, CBC 'Ideas', Toronto: Canadian Broadcasting Corporation (CBC Radio).

Alia, Valerie (1995a) Interviews conducted during research for CBC radio documentary, op. cit. (not all of these were used in the documentary and therefore, do not appear in the published transcript).

Alia, V. (1999) *Un/Covering the North: News, Media, and Aboriginal People*, Vancouver: University of British Columbia Press.

Alia, V. (2000) 'The Boundaries of Liberty and Tolerance in the Canadian North: Media, Ethics, and the Emergence of the Invit Homeland of Nunavut', in Cohen-Almagov, R. (ed.), *Challenges to Democracy: Essays in Honour and Memory of Isaiah Berlin*, Aldershot: Ashgate, 275–95.

Alia, V. (2000–2001) Interviews conducted for research project funded by the Canadian High Commission in the UK.

Alia, V. (2002) 'Scattered Voices, Global Vision: Indigenous Peoples and the

New Media Nation', in Karim, Karim H. (ed.), *The Media of Diaspora*, London and New York: Routledge, 36–50.

Alia, Valerie (2004) 'Opening the Windows', *Media Ethics*, vol. 15, no. 2, Spring, 17–19.

Alia, Valerie (2004a) Letter to the editor of *The Independent on Sunday*, unpublished.

Alia, Valerie (2004b) Journal (notes on ethnicity), unpublished.

Alia, Valerie (2004c) *Media Ethics and Social Change*, Edinburgh: Edinburgh University Press.

Alia, Valerie (2005) 'Inuit Naming: The People Who Love You', in Newhouse, David, Voyageur, Cora and Beavon, Daniel (eds), *Hidden in Plain Sight: Contributions of Aboriginal Peoples to Canadian Identity and Culture*, Toronto: University of Toronto Press, 252–66.

Alia, Valerie, Brennan, Brian and Hoffmaster, Barry (eds) (1996) *Deadlines and Diversity: Journalism Ethics in a Changing World*, Halifax: Fernwood.

Alibhai-Brown, Yasmin (2002) 'No Room at the Inn', *New Internationalist*, October, 16–17.

Alibhai-Brown, Yasmin (2004) *Some of my Best Friends are . . . Collected Writings 1989–2004*, London: Politico's.

Allison, P. (1989) 'Stranger than Fiction: The Way the Media and the Cops Paint a Picture of Violent Crime', *Metro Magazine*, September, 98–104.

American Anthropological Association (1997) *Code of Ethics of the American Anthropological Association*.

Ames, M. M. (1992) *Cannibal Tours and Glass Boxes: The Anthropology of Museums*, Vancouver: UBC Press.

ASA News online (2002) American Sociological Association, 20 August, unpaginated.

Anthropology Newsletter 39 (1998) vol. 6, no. 3, September.

Ang, Ien (1996) *Living Room Wars: Rethinking Media Audiences for a Postmodern World*, London: Routledge.

Anti Nazi League (1999) *Fighting the Nazi Threat Today*, London: Anti Nazi League.

Appadurai, Arjun (1996) *Modernity at Large: Cultural Dimensions of Globalization*, Minneapolis, MN: University of Minnesota Press.

Appiah, Kwame Anthony (1998) 'Cosmopolitan Patriots', in Cheah, Pheng and Robbins, Bruce (eds), *Cosmopolitics: Thinking and Feeling beyond the Nation*, Minneapolis: University of Minnesota Press, 91–114.

Appleton, J. (2002) 'Battle of the bones', 12 December 2002, <www.spiked-online.com>

Archer, D. and Archer, M. (1970) 'Race, Identity, and the Maori People', *Journal of the Polynesian Society*, vol. 79, no. 2, 201–18.

Archer, D. and Archer, M. (1971) 'Maoris in Cities', *Race*, vol. XIII, no. 2, 179–85.

Arctic Circle (1991) 'ALL YOU QALLUNAAT, GET REGISTERED', July/Aug., 13.

Asad, T. (1973) 'Two European Images of Non-European Rule', in Asad, T. (ed.), *Anthropology and the Colonial Encounter*, London: Ithaca Press, 104–18.

Awatere, D. (1996) *My Journey*, New Zealand: Seaview Press.

Baird, V. (2002) 'Fear Eats the Soul', *New Internationalist*, October, 9–12.

Ballara, A. (1991) 'Hinematioro', in Orange, C. (ed.), *The People of Many Peaks: The Maori Biographies from the Dictionary of New Zealand Biography*, Wellington: Bridget Williams Books/Department of Internal Affairs, 13–14.

Ballara, A. (1993) 'Pakeha Uses of Takitimutanga – Who Owns Tribal Tradition?', *Stout Centre Review*, March, 17–21.

Bannerji, H. (2000) *The Dark Side of the Nation: Essays on Multiculturalism, Nationalism and Gender*, Toronto: Canadian Scholars' Press.

Banton, Michael (1983) *Racial and Ethnic Competition*, Cambridge: Cambridge University Press.

Barclay, Barry (1996) 'Amongst Landscapes' in Dennis, J. and Bieringa, J. (eds), 2nd edn, *Film in Aotearoa New Zealand*, Wellington: Victoria University Press, 116–29.

Barkham, P. (2002) 'Refugees dig their own graves in Australian detention protest', *The Guardian*, 3 August, 17.

Barnouw, Erik (1974) *Documentary: A History of the Non-Fiction Film*, London: Oxford University Press.

Barrington, J. M. and Beaglehole, E. (1974) *Maori Schools in a Changing Society*, Wellington: Council for Educational Research.

Barth, Frederic (1969) *Ethnic Groups and Boundaries*, Boston, MA: Little, Brown and Company.

Basso, Keith H. (1996) *Wisdom Sits in Places: Landscape and Language among the Western Apache*, Albuquerque, NM: University of New Mexico.

Baudrillard, J. (1981) *Simulacra and Simulation*, Ann Arbour: University of Michigan Press.

BBC (2001) 'Lego game irks Maoris', http://news.bbc.co.uk/1/hi/world/asia-pacific/1362435.stm

BBC (2004) 'NZ launches first Maori TV station', 28 March, http://news.bbc.co.uk

BBC (2004a) 'Maori march to defend beaches', 5 May http://news.bbc.co.uk

BBC (2004b) BBC Website, www.bbc.co.uk

BBC (2004c) 'Tribe challenges American origins', 7 September, http://news.bbc.co.uk

Becker, H. S. (1963) *Outsiders: Studies in the Sociology of Deviance*, New York: Free Press.

Belich, J. (1996) *Making Peoples – A History of the New Zealanders from Polynesian Settlement to the End of the 19th Century*, Auckland: Penguin Books (NZ) Ltd.

Belich, J. (1997) 'Myth, Race, and Identity in New Zealand', *New Zealand Journal of History*, vol. 31, no. 1, 9–22.

Bell, Diane (1998) *Ngarrindjeri Wurruwarrin: A World That Is, Was and Will Be*, Melbourne: Spinifex Press Pty Ltd.

Berger, P. (1963) *Invitation to Sociology*, New York: Bantam Books.

Berlitz Guides (1990–1) *Berlitz Travel Guide: Ireland*, Lausanne: Berlitz Guides/Macmillan S.A.

Biggs, B. (1964) 'The Oral Literature of the Polynesians', *Te Ao Hou*, vol. 49, 23–5, 42–7.

Binney, J. (1984) 'Myth and Explanation in the Ringatu Tradition: Some Aspects of the Leadership of Te Kooti Arikirangi Te Turuki and Rua Kenana Hepetipa', *Journal of the Polynesian Society*, vol. 93, no. 4, 345–98.

Binney, J. (1987) 'Maori Oral Narratives, Pakeha Written Texts: Two Forms of Telling History', *New Zealand Journal of History*, vol. 21, no. 1, 16–28.

Blythe, M. (1994) *Naming the Other: Images of the Maori in New Zealand Film and Television*, Metuchen, NJ: Scarecrow Press, Inc.

Boneart Place (2005) http://www.boneart.co.nz

Bourdieu, Pierre (1991) *Language and Symbolic Power*, Cambridge, MA: Harvard University Press.

Bowling, B. and Phillips, C. (2002) *Racism, Crime and Justice*, London: Longman.

Brecher, Jeremy, Costello, Tim and Smith, Brendan (2000) *Globalization from Below: The Power of Solidarity*, Boston, MA: South End Press.

Brincker, Benedikte (undated) *Clash of Communities: A Study of the LEGO product Bionicle*, www.lse.ac.uk/collections/EMTEL/Conference/papers/Brincker.doc

Bristow, G., Condon, R. and Kuptana, R. (1992) unpublished letter to the editor of the *Telegraph Magazine*, sent from Holman Island, Canada.

Brody, Hugh (1987) *Living Arctic: Hunters of the Canadian North*, Vancouver and Toronto: Douglas and McIntyre.

Brown, Y.-A. (2002) *No Room at the Inn*, New Internationalist, October, 16–17.

Bull, S. (2004) 'The Land of Murder, Cannibalism and All Kinds of Atrocious Crimes? Maori and Crime in New Zealand, 1853–1919', *British Journal of Criminology*, vol. 44, no. 4, 496–519.

Bull, S. and Alia, V. (2004) 'Unequalled Acts of Injustice? Pan-Indigenous Encounters with Colonial School Systems', *Contemporary Justice Review*, vol. 7, no. 2, June, 171–82.

Bungay, M. and Edwards, B. (1983) *Bungay on Murder*, Christchurch: Whitcoulls Publishers.

Bungay, R. (1998) *Scarecrows: Why Women Kill*, Auckland: Random House New Zealand Ltd.

Burgess, M. and Valaskakis, G. G. (1995) *Indian Princesses and Cowgirls: Stereotypes from the Frontier*, Montreal: OBORU.

Burne, Jerome (2003) 'The hidden power to heal', *The Independent Review*, 22 April, 8.

Butler, E. (2003) 'Fighting back – the Inuit forced from their homes to protect the US', *The Independent*, 13 November, http://www.news.independent.co.uk/world/americas/story.jsp?story=463225

Cahn, Claude (ed.) (2002) *Roma Rights: Race, Justice, and Strategies for Equality*, New York: International Debate Education Association, IDEA Sourcebooks in Contemporary Controversies. Available from IDEA, 4th Floor, 400 West 59th Street, 4th New York, NY 10019, USA.

Calder, P. (1991) *New Zealand Herald*, 22 November, http://www.film.society. tripod.com/nzffs/te-rua.htm

Calder, P. (1996) 'Would-be Warriors – New Zealand Film since *The Piano*', in Dennis, J. and Bieringa, J. (eds), *Film in Aotearoa New Zealand*, 2nd edn, Wellington: Victoria University Press, 183–90.

Callinicos, A. (2002) 'Race and Class', *International Socialism Journal*, vol. 55, no. 3, page not available.

Campbell, R. (1996) 'Nine Documentaries', in Dennis, J. and Bieringa, J. (eds), *Film in Aotearoa New Zealand*, 2nd edn, Wellington: Victoria University Press.

Canadian Daily Newspaper Association (1977) *Code of Conduct*. Toronto Canadian Daily Newspaper Association.

Carmichael, S. and Hamilton, C. V. (1967) *Black Power: The Politics of Liberation in America*, New York: Penguin.

Cassidy, Sarah (2005) 'Black boys do better', *The Independent, Education and Careers*, 13 January, 1, 4–5.

CBC (2003) 'Highway into Oka blocked by protest', WebPosted on CBC News online, 31 March 31, http://cbc.ca/news

CBC (2003a) 'Canada's first aboriginal-run university opens', News online, 21 June, http://cbc.ca/news

CBC (2005) 'Prince Harry's Nazi costume draws international fire', News online 13 January, http://cbc.ca/news

Cernetig, M. (1992) *The Globe and Mail*, A1, D1, D5.

Chapman, Murray (1978) 'On the Cross-Cultural Study of Circulation', *International Migration Review*, vol. 12: 559–69.

Chapple, S. (2000) 'Maori Socio-Economic Disparity', unpublished paper for the Ministry of Social Policy Seminar, 15 September, http://www.act.org.nz/content/20887/maorisocioeconomicdisparity.pdf

Clifford, James (1989) 'Notes on Travel and Theory', *Inscriptions*, vol. 5, 177–88.

Clifford, James (1997) *Routes: Travel and Translation in the Late Twentieth Century*, Cambridge and London: Harvard University Press.

Clifford, James (2001) 'Indigenous Articulations', *The Contemporary Pacific*, vol. 13, no. 2, 468–90.

Cohen, S. (1972) *Folk Devils and Moral Panics*, Oxford: Blackwell.

Cohen, S. (1993) 'Crimes of the State: The Culture of Denial', *Australian and New Zealand Journal of Criminology*, vol. 26, 97–115.

Colling, Linda (2003) 'Celebrating the difference', *Sunderland Echo*, 22 July, Lifestyle section, 6, 7.

Committee to Defend Asylum Seekers (2002) *Everybody has the Right to Seek Asylum from Persecution: But not in Blunkett's Britain*, London: East End Offset Ltd.

Condon, Richard (1992) Bristow, personal communication.

Connell, R. (1987) *Gender and Power: Society, the Person and Sexual Politics*, Cambridge: Polity Press.

Conton, Leslie (1996) 'Experiential Shamanism in the College Classroom: Rewards and Challenges', *Anthropology of Consciousness* vol. 7, no. 1, American Anthropological Association, 39–47.

Crow Dog, Mary and Erdoes, R. (1992) *Lakota Woman*, New York: Grove Press.

Crowe, Keitt (1991) *A History of the Original Peoples of Northern Canada*, revd edn, Montreal: McGill-Queen's University Press.

CRTC (1980) *The 1980s. A Decade of Diversity: Broadcasting, Satellites and Pay-TV*, Hull: Canadian Government Publishing Centre.

Cunneen, C. (1999) 'Criminology, Genocide and the Forced Removal of Indigenous Children from their Families', *The Australian and New Zealand Journal of Criminology*, vol. 32, no. 2, 124.

Curnow, J. (1983) *Wiremu Maihi Te Rangikaheke: His Life and Work*, Master of Arts Thesis, University of Auckland.

Daes, Erica-Irene (1993) *Discrimination against Indigenous Peoples – Study on the Protection of the Cultural and Intellectual Property of Indigenous Peoples*, Geneva: Office of the United Nations High Commissioner for Human Rights [E/CN.4/Sub.2/1993/28].

Dennis, J. and Bieringa, J. (eds) (1996) *Film in Aotearoa New Zealand*, 2nd edn, Wellington: Victoria University Press.

Deschênes, Jules (1985) 'Proposal Concerning a Definition of the Term "Minority"', UN document E/CN.4/Sub.2/1985/31.

Dietz, Mary Lorenz, Prus, Robert and Shaffir, William (eds) (1994) *Doing Everyday Life: Ethnography as Human Lived Experience*, Toronto: Copp Clark Longman.

Dior, Christian (2001) Photograph from 2001 collection, *The Guardian*, 26 January, 11.

District Court (1998) Whakatane, T980938, 18 December, Thorburn, J.

Ditton, J. and Duffy, J. (1983) 'Bias in the Newspaper Reporting of Crime News', *British Journal of Criminology*, vol. 23, no. 2, April 159–66.

Douglas, M. (1992) *Risk and Blame*, London: Routledge.

Douglas, M. (1999) *Purity and Danger – An Analysis of the Concepts of Pollution and Taboo*, 2nd edn, London: Viking.

Dowds, L. and Young, K. (1996) 'National Identity', in Jowell, R. et al. (eds), *British Social Attitudes*, 13th report, Hants: Dartmouth, 141–59.

Du Bois, W. E. (1987) [1903] *The Souls of Black Folks*, New York: Vintage.

Duff, A. (1990) *Once Were Warriors*, Auckland: Tandem Press.

Duff, A. (1993) *Maori – The Crisis and the Challenge*, Auckland: HarperCollins Publishers (New Zealand) Ltd.

Duff, A. (1996) *What Becomes of the Broken Hearted?*, Auckland: Vintage.

Duff, A. (1999) *Out of the Mist and Steam: A Memoir*, Auckland: Tandem Press.

Duncan, L. S. W. (1972) 'Racial Considerations in Polynesian Crime', in Vaughan, G. (ed.) *Racial Issues in New Zealand*, Auckland: Akarana Press.

Durie, M. (1994) *Whaiora – Maori Health Development*, Auckland: Oxford University Press.

Durie, M. (1998) *Te Mana Te Kawanatanga-The Politics of Maori Self-Determination*, Auckland: Oxford University Press.

eBay (2003) Maori artefacts on Website, 27 August.

Ellison-Loschmann, Liz (2004) *Irihapeti Merenia Ramsden 24 February 1946–5 April 2003*, http://culturalsafety.massey.ac.nz/

Erickson, M. and Williams, S. (eds) (1995) *Social Change in Tyne and Wear*, Sunderland: Black Cat Publications.

Eriksen, Thomas Hylland (2002) *Ethnicity and Nationalism: Anthropological Perspectives*, new, expanded version, London: Pluto Press.

Ernerk (also Irniq), Peter, 'The Inuit as Hunters and Managers', in *The Beaver* 67(1), Feb/March 1987:62), (Petrone 1988: 283).

Étienne, M. and Leacock, E. (eds) (1980) *Women and Colonization: Anthropological Perspectives*, New York: Praeger [out of print; subject to availability].

Evans, J., Grimshaw, P., Philips, D. and Swain, S. (2003) *Equal Subjects, Unequal Rights: Indigenous Peoples in British Settler Colonies, 1830–1910*, Manchester and New York: Manchester University Press.

Evening Post (1997) Editorial, 15 May.

Fairhaven College (2005) http://www.wwu.edu/depts/fairhaven

Fanon, Franz (1963) *The Wretched of the Earth*, London: Paladin.

Fanon, Franz (1965) *Black Skin, White Masks*, New York: Grove.

Farb, Peter (1974) *Word Play: What Happens When People Talk*, New York: Knopf.

Ferguson, N. (2003) *Empire: How Britain Made the Modern World*, London: Allen Lane, an imprint of Penguin Books Ltd.

Fforde, C., Hubert, J. and Turnbull, P. (eds) (2002) *The Dead and their Possessions: Repatriation in Principle, Policy and Practice*, London: Routledge.

Fickling, D. (2003) 'The return of the native', *The Guardian*, 10 July, http://www.film.guardian.co.uk/featurepages/0,4120,995725,00.html

Fienup-Riordan, Ann (1995) *Freeze Frame: Alaska Eskimos in the Movies*, Seattle and London: University of Washington Press.

Flaherty, Robert, in collaboration with Flaherty, France, Hubbard (1924) *My Eskimo Friends: Nanook of the North*, New York: Doubleday, Page and Company.

Fleras, A. and Spoonley, P. (1999) *Recalling Aotearoa – Indigenous Politics and Ethnic Relations in New Zealand*, Auckland: Oxford University Press.

Fonseca, Isabel (1995) *Bury Me Standing: The Gypsies and Their Journey*, New York: Vintage.

Foucault, Michel (1977) *Discipline and Punish: The Birth of the Prison*, London: Penguin Books Ltd.

Foucault, Michel (1980) *Power/Knowledge: Selected Interviews and Other Writings 1972–1977*, ed. Colin Gordon, New York: Pantheon Books.

Fournier, S. and Crey, E. (1997) *Stolen from our Embrace: The Abduction of First Nations Children and the Restoration of Aboriginal Communities*, Vancouver and Toronto: Douglas and McIntyre.

Fullard-Leo, B. (1998) 'Sacred Burial Practices', *Coffee Times*, February, Hawaii: Les Drent.

Fung, Richard (1993) 'Working through Cultural Appropriation', *Fuse*, vol. 16, no. 5/6, Summer, 16–27.

Galtung, Johan and Ikeda, Daisaku (1995) *Choose Peace*, London: Pluto Press.

Gaski, Harald (1997) 'Voice in the Margin: A Suitable Palce for a Minority Literatures', in Gaski, H (ed.), *Sámi Culture in a New Era: The Norwegian Sámi Experience*, Karasjok: Davvi Girji, OS, 199–220.

Gault, John (1984) 'The Stranger Among Us', *Toronto Life*, July, 11–14.

George, Jane (2001) 'All Nunavik Communities Will Soon Get Access to the Internet', *Nunatsiaq News*, 9 March, 25, 31.

George, Jane (1996) *Nunatsiaq News*, 'Who should talk about shamanism?', 23 Aug., 11.

Gheorghe, N. (1991) 'Roma-Gypsy Ethnicity in Eastern Europe', *Social Research*, vol. 58, no. 4, Winter, 829–44.

Giddens, Anthony (1997) *Sociology*, London: Polity Press.

Giddens, Anthony (1999) 'Runaway World: The Reith Lectures Revisited', *The Director's Lectures*, Lecture 3, 24 November, www.polity.co.uk

Gilbert, Jenny (2004) 'Strike a pose', *The Independent on Sunday*, 21 March, 14–15.

Gillan, Audrey (2003) 'Brutal death of a travelling child', *The Guardian*, 10 June, 9.

Gilroy, P. (1987) *There Ain't No Black in the Union Jack*, London: Unwin Hyman Ltd.

Glazer, Nathan and Moynihan, Daniel Patrick (eds) (1975) *Ethnicity: Theory and Experience*, Cambridge, MA: Harvard University Press.

Glover, M. (1993) *Maori Women's Experience of Male Partner Violence: Seven Case Studies*, Master of Social Science Thesis, University of Waikato.

Gluckman, L. (1964) 'Kereopa: The Psychodynamics of a 19th-Century Murder', *New Zealand Medical Journal*, vol. 63, August, 486–91.

Godfrey, Stephen (1993) 'Cultural Appropriation in Dance', *Step Text*, vol. 2, no. 2, March, 16.

Goffman, Erving (1959) *The Presentation of Self in Everyday Life*, New York: Doubleday.

Goldson, A. (1996) 'Piano Lessons', in Dennis, J. and Bieringa, J. (eds), *Film in Aotearoa New Zealand*, Wellington: Victoria University Press, 197.

Goodchild, Sophie (2004) 'Two-thirds of whites say they are biased against minorities', *Independent on Sunday*, 14 November, 4.

Grace, Sherrill E. (1996) 'Exploration as Construction: Robert Flaherty and *Nanook of the North*, *Essays on Canadian Writing*, no. 59 (fall), 123–46.

Greenland, H. (1984) 'Ethnicity as Ideology: The Critique of Pakeha Society', in Spoonley, P., MacPherson, C., Pearson, D., and Sedgwick, C. (eds), *Tauiwi – Racism and Ethnicity in New Zealand*, Palmerston North: The Dunmore Press Ltd, 86–102.

Greer, Germaine (2004) *Whitefella Jump Up: The Shortest Way to Nationhood*, London: Profile Books (excerpt published online in 'Special Report – Australia', *The Guardian Unlimited*, 19 June, unpaginated).

Grey, G. (1854) *Ko Nga Mahinga a Nga Tupuna Maori He Mea Kohikohi Mai*, London: G. Willis.

Grey, G. (1855) *Polynesian Mythology and Ancient Traditional History of the New Zealanders (as Furnished by their Chiefs and Priests)*, London: John Murray.

Griffith, Richard (1953) The *World of Robert Flaherty*, New York: Duell, Sloan and Pearce.

Guemple, Lee (1965) '*Saunik*: Name Sharing as a Factor Governing Eskimo Kinship Terms', *Ethnology* vol. 4, no. 3, 323–35.

Gumbel, A. (2003) 'Race Row Over "Negro For Hire" Web Spoof', *The Independent*, 1 June, http://news.independent.co.uk/world/americas/story/jsp'. story=41122

Gunew, Sneja (2004) *Haunted Nations: The Colonial Dimensions of Multiculturalisms*, London and New York: Routledge.

Gunnison, R. B. (1999) 'Ishi May Not Have Been Last Member of His Tribe – Smithsonian Could Return Remains to Indians', *Chronicle Sacramento Bureau*, 6 April, http://sfgate.com

Haig-Brown, Celia (1988) *Resistance and Renewal: Surviving the Indian Residential School*, Vancouver: Arsenal Pulp Press.

Hall, S., Critcher, C., Jefferson, T., Clarke, J. and Roberts, B. (1978) *Policing the Crisis: Mugging, the State and Law and Order*, London: Macmillan.

Hall, Stuart (ed.) (1997) *Representation: Cultural Representations and Signifying Practices*, London: Sage/Open University.

Hall, Stuart (1997a) 'Culture, Identity and Diaspora', in McDowell, L. (ed.) *Undoing Place? A Geographical Reader*, London: Arnold, 231–42.

Hancock, Ian (2002) *We are the Romani People – Ame sam e Rromane Dzene*, Hatfield: University of Hertfordshire Press.

Hancock, Ian, Dowd, Siobhan and Djuric, Rajko (1998) *The Roads of the Roma*, Hatfield: University of Hertfordshire Press.

Hanson, A. (1989) 'The Making of the Maori: Culture Invention and its Logic', *American Anthropologist*, vol. 91, 890–902.

Hanson, F. A., and Hanson, L. (1983) *Counterpoint in Maori Culture*, London: Routledge and Kegan Paul.

Harjo, Joy and Bird, Gloria (1997) *Reinventing the Enemy's Language: Contemporary Native Women's Writings of North America*, New York and London: W. W. Norton.

Harper, K. (2000) *Give me my Father's Body – The Life of Minik, the New York Eskimo*, South Royalton, VT: Steerforth Press.

Hau'ofa, Epili (1993) 'Our Sea of Islands…A Beginning', in Hau'ofa, E., Naidu, V. and Wadell, E. (eds), *A New Oceania: Rediscovering our Sea of Islands*, Suva: University of the South Pacific, School of Social and Economic Development, 4–19, 126–39.

Hau'ofa, Epeli (2000) '*Pasts to Remember*' in Remembrance of Pacific Pasts, ed. Robert Borofsky, Honolulu: University of Hawai'i Press, 453–71.

Hayter, T. (2001) *Open Borders: The Case against Immigration Controls*, London: Pluto Press.

Hayter, T. (2002) 'The New Common Sense', *New Internationalist*, October, 14–15.

Hecht, Jeff (2004) 'Kennewick Man Ruling – Politics or Science?' *New Scientist*, no. 2434, 14 February, http://www.newscientist.com/article.ns?id= dn4666

Hechter, Michael (1975) *Internal Colonialism: The Celtic Fringe in British National Development, 1536–1966*, Berkeley, CA: University of California Press.

Hechter, Michael (1986) Rational Choice Theory and the Study of Race and Ethnic Relations', in Rex, John and Mason, David (eds), *Theory of Race and Ethnic Relations*, Cambridge: Cambridge University Press.

Heim, O. (1998) *Writing along Broken Lines – Violence and Ethnicity in Contemporary Maori Fiction*, Auckland: Auckland University Press.

Hilliard, C. (1997) 'James Cowan and the Frontiers of New Zealand History', *New Zealand Journal of History*, vol. 31, no. 2, 219–33.

Hobsbawm, Eric J. and Ranger, T. (1983) *The Invention of Tradition*, Cambridge: Cambridge University Press.

Home Office of the Government of the United Kingdom (2002) www.homeoffice.gov.uk/rds/immigration1.html

Home Office of the Government of the United Kingdom (2003) www.homeoffice.gov.uk/rds/immigration1.html

hooks, b. (1995) *Killing Rage: Ending Racism*, New York: Henry Holt and Company.

Horowitz, D. (1985) *Ethnic Groups in Conflict*, Berkeley, CA: University of California Press.

Horrocks, R. (1996) 'Alternatives – Experimental Film Making in New Zealand', in Dennis, J. and Bieringa, J. (eds), *Film in Aotearoa New Zealand*, Wellington: Victoria University Press, 55–88.

Hulme, K. (1983) *The Bone People*, New York: Penguin.

Ihimaera, W. (1972) *Pounamu Pounamu*, Auckland: Heinemann Reed.

The Independent (2005) 12 February, 36.

Indigenous Arts Reference Group (1998) *Discussion Paper: Indigenous Arts Protocols*, Sydney: Australian Ministry of the Arts.

Isaacs, Harold R. (1989) *Idols of the Tribe: Group Identity and Political Change*, Cambridge, MA: Harvard University Press.

Jackson, M. D. (1975) 'Literacy, Communications and Social Change: A Study of the Meaning and Effect of Literacy in Early Nineteenth Century Maori Society', in Kawharu, I. H. (ed.), *Conflict and Compromise: Essays on the Maori since Colonisation*, Wellington: A. H. and A. W. Reed, 27–54.

Jacobs, Alex Karoniaktatie (1986) 'The Politics of Primitivism: Concerns and Attitudes in Indian Art', *Akwekon*, vol. 2, no. 3 (no page number).

Jenkins, K. E. H. (1991) *Te Ihi, te Mana, te Wehi o te Ao Tuhi. Maori Print Literacy from 1814 to 1855: Literacy, Power and Colonisation*, Master of Arts Thesis, University of Auckland.

Jocks, Conway (1996) 'Talk of the Town: Radio Talk Shows', in Alia, Valerie, Brennan, Brian and Hoffmaster, Barry (eds), *Deadlines and Diversity: Journalism Ethics in a Changing World*, Halifax: Fernwood, 151–72.

Joe, Rita (1996) *Song of Rita Joe: Autobiography of a Mi'kmaq poet*, Charlottetown: Ragweed Press.

Jones, L. (1998) *Images of Maori in the Pakeha Press – Pakeha Representations of Maori in the Popular Print Media 1935–1965*, Master of Arts Thesis, Auckland: University of Auckland.

Kakfwi, Stephen (1989) *Dehcho: Mom, We've Been Discovered* (back cover), Yellowknife: Dene Cultural Institute.

Karetu, S. (1975) 'Language and Protocol of the Marae', in King, M. (ed.), *Te Ao Hurihuri – The World Goes On*, Wellington: Hicks, Smith and Sons Ltd, 35–54.

Karpf, A. (2002) 'We've been here before' *The Guardian Weekend*, 8 June, 26–8.

Kassem, Mia (2003) 'Contemporary Manifestations of *Ta Moko*', *NZArt-Monthly*, March, <www.nzartmonthly.co.nz/kassem_001.html>

Kauzlarich, D., Matthews, R. A. and Miller, W. J. (2001) 'Toward a Victimology of State Crime', *Critical Criminology*, vol. 10, 173–94.

Keeshig-Tobias, Lenore (1990) 'White Lies?', *Saturday Night*, October, 67–8.

Kelbie, P. (2004) 'Maoris win return of preserved heads hidden away in museum', *The Independent*, 24 June, http://www.independent.co.uk/low_res/story.jsp?story=534614$host=3$dir=65

Kernot, B. (1990) 'Race-tagging: The Misuse of Labels and the Press Council', in Spoonley, P. and Hirsh, W. (eds), *Between the Lines – Racism and the New Zealand Media*, Auckland: Heinemann Reed, 53–5.

Kershaw, Sarah and Davey, Monica (2004) 'Plagued by drugs, some tribes revive the ancient penalty of banishment', *New York Times*, 18 January, http://www.nytimes.com/2004/01/18/national/18BANI.html?ex=1110690000$en=bd53cb78320f8970$ei=5070

King, J. C. H. and Lidchi, H. (1998) *Imaging the Arctic*, Vancouver: UBC Press.

King, M. (1978) 'New Zealand Oral History: Some Cultural and Methodological Considerations', *New Zealand Journal of History*, vol. 12, no. 2, 104–23.

King, M. (1985) *Being Pakeha*, Auckland: Hodder and Stoughton.

King, M. (1997) *Nga Iwi o te Motu: One Thousand Years of Maori History*, Auckland: Reed Publishing (New Zealand) Ltd.

Kipling, R. (1940) *Rudyard Kipling's Verse: Definitive Edition*, New York: Doubleday.

Kirby, A. (2000) 'Norway's other nation demands land', 8 September, http://news.bbc.co.uk

Kirikiri, R. and Wrighton, N. (1990) *A Beginner's Guide to Cultural Identity – A Resource for Teachers*, Wellington: Ministry of Education.

Kroeber, Theodora (1961) *Ishi in Two Worlds: A Biography of the Last Wild Indian in North America*, Berkeley, CA: University of California Press.

Kroeber, Theodora (1964) *Ishi, Last of his Tribe*, Berkeley, CA: Parnassus Press.

Lavenders Blue Ltd (2004) 'Handmade gypsy caravans for [children's] play' (advertisement), *The Independent Review*, 16 August.

Lawson, Mark (2005) 'The very nasty party', *The Guardian*, 15 January, 19.

Lehtola, V-P. (2002) *The Sámi People – Traditions in Transition*, Jyvaskyla: Kustannua-Puntsi.

Levine, H. B. (1991) 'Comment on Hanson's *The Making of the Maori*', *American Anthropologist*, vol. 93, 444–6.

Lianos, M. and Douglas, M. (2000) 'Dangerization and the End of Deviance', *British Journal of Criminology*, vol. 40, 261–78.

Loewen, J. W. (1995) *Lies my Teacher Told me – Everything your American History Textbook Got Wrong*, New York: Touchstone, Simon and Schuster Inc.

Lynott, Mark J. and Wylie, Alison (1995) *Ethics in American Archaeology: Challenges for the 1990s*, Washington, DC: Society for American Archaeology.

Maalouf, Amin (2000) *On Identity*, London: The Harvill Press.

Mahamdallie, H. (2001) 'Refugees are not to blame', *Socialist Worker* 1765: front page.

Mahamdallie, H. (2002) 'Racism: Myths and Realities', *International Socialism Journal*, vol. 95, http://www.pubs.socialistreviewindex.org.uk/isj95/mahamdallie.htm

Mahoney, P. D. (2003) *The Response to Family Violence in New Zealand – The Role of the Family Court*, Wellington, NZ: Ministry of Justice, www.justice.govt.nz

Malinowski, Bronislaw (1922) *The Argonauts of the Western Pacific*, New York: E. P. Dalfon.

Marks, K. (2004) 'Thousands of Maoris march to defend "their" beaches', *The Independent*, 6 May, http://www.independent.co.uk

Martinez Cobo, Jose R. (1986) *Study on the Problem of Discrimination against Indigenous Populations*, E/CN.4/Sub.2/1986/Add.4 paragraphs 379–82, United Nations.

Masterson, A. (2003) 'More than once were warriors out of their tiny minds', *The Age*, 21 January, www.theage.com.au

Mattes, Catherine and Racette, Sherry Farrell (2001) *Rielisms*, Winnipeg: Winnipeg Art Gallery.

McGregor, J. (1991) 'Te Orenga Waha Ki – "In Search of a Voice" ', *New Zealand Journalism Review*, vol. 4, Winter, 43–6.

McGregor, J. (1993) *Crime News as Prime News in New Zealand's Metropolitan Press*, Publication No. 36, Auckland: Legal Research Foundation.

McGregor, J. and Comrie, M. (1995) *Balance and Fairness in Broadcasting News (1985–1994)*, Wellington: Broadcasting Standards Authority and New Zealand On Air.

McMaster, D. (2001) *Asylum Seekers: Australia's Response to Refugees*, Melbourne: Melbourne University Press.

McMaster, Gerald (1998) *Reservation X: The Power of Place in Contemporary Aboriginal Art*, Seattle, WA: University of Washington Press.

McMaster, Gerald and Martin, Lee-Ann (eds) (1992) *Indigena: Contemporary Native Perspectives*, Vancouver: Douglas and McIntyre.

McRobbie, A. and S. Thornton (1995) 'Rethinking Moral Panic for Multi-Mediated Social Worlds', *British Journal of Sociology*, vol. 46: 559–74.

Memmi, A. (1965) *The Colonizer and the Colonized*, New York: Orion Press.

Messerschmidt, J. W. (1993) *Masculinities and Crime: Critique and Reconceptualization of Theory*, Lanham, MD: Rowman and Littlefield.

Mill, A. (1997) *Maori Television: A Summary of Views*, Wellington: Ministry of Commerce.

Minde, Harold (1995) 'The International Movement of Indigenous Peoples: An Historical Perspective', in Brantenberg, T., Hansen, J. and Minde, H. (eds),

Becoming Visible – Indigenous Politics and Self-Government, Tromsø: University of Tromsø, Sámi dutkamiid guovddás – Centre for Sámi Studies, 90–128.

Mita, M. (1996) 'The Soul and the Image', in Dennis, J. and Bieringa, J. (eds), *Film in Aotearoa New Zealand*, 2nd edn, Wellington: Victoria University Press, 36–54.

Mollard, C. (2001) 'Asylum: The truth behind the headlines', Oxfam UK, http://www.oxfam.org.uk/what_we_do/issues/conflict_disasters/asylum_truth.htm

MORI Social Research Institute (2003) 'Refugee Week 2003: A Survey of 15–24 Year Olds', London: Amnesty International UK, The Commonwealth Institute, RefAid, Refugee Action, Refugee Council, Save the Children UK, United Nations High Commissioner for Refugees.

Moscovici, S. and Lage, E. (1976) 'Studies in Social Influence III: Majority versus Minority Influence in a Group', *European Journal of Social Psychology*, vol. 6, 149–74.

Mowlana, Hamid (1989) 'Communication, Ethics, and the Islamic Tradition', in Cooper, Thomas (ed.), *Communication, Ethics, and Global Change*, White Plains, NY: Longman, 147–58.

Muncie, J. and McLaughlin, E. (eds) (2001) *The Problem of Crime*, 2nd edn, London: Sage Publications.

Nader, L. (1990) *Harmony Ideology – Injustice and Control in a Zapotec Mountain Village*, Stanford, CA: Stanford University Press.

Nasim, K. (2002) 'Road To Freedom', *New Internationalist*, October, 18–19.

Neleman, H. (photography), Iti, T. W., Turei, P., and MacDonald, N. (text) (1999) *Moko: Maori Tattoos*, Zurich: Edition Stemmle.

New Zealand Film Archive (2003) www.filmarchive.org.nz

New Zealand Government (1847) *Education Ordinance*, Auckland: New Zealand Government Printer.

New Zealand Government (1867) *New Zealand Parliamentary Debates*, Auckland: New Zealand Government Printer.

New Zealand Government (1867b) *The Native Schools Act 1867*, Auckland: New Zealand Government Printer.

New Zealand Government (1880) *The Native Schools Code 1880*, Wellington: New Zealand Government Printer.

New Zealand Government (1888) *Appendices to the Journals of the House of Representatives*, Wellington: New Zealand Government Printer.

New Zealand Government (1902) *The School Attendance Act 1901*, Wellington: New Zealand Government Printer.

New Zealand Government (1903) *The School Attendance Act, section VX – School Attendance of Native Children [Regulations of the Minister]*, Wellington: New Zealand Government Printer.

New Zealand Government (1906) *Appendices to the Journals of the House of Representatives*, Wellington: New Zealand Government Printer.

New Zealand Government (1908) *The Education Act 1908*, Wellington: New Zealand Government Printer.

New Zealand Government (1853–1980) *Statistics of New Zealand*, Auckland and Wellington: New Zealand Government Printer.

New Zealand Government (2003) press release 'Maori Radio goes global', 11 November, http://www.scoop.co.nz/stories/PA0311/S00230.htm

New Zealand Herald (1935) 'Probation for Maori', 13 March, 14.

New Zealand Herald (1950) 'Maori guilty of murder', 11 February, 8.

New Zealand Truth (1947) 'Maori guilty of murder', 27 August, 9, 22.

Noyce, Phillip (2002) *Rabbit-Proof Fence* (feature film), Australia.

Nunatsiaq News (2003) 7 February, 20.

Oakeshott, M. (ed.) (1962) *Leviathan*, New York: Macmillan Publishing Co., Inc. *The Observer* (2002) 21 July, 12.

Okely, Judith (1983) *The Traveller-Gypsies*, Cambridge: Cambridge University Press.

O'Malley, P. (1973) 'The Influence of Cultural Factors on Maori Crime Rates', in Webb, S. D. and Collette, J. (eds), *New Zealand Society – Contemporary Perspectives*, Sydney: John Wiley and Sons Australasia Pty Ltd, 386–96.

Parsonson, A. (1980) 'The Expansion of a Competitive Society – A Study in 19th Century Maori Social History', *New Zealand Journal of History*, vol. 14, no. 1, 45–60.

Pearsall, Judy and Trumble, Bill (eds) (1966) *The Oxford English Reference Dictionary*, 2nd edn, Oxford: Oxford University Press.

Pearson, G. (1983) *Hooligan. A History of Respectable Fears*, London: Macmillan.

Penrose, J. (2002) *Poverty and Asylum in the UK*, London: Oxfam and Refugee Council.

Pere, J. (1991) 'Hitori Maori', in Davis, C. and Lineham, P. (eds), *The Future of the Past – Themes in New Zealand History*, Palmerston North: Massey University, 29–48.

Perrot, Michel (1993) 'L'état des médias en Tchoukotka', *Sibérie III: Questions sibériennes, Paris*, 149–57.

Petrone, Penny (1988) *Northern Voices: Inuit Writing in English*, Toronto: University of Toronto Press.

Philipp, E. (1946) *Juvenile Delinquency in New Zealand – A Preliminary Study*, Wellington: New Zealand Council for Educational Research.

Pickering, S. (2002) 'Editorial', *Current Issues in Criminal Justice* vol. 14, no. 1, 7–8.

Pihama, L. (1996) 'Repositioning Maori Representation – Contextualising Once Were Warriors', in Dennis, J. and Bieringa, J. (eds), *Film in Aotearoa New Zealand*, 2nd edn, Wellington: Victoria University Press, 191–3.

Pilger, John (1998) *Hidden Agendas*, London: Vintage.

Pilkington, Doris (1996) *The Long Walk Home*, Brisbane: University of Queensland Press.

Poata-Smith, E. S. Te Ahu (1996) '*He Pokeke Uenuku i Tu Ai* – The Evolution of Maori Protest', in Spoonley, P., Pearson, D. and MacPherson, C. (eds), *Nga Patai: Racism and Ethnic Relations in Aotearoa/New Zealand*, Palmerston North: The Dunmore Press Ltd, 97–116.

Poynting, S. (2002) 'Bin Laden in the Suburbs: Attacks on Arab and Muslim Australians before and after 11 September', *Current Issues in Criminal Justice*, vol. 14, no. 1, July, 43–64.

Pratt, J. (1992) *Punishment in a Perfect Society: The New Zealand Penal System 1840–1939*, Wellington: Victoria University Press.

Pratt, Mary Louise (1992) *Imperial Eyes: Travel Writing and Transculturation*, London: Routledge.

Ramamurthy, A. (2003) *Imperial Persuaders – Images of Africa and Asia in British Advertising*, Manchester: Manchester University Press.

Reedy, A. (1993) (translator, editor, annotator) *Nga Korero a Mohi Ruatapu*, Christchurch: Canterbury University Press.

Reedy, A. (1997) (translator, editor, annotator) *Nga Korero a Pita Kapiti*, Christchurch: Canterbury University Press.

Reilly, M. (1985) *John White: An Examination of his Use of Maori Oral Tradition and the Role of Authenticity*, Master of Arts Thesis, Victoria University of Wellington.

Reilly, M. (1990) 'John White Part II: Seeking the Elusive Mohio: White and his Maori Informants', *New Zealand Journal of History*, vol. 24, no. 1, 45–55.

Reilly, M. (1995) 'An Ambiguous Past – Representing Maori History', *New Zealand Journal of History*, vol. 29, no. 1, April, 19–39.

Rickard, J. (1995) 'Sovereignty: A Line in the Sand', *Aperture*, no. 139, Spring, 51.

Rincon, Paul (2004) 'Tribe challenges American origins', 7 September, http://news.bbc.co.uk

Ritter, R. M. (ed.) (2000) *The Oxford Dictionary for Writers and Editors*, 2nd edn, Oxford: Oxford University Press.

Rive, Richard (1970) *Emergency*, London: Collier.

Robinson, J. (1984) 'Canterbury's Rowdy Women: Whores, Madonnas and Female Criminality', *New Zealand Women's Studies Journal*, vol. 1, no. 1, 6–25.

Ross, L. (1998) *Inventing the Savage: The Social Construction of Native American Criminality*, Austin, TX: University of Texas Press.

Roth, Lorna (1991) *CBC Northern Service and Electoral Reform*, Ottawa: Royal Commission on Electoral Reform and Party Financing.

Roth, Lorna (1993) 'Mohawk Airwaves and Cultural Challenges: Some Reflections on the Politics of Recognition and Cultural Appropriation after the Summer of 1990', *Canadian Journal of Communications – Special Thematic Issue on Indigenous Peoples and Communications*, vol. 18, no. 3, Summer, 315–31.

Roth, Lorna (1995) '(De)romancing the North', *BorderLines*, vol. 36, 36–43.

Roth, Lorna (1996) 'Cultural and Racial Diversity in Canadian Broadcast Journalism', in Alia, Valerie, Brennan, Brian and Hoffmaster, Barry (eds), *Deadlines and Diversity: Journalism Ethics in a Changing World*, Halifax: Fernwood, 72–91.

Roth, Lorna (2000) 'By passing of Borders and Building of Bridges: Steps in the Construction of the Aboriginal Peoples' Television Network in Canada', *Gazette*, vol. 62, no. 3–4, July.

Roth, Lorna, with Bev Nelson and Marie David (1995) 'Three Women, a Mouse, a Microphone, and a Telephone: Information (Mis)Management during the Mohawk/Canadian Governments' Conflict of 1990', in Angara Valdivia (ed.), *Feminism, Multiculturalism, and the Media: Global Diversities*, Pennsylvania, PA: Pennsylvania State University Sage Publication, 48–81.

Rothschild, J. (1981) *Ethnopolitics: A Conceptual Framework*, New York: Columbia University Press.

Rutherford, Jonathan (1990) 'A Place Called Home: Identity and the Culture Politics of Difference', in Jonathan Rutherford (ed.), *Identity: Community, Culture, Difference*, London: Lawrence and Wishart, 9–27.

Saeed, A. (2002) 'A Community under Suspicion: Riots and British Asians', *Scottish Left Review*, vol. 12, 17–19.

Saeed, A., Blain, N. and Forbes, D. (1999) 'New Ethnic and National Questions in Scotland: Post-British Identities among Gasgow Pakistani Teenagers', *Ethnic and Racial Studies*, vol. 22, September, 824–44.

Said, Edward (1979) *Orientalism*, New York: Vintage.

Said, Edward (1986) 'An Ideology of Difference', in Gates, L. H., Jr (ed.), *"Race," Writing, and Difference*, Chicago, IL: University of Chicago Press, 38–58.

Said, Edward (1994) *Culture and Imperialism*, London: Chatto and Windus; New York: Alfred A. Knopf.

Sainte-Marie, Buffy (1998) 'Honoring or Exploitation?' *Aboriginal Voices*, July/August, 7.

Salmond, A. (1983) 'The Study of Traditional Maori Society: The State of the Art', *Journal of the Polynesian Society*, vol. 92, no. 3, 309–31.

Salmond, A. (1985) 'Maori Epistemologies', in Overing, J. (ed.), *Reason and Morality*, London and New York: Tavistock Publications.

Sampson, Anthony (1997) *The Scholar Gypsy: The Quest for a Family Secret*, London: John Murray.

Sercombe, H. (1995) 'The face of the criminal is aboriginal', in Bessant, J., Carrington, K. and Cook, S. (eds), *Cultures of Crime and Violence: The Australian Experience*, Bundoora: Latrobe University Press, 76–92.

Shand, Peter (2000) 'Can Copyright be Reconciled with First Nations' Interests in Visual Arts?', a Paper for Protecting Knowledge: Traditional Resource Rights in the New Millennium organised by the Union of British Columbia Indian Chiefs, February, Vancouver: University of British Columbia.

Sharples, P. (1993) 'A Maori Perspective', *Community Mental Health in New Zealand*, vol. 7, no. 2, 10–17.

Sheffield, M. C. (1958) *Maori Theft: A Study of Crime and Acculturation Stress*, Master of Arts Thesis, University of New Zealand.

Shipman, T. (2002) 'Asylum: the real cost', *The Sunday Express*, 8 December, 1.

Simmons, D. (1963) *The New Zealand Myth*, Master of Arts Thesis, University of Auckland.

Simmons, D. (1966) 'The Sources of Sir George Grey's Nga Mahi a Nga Tupuna', *Journal of the Polynesian Society*, vol. 75, no. 2, 177–88.

Simmons, D. (1969) *A New Zealand Myth – Kupe, Toi and the 'Fleet'*, New Zealand *Journal of History*, vol. 3, no. 1, April, 14–21.

Simmons, D. R. (1976) *The Great New Zealand Myth: A Study of the Discovery and Origin Traditions of the Maori*, Wellington: A. H. and A. W. Reed.

Sinclair, John and Cunningham, Stuart (2000) 'Diasporas and the Media', in Cunningham, S. and Sinclair, J., *Floating Lives: The Media and Asian Diasporas*, Brisbane: University of Queensland Press, 1–34.

Sissons, J. (1991) *Te Waimana: The Spring of Mana: Tuhoe History and the Colonial Encounter*, Dunedin: University of Otago Press.

60 Minutes (1998) TV interview, 19 December.

Sjöden, Gudrun (2003) *Spring 2003: The Four Elements, Part One*, Stockholm: Gudrun Sjöden.

Smith, Linda Tuhiwai (1999) *Decolonizing Methodologies: Research and Indigenous Peoples*, London and New York: Zed Press/Dunedin; NZ: University of Otago Press.

Smith, S. P. (1900) 'On the Tohunga Maori', *Transactions and Proceedings of the New Zealand Institute*, vol. 32, 253–70.

Smith, L. and Smith, G. (1990) *Myths and Realities: Schooling in New Zealand*, Palmerston North: The Dunmore Press.

Smithyman, K. (1979) 'Making History: John White and S. Percy Smith at Work', *Journal of the Polynesian Society*, vol. 88, no. 4, 375–413.

Socialist Worker (2003) 'Resist the attacks on asylum seekers, 15 February, 26.

Solbakk, J. T. (1997) 'Sámi Mass Media: Their Role in a Minority Society', in Gaski, H. (ed.), *Sámi Culture in a New Era: The Norwegian Sámi Experience*, Karasjok: Davvi Girgi OS, 172–220.

Soutar, M. (1994) 'Tribal History in History', *Oral History in New Zealand*, vol. 6, 29–40.

Spivak, G. (1988) 'Can the Subaltern Speak?', in Cary Nelson and Lawrence Grossberg (eds), *Marxism and the Interpretation of Culture*, Urbana, IL: University of Illinois Press.

Spoonley, P. (1990) 'Racism, Race Relations and the Media', in Spoonley, P. and Hirsh, W. (eds), *Between the Lines – Racism and the New Zealand Media*, Auckland: Heinemann Reed, 26–37.

Spoonley, P. (1993) *Racism and Ethnicity*, revised edition, Auckland: Oxford University Press.

Spoonley, P. (1994) 'The Political Economy of Racism', in Green, P. F. (ed.), *Studies in New Zealand Social Problems*, 2nd edn, Palmerston North: The Dunmore Press Ltd, 171–89.

Starn, O. (2004) *Ishi's Brain – In Search of the Last 'Wild' Indian*, New York: Norton.

Statistics Department of the Government of the United Kingdom (2001) www.statistics.gov.uk/census2001/pop2001/sunderland.asp

Stordahl, Vigdis (1993) 'How to be a real Sami? Ethnic identity in a context of (inter)national integration', *Études/Inuit/Studies* vol. 17, no. 1, 127–30.

Stuart, I. (2002) 'Maori and Mainstream: Towards Bicultural Reporting', *Pacific Journalism Review* 8, 42–58.

The Sun (2005) 'HARRY THE NAZI' 13 January, 1.

Sunderland Echo (2003) 15 March, 6.

Sutherland, J. (2002) *Colonialism, Crime, and Dispute Resolution: A Critical Analysis of Canada's Aboriginal Justice Strategy*, Boskey Dispute Resolution Essay Competition, www.acresolution.org/research.nsf

Suzuki (2002) 'Room for the tribe' (advertisement), Japan: Suzuki.

Sykes, G. M. and Matza, D. (1957) 'Techniques of Neutralization: A Theory of Delinquency', *American Sociological Review*, vol. 22, 664–70.

Tamahori, Lee (2003) An interview with *Once Were Warriors* director Lee Tamahori, www.finelinefeatures.com

Tarver, Marsha, Walker, Steve and Wallace, Harvey (2002) *Multicultural Issues in the Criminal Justice System*, Boston, MA: Allyn and Bacon.

Te Awekotuku, Ngahuia (1996) 'Who Called this a Club? Issues of Power, Naming and Provenance in Maori Collections Held Overseas', keynote paper, plenary session 3, 1 November 1, conference on 'Power and Empowerment – Preparing for the New Millennium', organised by Museums Australia Inc.

Te Awekotuku, Ngahuia (1998) personal communication.

Te Awekotuku, Ngahuia (1999) personal communication.

Te Awekotuku, Ngahuia (2001) personal communication.

Te Awekotuku, Ngahuia, Neich, Roger and Davidson, Janet (1996) *Maori: Art and Culture*, London: David Bateman/British Museum Press.

Television New Zealand (1999) *Millennium Moments – Once Were Warriors*.

Te Whaiti, P. and Roguski, M. (1998) *Maori Perceptions of the Police*. A Report to the New Zealand Police and the Ministry of Maori Development (Te Puni Kokiri), Wellington: He Parekereke/Victoria Link, Victoria University of Wellington.

Thomas, D. H. (2000) *Skull Wars: Kennewick Man, Archaeology, and the Battle for Native American Identity*, New York: Basic Books.

Thompson, R. H. T. (1953) 'Maori Affairs and the New Zealand Press', Part One, *Journal of the Polynesian Society*, vol. 62, no. 4, December, 366–83.

Thompson, R. H. T. (1954) 'Maori Affairs and the New Zealand Press', Parts Two and Three, *Journal of the Polynesian Society*, vol. 63, no. 1, March, 1–6.

Thompson, R. H. T. (1955) 'Maori Affairs and the New Zealand Press', Part Four, *Journal of the Polynesian Society*, vol. 64, no. 1, March, 22–34.

Thompson (1992) Francis (1992) 'British Newspaper Article Deserves "Harsh Rebuttal" – Holman Mayor', *News/North*, vol. 2, Nov., A3, A30.

Thornton, A. (1985) 'Two Features of Oral Style in Maori Narrative', *Journal of the Polynesian Society*, vol. 94, no. 2, pp. 149–77.

Thornton, R. (ed.) (1998) *Studying Native America: Problems and Prospects*, city WI: Russell University of Wisconsin Press.

Trowler, P. (1991) *Investigating the Media*, London: Collins Educational.

United Nations Draft Declaration of the Rights of Indigenous Peoples, 1993

Urdang, Stephanie (1979) *Fighting Two Colonialisms: Women in Guinea-Bissau*, New York: Monthly Review.

Vaggioli, Dom Felice (2000) [1896] *History of New Zealand and its Inhabitants*, Dunedin: University of Otago Press.

Valaskakis, Gail Guthrie (1988) 'The Chippewa and the Other: Living the Heritage of Lac du Flambeau', *Cultural Studies*, vol. 2, no. 3, October, unpaginated.

Valaskakis, Gail Guthrie (1993) 'Dance Me Inside: Pow Wow and Being "Indian"', *Fuse* vol. 16, no's 5/6, Summer, 39–44.

Valaskakis, Gail Guthrie (1995) 'Sacajawea and her Sisters: Images and Indians', in Burgess, Marilyn and Valaskakis, Gail Guthrie, *Indian Princesses and Cowgirls: Stereotypes from the Frontier*, Montreal: OBORO, 11–39.

van den Berghe, Pierre (1978) *Race and Racism: A Comparative Perspective*, New York: John Wiley.

van den Berghe, Pierre (1981) *The Ethnic Phenomenon*, New York: John Wiley.

Verrengia, J. (2002) 'Global warming forces Inuits to abandon swamped homes', *The Independent*, 20 September, www.independent.co.uk/world/environment/story.jsp?story=334857

Waitangi Tribunal (1986) *Report of the Waitangi Tribunal on the Te Reo Maori Claim*, *WAI11*, http://www.waitangi.tribunal.govt.nz/reports/generic/wai11/

Waitangi Tribunal (1990) *Report of the Waitangi Tribunal on Claims Concerning the Allocation of Radio Frequencies*, *WAI 26/150*, http://www.waitangi-tribunal.govt.nz/about/publications/published_reports.asp

Waite, Maurice (ed.) (1966) *The Oxford Colour Spelling Dictionary*, Oxford: Clarendon Press.

Walker, Alice (1982) *The Color Purple*, New York: Simon and Schuster.

Walker, R. J. I. (1975) 'The Politics of Voluntary Association', in Kawharu, I. H. (ed.), *Conflict and Compromise: Essays on the Maori since Colonisation*, Wellington: A. H. and A. W. Reed, 167–86.

Walker, R. (1992) 'Sovereignty: *Te Tino Rangatira*', in Novitz, D. and Willmott, B. (eds), *New Zealand in Crisis – A Debate about Today's Critical Issues*, Wellington: GP Publications Ltd, 17–25.

Walker, R. (2001) *He Tipua – The Life and Times of Sir Apirana Ngata* Auckland: Penguin Books.

Wall, M. (1997) 'Stereotypical Constructions of the Maori "Race" in the Media', *New Zealand Geographer*, vol. 53, no. 2, 40–5.

Waltz, Jay (1969) 'Canada promotes nationalism in the Arctic', *New York Times*, 5 May, 14.

Ward, A (1980) 'Documenting Maori History: The Arrest of Te Kooti Rikirangi Te Turuki, 1889', *New Zealand Journal of History*, vol. 14, no. 1, 25–44.

Ward, A. (1990) 'History and Historians before the Waitangi Tribunal-Some Reflections on the Ngai Tahu Claim', *New Zealand Journal of History*, vol. 24, no. 2, 150–67.

Ward, Chrissie (1998) 'The Stone', in Hancock, Ian, Dowd, Siobhan and Djuri¢, Rajko (eds), *The Roads of the Roma: A PEN Anthology of Gypsy Writers*, Hatfield: University of Hertfordshire Press, 119–20.

Wearne, P. (1996) *Return of the Indian: Conquest and Revival in the Americas*, Philadelphia, PA: Temple University Press.

Weber, L. (2002) 'The Detention of Asylum Seekers: Twenty Reasons why Criminologists should Care', *Current Issues In Criminal Justice* vol. 14, 9–30.

Weber, L. and Bowling, B. (2002) 'The Policing of Immigration in the New World Disorder', in Scraton, P. (ed.), *Beyond September 11th: An Anthology of Dissent*, London: Pluto Press, 123–9.

Weber, L. and Gelsthorpe, L. (2000) 'Deciding to Detain: How Decisions to Detain Asylum Seekers are Made at Ports of Entry', Cambridge: University of Cambridge, Institute of Criminology.

Webster, S. (1998) *Patrons of Maori Culture: Power, Theory and Ideology in the Maori Renaissance*, Dunedin: University of Otago Press.

West Australian (1990) 'Aboriginal gangs terrorise suburbs', West Australian, 28 February, http://www.presscouncil.org.au/pcsite/activities/studs/case2.htme#article

Wetherell, M. and Potter, J. (1992) *Mapping the Language of Racism: Discourse and the Legitimation of Exploitation*, Hemel Hempstead: Harvester Wheatsheaf.

White, J. (1889) *The Ancient History of the Maori: His Mythology and Tradition*, Wellington: New Zealand Government Printer.

White Eye, Bud (President) and Alia, Valerie (Advisory Board) (1992) *Communication and Journalism, a Brief to the Royal Commission on Aboriginal Peoples*, Toronto: Native News Network of Canada, 21 October.

Williams, P. and Dickinson, J. (1993) 'Fear of Crime: Read All About It? The Relationship between Newspaper Crime Reporting and Fear of Crime', *British Journal of Criminology*, vol. 33, no. 1, Winter, 33–56.

Wilson, R. (1997) *Bringing Them Home: Report of the National Inquiry into the Separation of Aboriginal and Torres Strait Islander Children from their Families*, Sydney: Sterling Press.

www.msnbc.msn.com (2004) 6 September, Microsoft.

Young, J. (1999) *The Exclusive Society*, London: Sage Publications.

Media resources

A selection of recommended television and radio programmes, documentary and feature films and music CDs created by and about minority people.

Films and videos

Aboriginal Peoples' Television Network (APTN) (1999) *Inaugural Live Broadcast* 1 September. Canada.

APTN promotional video (1998) November. Canada.

Acts of Defiance (1990) Director: Alec G. MacLeod. Non-indigenous director. The 'Oka Crisis' – government and Mohawk people in Québec. Canada.

Atanarjuat (The Fast Runner) (2000) Director: Zacharias Kunuk. Winner of Caméra d'or prize at Cannes. Canada.

Babakiueria (1986) Produced by Aboriginal Television. Drama. Australia.

The Chant of Jimmie Blacksmith (1977) Director: Fred Schepisi. Based on a novel by Thomas Keneally. Australia.

Dances with Wolves (1990) Director: Jake Eberts. Feature. USA.

Dersu Uzala (1975) Director: Akira Kurosawa. Set in Siberia. Relationship between scientist and indigenous man has parallels with that in *Ishi*. USSR/Japan.

Different Lenses (1996) TV documentary on Edward and Asahel Curtis produced by KCTS Television, Seattle. USA.

The Fiddlers of James Bay (1980) Director: Bob Rodgers. Scottish cultural legacy and indigenous Canadians National. Film Board of Canada. Canada.

Gadjo Dilo (1997) Director: Tony Gatlif (pen name of Michel Dahamani) [Roma and Algerian descent; French citizen]. Feature. France.

Grand Avenue (1996) Director: Daniel Sackheim. Book by Greg Sarris. Feature. USA.

Grey Owl (2000) Director: Richard Attenborough. A romanticised version of the life of Archibald Stansfeld Belaney, born 1888 in England, who emigrated to Canada and masqueraded as a Native American. Feature. UK.

Hands of History: Four Aboriginal Women Artists (1994) Director: Loretta Todd. National Film Board of Canada. Canada.

Healing the Mission School Syndrome (1994) Executive Producer: Vic Istchenko. Northern Native Broadcasting Yukon TV documentary. Canada.

Indian America: A Gift from the Past (1994) Director: Dave Warren. Narrator: Wes Studi. Makah culture. USA.

Ishi: The Last Yahi (1992) Directors: Jed Riffe, Pamela Roberts. Documentary released same year as the feature film on Ishi (see *The Last of His Tribe*). USA.

Kabloonak (1994) Director: C. Massot. Feature. France/Canada co-production.

Kanehsatake: 270 Years of Resistance (1993). Director: Alanis Obomsawin. Documentary. Director is of Abenaki descent. Subject concerns. Mohawk people in Québec and the 'Oka Crisis'. National Film Board of Canada. Canada.

The Last Dream (1988) Directors: John Pilger, A. Lowery and A. Morgan. ABC series. Australia.

The Last of His Tribe (1992) Director: Harry Hook. Feature dramatising the story of Ishi and A. L. Kroeber. Makes an interesting comparison to *Dersu Uzala*. USA.

Latcho Drom (1993) Director: Tony Gatlif (Michel Dahamanai) [Roma and Algerian descent; French citizen]. Magnificent feature film – geographic history of Roma told through music. France.

The Learning Path (1991) Director: Loretta Todd. Documentary. National Film Board of Canada. Canada.

The Lone Ranger: Message to Fort Apache (1954) Television series. USA. Released on video by Tamarack Productions, Ontario, Canada.

Lousy Little Sixpence (1982) Director: Alec Morgan. ABC documentary. Australia.

Magic in the Sky Peter Raymont. (1981) Director: Documentary on the beginnings of Inuit television in the Canadian eastern Arctic. National Film Board of Canada. Canada.

Map of the Human Heart (1997) Director: Vincent Ward. Feature film. USA.

A Matter of Survival: Old Crow, Yukon (1990) Executive Producer: Vic Istchenko. Gwich'in culture. TV documentary. Canada.

The Mission School Syndrome (1988) Executive Producer: Vic Istchenko. Northern Native Broadcasting Yukon TV documentary. Canada.

Nanook of the North (1922) Director: Robert Flaherty. Documentary. USA.

Ngati (1987) Director: Barry Barclay. Feature. Aotearoa.

Northern Exposure, First Episode (1990) Director: Joshua Brand. Television sitcom. USA.

The New Zealand Wars (1997) Director: James Belich. Landmark Productions Television New Zealand. New Zealand.

Nunavut: Changing the Map of Canada (1990?) Director: Ian Parker. Informational video produced for Indian and Northern Affairs Canada. Canada.

Nunavut: Our Land (1998?) Inuit inuksuit – sculptures which mark important features of the Arctic landscape. Documentary video by the Royal Bank of Canada. Canada.

Nunavut: Where Names Never Die (1995) Writer and presenter: Valerie Alia; producer: Alison Moss CBC radio documentary. Canada.

Old Crow: A Documentary (1990) Executive Producer: Vic Istchenko. Old Crow, Yukon. Television documentary. Canada.

Once Were Warriors (1994) Director: Lee Tamahori. Feature. Aotearoa.

Only the Devil Speaks Cree (2002) Producer: P. Matthews. CBC television documentary. Canada.

The Other Side of the Ledger: An Indian View of the Hudson's Bay Company (1972) Directors: Martin Defalco and Willie Dunn. Narrator: George Manuel. BBC–NFB co-production. UK and Canada.

The Piano (1993) Director: Jane Campion. Feature. Australia.

Picturing a People (1997) Director: Carol Geddes. Tlingit, Teslin, Yukon. Documentary film. National Film Board of Canada. Canada.

Pocahontas (1995) Directors: Mike Gabriel and Eric Goldberg. Walt Disney cartoon feature. USA.

Pow Wow Highway (1997) Director: Jonathan Wacks. Screenplay David Seals (based on his novel). Feature. USA.

Rabbit-Proof Fence (2003) Director: Phillip Noyce. Feature. Australia.

Rashomon (1951) Director: Akira Kurosawa. Feature. Japan.

Sananguagat: Inuit Masterworks (1994) Director: Derek May. Inuit art; scenes of Igloolik. Canada.

Smilla's Sense of Snow (also titled *Miss Smilla's Feeling for Snow*) (1997) Director: Bille August. Denmark/Germany/Sweden.

Smoke Signals (1999) Director: Chris Eyre. Feature. USA.

The Story of Joe and Elise (1995) Director: Halya Kuchmij. *Man Alive* series. CBC. Canada.

The Story of Joe and Elise (1995) Director: Halya Kuchmij. CBC TV documentary. Canada.

Television Northern Canada (TVNC) promotional video (1993) Produced by TVNC. Canada.

Voice of the West: M. Scott Momaday (1993) Producer: Jean Walkinshaw KCTS TV. Portrait of distinguished Native American writer. Television documentary. USA.

Walkabout (1970) Director: Nicolas Roeg. Non-indigenous Australians encounter an Aboriginal in the outback. Feature. Australia.

Music – audio CDs and cassettes

Aglukark, Susan (1999) *Unsung Heroes*, Canada: EMI Music.

Alfred, Jerry and the Medicine Beat (1996) [Northern Tutchone, Selkirk First Nation, Pelly Crossing, Yukon] *Nendaä – Go Back*, Redhouse Records, and any other of his albums.

Boine, Mari (1996) [Norwegian Sámi] *Radiant Warmth*, Poly Gram [liner notes by Harald Gaski] and any other of her albums.

Idlout, Lucie (2002) *E5-770 My Mother's Name*, Canada: Heart Wreck Records.

Herbs – contemporary Maori reggae group. See, in particular, their album *Herbs – The Very Best Of* (2002) Distributed by Warner Music NZ. Compiled and remastered by Jason Backhouse.

Internationally acclaimed Maori opera performers Kiri Te Kanawa and Inia Te Wiata have albums sung in Maori. These are *Maori Songs* ((1999) EMI Records) and *A Festival of Maori Song* ((1992) produced by Kiwi Pacific), respectively.

Kristiansen, Ole (1988) [Kalaallit (Greenlandic Inuit)] *Isimiit Iikkamut (From the Eye to the Wall)*, Greenland: ULO.

Lyberth, Rasmus (1989) [Kalaallit] *Ajorpiang* Greenland: Lyberth Music (LRC).

Moana and the Moa Hunters – a contemporary Maori group who sing in both English and Maori.

Patea Maori Club – a more 'traditional' Maori performing arts group, famous for the hit song and music video *Poi E*.

A Native American Odyssey (1992) [musicians from many Native American cultures] Putumayo: PUTU 1542.

Robertson, Robbie (1994) *Robbie Robertson and the Red Road Ensemble: Music for the Native Americans*, featuring Rita Coolidge, Kashtin, The Silvercloud Singers, Douglas Spotted Eagle, Ulali, and Jim Wilson, Canada: Capitol.

Robertson, Robbie (1998) [Six Nations Iroquois, Ontario, Canada, US], *Contact From the Underworld of Redboy*, Canada: Capitol.

The Rough Guide: Australian Aboriginal music, World Music.

Seblon, Kunuut (1990) [*Kalaallit*] *Ilinniut* (classical guitar), Greenland: ULO.

Shenandoah, Joanne (1994) [Oneida Six Nations Iroquois, Ontario, Canada, US] *Once in a Red Moon*, Canada: Canyon Records.

Tagoona, William (1992) [Canadian Inuit] *Memories*. Privately produced and dedicated to his father, Armand Tagoona. Canada.

Tocker, Mahinarangi – contemporary Maori solo artist. See the album, *Te Ripo* (1997), produced by Columbia.

Upper Hutt Posse – contemporary Maori rap group.

Ware, Tom (1990) [Native American] *Tom Ware and Blues Nation*, University of Oklahoma, recorded at the American Indian Music and Dance Show, Anadarko, Oklahoma.

Westerman, Floyd Red Crow (1993) *The Land is Your Mother/Custer Died for your Sins*, audio CD (remastered from original vinyl), Germany: Trikont (Indigo).

Yothu Yindi (1992) [Yoingu Aboriginal, NE Arnhem Land, Australia] *Tribal Voice*, Mushroom Records. Album is dedicated to masters of Djatpangarri popular Yoingu music: Balun Yunupingu, Dhambutjawa Burrwanga and Rrikin Burarrwanga.

Zikaza, vocals and guitar: Siiva Fleischer vocals and composer (1988) [Kalaallit] *Miki goes to Nuussuaq* Greenland: ULO.

Internet resources

Aboriginal People's Television Network (APTN): http://www.aptn.ca/en/

Ajjte (Sámi): http://jokkmokk.se/ajjte/index.htm

AIROS (The American Indian Radio on Satellite network distribution system): http//airos.org/

Brisbane Indigenous Media Association

Canada and the Circumpolar World: http://www.dfait-maeci.gc.ca/circumpolar/

Canadian Broadcasting Corporation (CBC): http://cbc.ca/news

The Center for World Indigenous Studies: http://www.cwis.org/

Finnish Ministry of Foreign Affairs, Websit for the Sami of Finland: http://www.formin.finland.fi/english/

Forsgren's Aanta (Sámi): http://www.itv.se/boreale/samieng.htm

The Independent: http://www.independent.co.uk

Inuit Circumpolar Conference (ICC): http://www.inuitcircumpolar.com

Maori performing arts: http://www.maori.org.nz/waiata/

Messagestick, Australian Broadcasting Corporation (ABC): http://www.abc.net.au/message

National Aboriginal Communications Society : http://www.ammsa.com/ams/amscanadapubs.html

National Indigenous Media Association of Australia: http://www.nimaa.au.org

Native American Communication Resources on the Internet: http://hanksville.phast.umass.edu/misc/NAmedia.html

Native Eyes Distance Education Program: http://www.iaiancad.org/nep/about/about-index.html

NativeWeb: http://www.nativeweb.org/

Nunatsiaq News: http://www.nunatsiaq.com/

Radio and Television Greenland: randburg.com

Refugee Council: www.refugeecouncil.org.uk

Samefolket (on-line version of world's oldest indigenous-controlled publication; monthly magazine, Sweden): http://www.samefolket.se/

Sámi-net discussion area: http://www.student.oulu.fi/~tryhanen/saminet /english.html

Sámi Parliament in Sweden: http://www.sametinget.se/english/index. html

Sámi Radio (based in Finland): http://www.ylefi/samiradio/contents.htm

Scott Polar Research Institute: http://www.spri.cam.ac.uk/

Taiga Communications: http://www.firstperspective.ca

Television New Zealand (TVNZ) c/o Nga Matatiki Rorohiko: Maori Electronic Resources, television/radio: http://www.tvnz.co.nz

UNESCO (addressing the status of the Sámi languages): http://amacrine. berkeley.edu/finnugr/uralic-table.html

Appendix. Ethnic minority media in the UK

Newspapers, Magazines and Periodicals

The Asian Post English language weekly
779 Leytonstone High Road
Leytonstone, London E11 4QS
Tel.: 0208 558 9127

Asian Telegraph and *Telegraph On-line* English language daily
21a Park Road
London NWI 6XN
Tel.: 0107 723 5042

Asian Times English language weekly
Unit 201
Whitechapel Technology Centre
65 Whitechapel Road
London E1 1DU
Tel.: 0107 650 2000

Black Perspective English language quarterly
PO Box 246
London SE13 7DL
Tel.: 0208 692 6986

Caribbean Times English language weekly
Unit 201 Whitechapel Technology Centre
65 Whitechapel Road
London E1 1DU
Tel.: 0207 650 2000

Patagonian Heights Bi-monthly, multi-ethnic readership
15/17 Belmont Street
Aberdeen AB10 1JR
Tel.: 01224 645268/645200

Indobrit Bi-monthly English language magazine
20 Kingsley House
25 Beaufort Street
London SW3 5BD
Tel.: 0207 352 2071

Irish Post English language weekly
Cambridge House
Cambridge Grove
Hammersmith
London W6 OLE
Tel.: 0208 741 0649

Irish World English language weekly
934 North Circular
London NW2 7RJ
Tel.: 0208 453 7800

Jewish Chronicle English language weekly
25 Furnival Street
London EC4 A1JT
Tel.: 0207 415 1500

Jewish Tribune English language weekly
95–7 Stamford Hill
London N16 5RE
Tel.: 0208 800 6688

La Voce Degli Italiani Italian fortnightly
20 Brixton Road
London SW9 6BU
Tel.: 0207 793 0385

London Irish Press English language
Unit 8
Concord Business Centre

Concord Road
London W3 OTR
Tel.: 0208 752 1202

London/Midland/Northern Asian/Black African quarterly
Wild Rose Publishing
10a Ellinfort Road
London
Tel.: 0208 985 4070

New Horizon English language monthly
ICIS House
144–6 Kings Cross Road
London
Tel.: 0207 833 8275

New Impact English language bi-monthly
Courtyard Offices
3 High Street
Marlow
Tel.: 01628 481 581

New Nation English language weekly for Black African-Caribbean
readership
1st Floor
148 Cambridge Heath Road
London E1 5QJ
Tel.: 0207 702 8012

New World English language fortnightly
234 Holloway Road
London N7 8DA
Tel.: 0207 700 2673

Opportunity English language quarterly for multi-ethnic readership,
aged 16–25
Independent Educational Publishing
Independent House
191 Marsh Wall
London E14 9RS
Tel.: 0207 005 2250

Pride Magazine English language monthly magazine for black african, black Caribbean, and mixed race readership
Hamilton House
55 Battersea Bridge Road
London SW11 3AX
Tel.: 0207 228 3110

Shang Ye Xian Feng Chinese language bi-monthly
194 Old Brompton Road
London SW5 OAW
Tel.: 0207 835 2183

Ta Nea Greek language weekly
8–10 Stamford Hill
London N16 6XS
Tel.: 0208 806 0169

Teamwork English language bi-monthly magazine
The West Indian Standing Conference
5 Westminister Bridge Road
London
Tel.: 0207 928 7861/2

Travellers' Times English language quarterly magazine for Gypsies and Travellers
c/o The Rural Media Company
Sullivan House
72–80 Widemarsh Street
Hereford HR4 9HG
Tel.: 01432 344039

The Voice English language weekly
Blue Star House
234–44 Stockwell Road
London
Tel.: 0207 737 7377

Radio and Television Stations

Choice FM (South London Radio) Multi-ethnic audience
291–9 Borough High Street
London SE1 1JG
Tel.: 0207 378 3969

Spectrum Radio Broadcasts 24 hours a day, digital and analogue, in
15 languages to listeners in 24 communities
204–6 Queenstown Road
London SW8 3NR
Tel.: 0207 627 4433

Index